VIVO BENNETT / CRICKET CLAGETT

1001 DISCARD

ways to avoid getting mugged, murdered, robbed, raped, or ripped off

 VAN NOSTRAND REINHOLD COMPANY
NEW YORK   CINCINNATI   TORONTO   LONDON   MELBOURNE

Printed in the United States of America.

Published by Van Nostrand Reinhold Company
A division of Litton Educational Publishing, Inc.
135 West 50th Street, New York, NY 10020, U.S.A.

Van Nostrand Reinhold Limited
1410 Birchmount Road
Scarborough, Ontario M1P 2E7, Canada

Van Nostrand Reinhold Australia Pty. Ltd.
17 Queen Street
Mitcham, Victoria 3132, Australia

Van Nostrand Reinhold Company Limited
Molly Millars Lane
Wokingham, Berkshire, England

16 15 14 13 12 11 10 9 8 7 6 5 4 3 2

CONTENTS

THIS BOOK IS DEDICATED TO KAY SUNDAY

acknowledgments

The authors would like to thank Jeff Jouett for his patient cooperation in researching this book. Also, we extend our appreciation to our typist, Marilyn Sefcik, for her diligence in seeing the manuscript through to its completion.

INTRODUCTION

The third time it happened, he was lucky. Only a broken nose. The first two street holdups had earned our friend and neighbor a brain concussion and a bullet in the chest. After the third episode, the authors spent many an evening talking with him about his misadventures. Much of the discussion centered on why he had seemingly been singled out for these crimes. For although we lived in the same neighborhood and regularly frequented the same areas of town as our neighbor—often in the robbery-prone night and early-morning hours—we can't remember ever experiencing as much as an unkind word from a stranger, let alone three holdups.

After much analysis, we discovered that our friend was literally asking for trouble in three conspicuous ways. First, his elegant dress and his expensive ring and watch advertised his affluence. Second, when paying his tab in a restaurant or other public place, he would remove a large bankroll from his pocket with a flourish and peel bills from it. His third, and worst, blunder, however, lay in very foolishly resisting armed, sometimes desperate men. At first, he would try to talk them out of it. Then, when that didn't work, he would attempt to subdue them physically.

Fortunately for him, he subsequently toned down his dress and started paying his restaurant and bar bills by credit card. Since making these changes, and altering a few other potentially dangerous habits, he has never been in a situation that could call for his third foolhardy practice, but we hope he now has wiser behavior in mind if such a situation ever occurs.

This book began as an outgrowth of our conversations with this man. Our research into holdups naturally led us into the related areas of protection against rape, home and business burglary, pickpockets and pursesnatchers, consumer gyps, and dangers to children.

Studies by behavioral scientists indicate that just as many individuals are accident-prone, a large segment of our society is crime-prone. That is, people either attract the criminal element in some way not obvious to themselves, or they unknowingly put themselves into hazardous situations in which they become victimized.

The aim of this book is threefold: to make you as unattractive as possible to the criminal; to keep you out of his way; and to provide you with methods of keeping him out of your way. If you diligently follow the suggestions contained herein, it is unlikely that you will ever be mugged, murdered, robbed, raped, or ripped off.

January 10, 1977   Vivo Bennett
San Diego, California   Cricket Clagett

CHAPTER 1

Your home is your castle—but did you forget to raise the drawbridge?

The scene is all too common in today's America. You come home from work or after a night out, open the door to your house or apartment, flick on the light switch, and gaze at a pitiful sight.

It looks as if a cyclone has twisted through your living room. Your television and stereo are gone, and the debris strewn before the closet door tells you that the intruder found your hidden jewelry, too.

It's sad, and it's costly. You may blame yourself for not replacing that flimsy lock on the front door. Maybe a window left unlatched provided easy entry for a burglar, who was able to approach hidden from view behind tall bushes next to your house. However it happened, you've just become a burglary statistic.

If you've been fortunate enough to miss out on this calamity so far, congratulate yourself—but not too heartily. Your time may be coming. According to the FBI, a prowler pries a window or jimmies a lock somewhere in this nation every ten seconds. If you *were* a burglar's target recently, don't feel too bad—you've got plenty of company. In 1976, over 3 million Americans lost more than $1 billion to the burglar's wily ways.

Can today's homeowner and apartment dweller do anything about burglaries besides count his losses? Yes! You can use your head and a few dollars to make your home 99 percent burglarproof. In this chapter we'll discuss many preventive security measures. Most of them require nothing more than simple use of common sense. Some involve a small expense, and a few a substantial investment.

But think a minute about the nature of burglary before you begin your prevention program. For the most part, burglary is a crime of opportunity. The average burglar is an amateur who grabs at any chance. He's the acquaintance who covets your stereo and hears through the grapevine that you're leaving on an extended vacation. He's the teenager walking down your dark alley looking for houses with no lights and no car in the driveway. He's the door-to-door salesman who pokes his head through an unlocked door to see that no one's home. In most break-ins (85 percent) the intruder is under twenty-five years old. Many of the simple precautions that follow will foil these and other part-time prowlers.

The seasoned, professional burglar is another matter. Fortunately, police estimate that only 5 percent of the nation's burglars are in this category. If one of these practiced crooks is truly determined to enter your home and haul off your goods, nothing short of a crocodile-infested moat will stop him—and, given time, not even that. But a number of the sophisticated alarm systems and ingenious tactics we suggest will make your abode so much trouble that prowlers will choose easier pickings.

Take notes as you read our anti-burglary hints and resolve today to implement an effective theft-prevention program. It could very well keep you from becoming still another statistic in the FBI's steadily growing crime report.

FOR FURTHER INFORMATION:

Are You Safe from Burglars? Robert E. Barnes. Garden City, N. Y.: Doubleday, 1971.

Burglar-Proof Your Home and Car. Peter Arnold. Los Angeles: Nash, 1971.

Do-It Yourself Home Protection. Ralph Treves. New York: Harper & Row, 1972.

Fences, Walls and Hedges for Privacy and Security. Jack Kramer. New York: Charles Scribner's Sons, 1975.

Home and Apartment Security. Al Griffin. Chicago: Henry Regnery, 1975.

How to Avoid Burglary, Housebreaking and Other Crimes. Ulrich Kaufmann. New York: Crown, 1967.

How to Avoid Electronic Eavesdropping and Privacy Invasion. Los Angeles: Investigator Information Service.

How to Hide Almost Anything. David Krotz. New York: William Morrow, 1975.

How to Install Protective Alarm Devices. Donald R. Brann. Briarcliff Manor, N. Y.: Directions Simplified, 1972.

Practical Ways to Prevent Burglary and Illegal Entry. Val Moolman. New York: Cornerstone Library, 1970.

Security! Martin Clifford. New York: Drake, 1974.

To Stop a Thief. George C. Nonte, Jr. South Hackensack, N. J.: Stoeger, 1974.

SIMPLE BUT EFFECTIVE PRECAUTIONS

Free security check. The police departments of most large and medium-sized cities have special crime-prevention units whose duties, in part, consist of helping citizens make their homes secure against crime. One call is all that's needed to bring a security expert from this department to your home for a free security check. We suggest you do it today.

Metermania. If your gas, electric, and water meters are in your cellar or inside any other part of your house, arrange for your utility company to take *annual* readings, instead of taking them monthly.

This will greatly reduce the number of instances in which strangers will enter your premises, and will proportionately decrease your chances of getting ripped off. The best security, of course, is to have your utility lines relocated so that the utility company can place a meter *outside* your house.

A table trick. Keep a small table by your front door. Then, when you come home loaded down with packages, you can deposit them on the table and close the door immediately—instead of carrying them to another room, then coming back to close the door.

This may seem to you like a rather trivial measure, but the victim of burglary—and rape as well—is merely followed through an open door more often than you'd care to realize. Play it safe!

Less landscaping. Here's where you can profit by putting yourself in the burglar's place. Stand just outside your front door. Are you hidden from the street by plants, shrubs, an overhanging tree? A burglar would be, too. Circle the house. Stand by the various windows, the side and back doors. Are you shielded from your neighbors by shrubbery?

If so, you'll want to trim things down so as to provide as little cover as possible in these areas. By sacrificing one type of green, you may be saving another!

Fire!? If an intruder enters your home while you're on the premises, and you have access to a telephone, by all means call the police. But just in case the police are delayed, and if a true emergency exists, call the fire department as well. You can depend on them to be there

3

pronto. Worry about the legal consequences later. With a gang of ax-wielding firemen about to smash in your door, what housebreaker is going to stick around?

A biteless bark. If you want to have some fun with the prevention business, dub your dog's bark onto a repeating tape. If you have no dog, use a neighbor's. Or, for short errands, buy a 20 minute special-effects phonograph record of a dog's bark.

When you go out, simply turn on your "barking" tape player or phonograph loud enough to be distinctly heard within a few feet of the house. Guaranteed to dissuade all but the most stout-hearted and resolute housebreaker.

Chutes and ladders. Batten down the hatches and secure your gang-planks and your home will float safely through the rising tide of crime. Burglars will beat the best door locks by wedging their way through coal chutes, service-elevator shafts, and attic-to-roof openings. You must install a strong steel bar or hasp and padlock inside these openings to make your home 100 percent secure. Also keep ladders inside a locked garage or chained to an immovable object to prevent their use by climbing crooks to get at second-story windows and roof entry points.

Shinny sliders. Give the guttersnipes scaling toward your roof or second-story windows the slip by smearing axle grease or anti-climb paint and barbed wire along all drainpipes. Get the grease at an auto-parts store, the special paint at a roofing outlet, and the wire at a fence dealer. You can combine any two of the above safety measures and not spend more than $20.

"Just call me B.J." If you're a woman, you're probably proud of it. But if you're a single woman, it's bad business to advertise the fact on your mailbox or in the telephone book. Eliminate titles such as Miss, Mrs., or the more modern Ms. And unless your first name happens to be Harry or Walter, better stick to using initials.

Why? Letting on that you're a woman simply gives the potential burglar, rapist, or other criminal one more bit of information with which to do you in.

Neighbor number. The first thing that we do when moving into a new house or apartment is visit the neighbors. Not for social reasons, mind you, but with an offer. We promise to call the police or otherwise try to thwart any attempted burglary or vandalism involving their property. Of course we ask them to do the same for us in return.

You would be wise to make such arrangements with your neighbors. If you live in an apartment building, try to involve everyone on your floor. If yours is a single residence, make this agreement with your next-door neighbors as well as those in back of you and across the street from you.

Neighbor vigilance. The brochure entitled *Neighborhood Watch*, published by the Los Angeles Police Department, gives some valuable tips on how you and your neighbors can work together to reduce crime in your neighborhood. It's available free by writing to the Public Affairs Division of the Los Angeles Police Department at 150 North Los Angeles Street, Los Angeles, Calif. 90012.

Cabin comment. If you have a vacation cabin in some isolated area, you'll save money and trouble by following these two rules: Keep as few possessions in it as possible, and don't lock it too securely. The first rule is obvious. The reason for the second rule is that if someone wants to break into a deserted cabin in the wilderness, strong locks won't deter him. He'll break down a door or smash in a window if necessary. You might as well avoid such unnecessary damage.

The radio ruse. If you're leaving your home for the day or evening, put your radio in the middle of the house. Then turn it on loud enough so that anyone standing just outside any door or window can hear it clearly.

If you're going on vacation, hook your radio up to an automatic timer and set it to go on at 7:00 P.M. and off at midnight—the most likely hours for a burglar to strike.

Air snare. Residents of major cities and their suburbs can stay on top of crime by taking a clue from a group of Los Angeles dwellers. In cooperation with the city police department, and armed with paint brushes and ladders, a number of people in that Western crime capital climbed onto their roofs and painted their house numbers in huge figures across their shingles. The deterrent helps aid location by police helicopters in emergencies. Police credit it with snagging burglars and recovering stolen property.

The peeping Tom—or Dick or Harry. Who knows what his name is? All we know is that he exists. What are his motives? He can be meek as milk or he can be a potential rapist or burglar—or worse! It's certainly a simple enough matter to rid yourself of this creepy bird. Just make sure all your blinds are tightly drawn. Double-check by going outside at night and seeing if *you* can peep in.

5

The no-answer answer. You can't run and hook up an answering service to your phone every time you leave home for a few hours, a day, or a weekend. Yet the caller at your doorstep or the prowler casing your house while you're at work or otherwise away may hear your unanswered phone—a bell signaling nobody home, easy pickin's. Don't let Ma Bell tip potential burglars during short absences from home. Turn your phone to its lowest possible volume before you leave. Then pile a few heavy blankets over it, thereby silencing it till your return.

The non-alarm. As its name implies, the non-alarm is not really an alarm—it just looks like one. It's usually a silver or black box, with a warning label to intruders affixed. For under $10, one can be bought in any hardware or electronic supply store. Attach the "alarm" to the front of your house in a prominent location.

Only amateurs, of course, are fooled by these devices. To deter the dedicated thief, you'll need more sophisticated equipment.

Line logic. The *smart* burglar's first act, if he makes it inside your house while you're sleeping, will be to remove the receiver from the phone in your living room, thus apparently making it impossible for you to call for help from your telephone extension.

Outwit him by obtaining a two-line phone from your telephone company. A switch near the dial lets you change from line to line. Although your basic monthly service charge will double, you'll have an effective line of defense.

Surprise! It's 4:00 A.M. and you're sound asleep. Suddenly you find yourself awakened by a sound you've never heard before. A scratching, then a scraping, then the unmistakable sound of someone stepping on that loose floorboard in the dining room. "Good Lord," you say to yourself, "a burglar is in my house!"

What to do? *Nothing,* if you're smart. If you value your life more than your personal possessions, you'll stay in bed and let him help himself. When you can, call the police.

Telephone talk. In the foregoing case, if you had a telephone on the nightstand next to your bed, you could easily pick up the receiver, quietly dial the operator, cup your hand over your mouth, and whisper for help.

It is wise to have several telephone extensions throughout your home—not only in case of a night burglar, but for other emergencies which may arise. On each instrument, put a label containing the telephone numbers of the police, fire department, and ambulance service.

The peephole. Don't open your door without first seeing who your visitor is. A peephole viewer is a $2 gadget available in hardware stores that, when installed in your door, will allow you to see from the inside who is knocking on your door.

Installation, which requires drilling a small hole in the door, is simple. You can do it yourself in about five minutes.

Peephole pointer. Another advantage in having a peephole viewer is that if you don't recognize your visitor, you can ask him for identification before you open the door.

Officials from the police department, post office, utility company, and reputable private organizations all carry identification. Don't let a uniform fool you—it can be rented. If you don't recognize the face, always ask to have identification shown you through the peephole.

The automatic timer. This device ranks with the peephole viewer as provider of a heap of protection for less than $10.

If you're going to be away from home in the evening, simply set the timer to turn on a lamp automatically at dusk. If you're going to be out all night or going on vacation, use two or three timers in conjunction with as many lights.

Twenty-four-hour timers are available which can be set to activate/deactivate house lights every night during your absence. The potential housebreaker is given the illusion of an occupied home.

There is another device that operates on a light-sensitive photoelectric cell which screws into any light socket and will automatically turn that light on at night and off during the day.

These units are available in hardware stores and electronics-supply houses.

Door dodge. If you're a lone woman when your doorbell rings unexpectedly in the evening or late at night, your first action should be to stand near the door and shout, "I'll get it, Harry" (or some other male name). This will indicate to your caller that you are not alone. Then take all other necessary precautions, such as viewing your visitor through your peephole or using your chain guard in order to identify him before opening your door.

Open-shut case. The simple doorstop, which helps let breezes in, can also help wedge would-be intruders out of your house or apartment, should they get pushy at the door. Slide a wooden, metal, or plastic doorstop under the door before cracking it to check a caller's credentials. If the outsider uses muscle, the doorstop wedges tighter. Meanwhile, you can get help or beat it out the back door.

7

Bell bedevilment. More than a few homeowners, upon returning to their residence from an evening out, have been killed or injured because they surprised a panicky burglar in the act. Now this may sound silly, but it may save your life. Upon returning home to an empty house—day or night—ring your own doorbell or knock on your door before entering. Then pause and enter. This will give any unauthorized visitor a chance to make a speedy rear exit. After all, a burglar doesn't want a confrontation any more than you do.

Catastrophe caution. Never allow a stranger to entice you out of your home. A stranger may knock on your door asking you to come out because of an emergency: there has just been a terrible automobile accident, or some other catastrophe, and your help is desperately needed.

As convincing as the individual may sound, it may be a ruse. Don't open your door. Your best bet here is to use your telephone to summon the police or an ambulance.

Silent partner. Young and older women living alone are prime targets for the thief or the rapist *if* he finds out their circumstances. It won't cost much to fake a roommate, and you might fake a crook in the process. Put a fictitious name alongside yours on the mailbox and list the name with the same phone number as yours in the city directory.

Police protection. Your local police department is doing all it can to protect your home from burglars—it even publishes pamphlets on the subject. One such publication, entitled *Home Sweet Home,* gives advice on a variety of burglar-related topics, and is available by writing to the San Diego Police Department, 801 West Market Street, San Diego, Calif. 92101.

A stitch in time. Before another day goes by, obtain the emergency numbers of the police and fire departments and local ambulance service. Post them prominently near every telephone extension in your house.

Protection guide. A booklet entitled *How to Protect Your Home Against Burglary and Fire* is available for 50¢ from Flashguard Security Systems, 3801 Liberty Avenue, Pittsburgh, Pa. 15201. Covered are such topics as locks and bolts, keys, door viewing systems and alarm devices.

LOCKS, LATCHES, KEYS, AND CATCHES

King of the locks. From the standpoint of security, the Medeco lock is superlative: the cylinder is virtually unpickable, and the keys cannot be duplicated on ordinary key-cutting machines, but must be ordered from the lock company or one of its authorized representatives.

The cylinders cost $30 and can be ordered through Medeco Security Locks, Inc., U.S. 11 West and Alleghany Drive, Salem, Va. 24153.

Padlock prudence. A professional thief can cut through the average padlock with a bolt cutter or steel hacksaw in seconds. The padlock with a shackle of hardened steel, however, is almost impervious to these instruments.

These high-security padlocks are available in hardware stores for as little as $2.

Locking window latch. A variation on the conventional window latch, this device incorporates a lock, and is manufactured by Loxem Manufacturing Company of Richardson, Tex. It sells for $4.

The proof lock. If you've given out duplicate keys to people whose honesty you later come to doubt, consider installing the Proof Lock. You can set this very clever device to "trap" all duplicate keys inserted in its cylinder. The duplicate key will then be held until you release it with a control dial, giving you possession of the duplicate. In the meantime, the cylinder is able to accept your master key. Sells for $30.

The anonymous key ring. Never attach your name, address, or other identifying data to your key ring. This precaution is just common sense; thousands of burglaries happen each year because potential burglars find house keys with address attached.

If you lose your keys, it's far cheaper to have a set of duplicates made (from the spare keys you should already have) than to fall prey to a lucky burglar who found them.

Under the doormat. Never leave a duplicate house key outside the house. If there comes a time when you *must* leave a key for a friend, don't leave it in an obvious place—under a doormat or flower pot, or on a ledge over the door. These are the first places a burglar will look.

Worn locks. Your home-protection locks will be easy picking for burglars if you aren't alert for two common yet seldom-noticed lock malfunctions. If your key slips out when the cylinder core is turned only part of the way, you may leave the core half-turned, thinking the door locked. But it's not—*anyone* can open it by continuing the turn with a paper clip in the keyway. Also, a cylinder that turns when the key is not fully inserted is faulty. The tumblers are frozen in the "open" position by grit or grease. The lock should be fixed or changed.

Loaded with bar. The Schlage Charley-Bar is designed to ensure the security of a sliding glass door while matching the metal trim of the window. This unit is mounted about halfway up on the inside of the outer door and swings down into position into a bracket installed on the inside edge of the inner door. Because of its visibility, it serves as a deterrent to the potential housebreaker. Retails for $6.

Pushbutton lock. The pushbutton lock offers a high level of security to the homeowner and apartment dweller alike, for there are no keys to be lost or duplicated.

This lock, which may be either mechanical or electronic, consists of a set of buttons which must be punched according to a preset combination. The more expensive models require the use of a plastic identity card, which may or may not be used in conjunction with the buttons.

An inexpensive mechanical model ($25) is the Presto-matic, which can be installed by the home handyman in about two hours. The more elaborate electronic versions can cost up to several hundred dollars.

Counter power. The Toepfer lock incorporates a counter that tells how many times the lock has been opened and closed. Thus you are able to know whether others, to whom you may have given duplicate keys, have entered your residence, garage, storeroom, or other area.

These sell for $45 and are available through Edwin Toepfer Company, 1016 South 16th, Milwaukee, Wisc. 53204.

Tumbler juggling. Juggle the tumblers to rekey your door locks three times a day and you'll be safe, even if confused. While a three-key-a-day habit is a bit extreme, it's possible (as are less frequent key changes) with the U-Change Lock System available from most security-equipment dealers.

The system uses a special lock cylinder, an assortment of keys, and a tumbler-change tool. The cylinder plug is turned with its present key, the tumbler tool is inserted, and a new key is placed in the lock. Tumblers adjust to the new key, and any key you have lost or given someone you distrust will no longer work.

Casement case. An effective locking device for casement windows is called the Casement Window Key Lock. Manufactured by Ideal Security, it is available through most locksmiths at under $5.

Deadbolt deftness. The simple spring latch or snaplock is the common tapered latch which one sees on most doors. Because of its taper, a housebreaker can easily slip a knife or plastic credit card between the door and frame and push the latch back, thus allowing the door to open.

To prevent this, we recommend a deadbolt. These are not tapered and thus cannot be pushed back into the door. Many models are available. Some work in conjunction with a spring latch, others don't. For maximum security, the deadbolt should have at least a ¾-inch, and preferably a 1-inch, "throw"—the distance that the bolt extends into the door frame.

Vertical deadbolts. A step up from the standard deadbolt is the vertical deadbolt lock. This has a double cylinder, which means that it can be locked either from the inside or the outside. The stationary part of the lock is attached securely to the door frame. The bolt, when closed, passes vertically through several steel loops, as does the hinge pin of a door. Thus the door is securely locked to the door frame.

Since there is no knob on the inside with which to unlock the door, the intruder cannot simply smash his fist through the door and unlock it. In order to gain entry, he must practically smash the whole door in—a very noisy procedure. Costs only $6.

Lock collars. The jimmyproof deadbolt lock is the answer to most prying intruders, but not to all. Using such tools as vise-grip pliers, pincers, or gear pullers, some housebreakers yank the whole lock cylinder out, permitting access to the bolt.

The way to fool the well-tooled housebreaker is to install a lock collar, a ring of tough metal that fits around the outside lock cylinder. They are available from locksmiths. When the crook clamps on the pincers, the lock collar spins, but the cylinder stays firmly in place.

The chain guard. These consist of a short piece of chain anchored to the door jamb on one end and a metal button which slips into a groove on the door on the other end. This device allows the occupant to open the door a crack in order to identify the visitor.

The links of the chain should be heavy, and welded rather than merely bent into shape. The length of the chain should be short, allowing the door to be opened no more than an inch or so. The device should be anchored to solid wood with screws at least 2 inches long.

As a test of the chain guard's strength, open your door with the chain engaged, then have a burly friend throw a shoulder hard against it. If the device holds, it's doing the job. Costs just $3.

No-rob knob loop. A stronger and more convenient-to-use chain guard, called Door Guard, is made by Ajax Hardware Company. This consists of a welded-steel brass-plated loop of chain which is solidly mounted on your door frame at the height of the door knob by means of 2-inch screws. The loop slips over the doorknob, and if it is properly positioned, will allow the door to open only a slit, not enough for a hand to reach in and unhook it.

Window lock. The Yale window lock is screwed into the top of the lower window on one side. Holes are then drilled in the corresponding side of the upper window frame, positioned so that the window can be locked in the closed position or in a partially open position for ventilation. Costs $3.

Change that lock! Whenever you move into a new house or apartment, one of your first calls should be to your local *licensed* locksmith. Have him change all outside locks on the house, and install any new ones necessary for your security. Actually, it's not necessary for him to remove the whole lock. He'll just change the tumbler arrangement in each of the cylinders.

This may seem like a drastic measure, but you have no way of knowing how many keys to your front door are floating around. Better play it safe.

Tumbling around. A good pickman working on a standard lock is able to "rake" the row of tumblers, allowing them to fall into place for opening of the lock. The Chicago Ace lock, however, has its tumblers arranged in a circle instead of all in a row. Furthermore, since these locks are seldom found in residential areas, it's unlikely that a burglar will have the necessary tools for the job.

Priced at $8, these are manufactured by the Chicago Lock Company, 4311 West Belmont, Chicago, Ill. 60641.

For sliding windows. Sliding windows are indeed a thief's delight. He can easily remove the screen, apply pressure to the conventional clamping mechanism, and slide the window open. Not so with the Schlage Vent-lock. This mechanism clamps onto either the upper or lower rail and locks the window in either a closed or partially open position. Costs $3.

12

Bedroom bolt. If you live with children who may need access to your bedroom at night, this device isn't practical, but if there are no children in the household, you'll derive an extra measure of security by buying and installing a lock or heavy barrel bolt for your bedroom door. After you retire, this will serve as yet another obstacle between a nocturnal housebreaker and you, giving you valuable time in which to seize a weapon, call the police, or escape through a window.

The licensed locksmith. Even though you may get a break on the price, don't ever let a carpenter, handyman, or unlicensed locksmith install a lock in your home. The odds are against such a thing happening, but it's possible for him to make a duplicate key to the lock he's installed in order to gain unauthorized entry to your home.

Deal only with a licensed or bonded locksmith, or with one who is a member of a recognized locksmith association such as the Associated Locksmiths of America or California Locksmiths Association. Or call the burglary detail of your local police department for a recommendation.

Mortise lock. This is a combination lock-latch-deadbolt-knob affair and, as such, affords excellent door security. The deadbolt can be operated either by key from the outside or by a thumb turn on the inside. Built into the lock are two buttons. Depressing one of them will allow the latch to open by turning the outside knob. Depressing the other locks the latch. This lock retails for $30.

Double cylinders. Install a double cylinder lock on all your doors. This type of lock requires a key from both sides in order to open it, effectively preventing a burglar from opening the door by simply reaching a hand in (through a broken glass pane or other opening) and unlocking it from the inside. Warning: Because these locks must be unlocked with a key from the inside, they are outlawed in some areas as a fire hazard. Check with your city building inspection department before installing.

Heavy-duty bolts. The Fox Police Double-Bolt Lock attaches to the center of the door and contains arms that extend horizontally across it, securely deadbolting into both the right and left door jambs, so that the hinge side of the door is held as firmly as the lock side.

It's available for $35 from Fox Police Lock Company, 46 West 21st Street, New York, N. Y. 10010.

Sealing the super's key. If you're an apartment dweller, or about to become one, it's more likely than not that the management will insist on retaining a duplicate key to your apartment. Try to talk them out of it. After all, every additional key to your home represents a threat to your security.

If the super doesn't go for this, put the duplicate key in an envelope, seal it with sealing wax, and write your name in the wax before it hardens. Now instruct the super to let you know when and if he uses your key. With this system, he'll think twice about using it indiscriminately.

Brace yourself! A heavy crowbar may tear an ordinary lock loose from its connection to the door jamb, but the Fox Police Brace Lock is not connected to the jamb; it consists of a locking mechanism and a steel bar that is attached to the lock at one end and to the floor at the other. It's available at about $10 from Fox Police Lock Company, 46 West 21st Street, New York, N. Y. 10010.

File locks. While a filing cabinet is the most convenient place to store and organize personal records, stocks, certificates, and other valuables in your home office or den, it's also one of the first places a burglar will search. For from $7 to $25 (depending on the number of file drawers) you can gain extra protection for often irreplaceable documents.

The File-Guard, manufactured by Loxem Corporation (1201 Exchange Drive, Richardson, Tex. 75080), is a heavy steel bar that is bolted across the front of your file cabinet, making the drawers impossible to open when it's padlocked at the top. The apparatus swings out of the way when not in use. If you keep valuable papers about the house, the price is worth the protection.

Master keys. Lock systems in many of the more modern apartment buildings, rather than having a duplicate key for each door, have a master key which fits all the units in the building or all the apartments on each floor.

These are bad business. Crooked tenants have been known to move out, taking the cylinder to their lock with them, "decoding" it, then having their own master key made up. Later, in the manager's absence, they return to clean out the building.

If your apartment building uses a master key, call a locksmith and have a second lock of your own installed on your door. Then leave a duplicate key to this lock with a trusted neighbor, who will give it to the manager only in case of an emergency.

Idiot-box locks. There comes a crisis point in everyone's life when it seems the only thing that will help is a long talk with Ward Cleaver.

But you'll miss the therapeutic *Leave It to Beaver* reruns and your other favorite television shows if a boob-tube burglar swipes your set.

A device called TV-Tective ($15) helps guard against television theft. The small module attaches to your TV set and emits a warning squeal if the set is moved. The gadget can protect other electrical appliances, too. Write TV-Tective, Box 8860, Oak Park, Mich. 48237 for information on ordering.

Lockpicker protection. A new replacement cylinder lock is said to be impossible to open without a proper key. The pins are unreadable by any special tool because they give the tool a false reading by design, while the cylinder itself is armored and drill-resistant.

It's available as a mortise cylinder for use with mortise entry locks and as a rim cylinder for surface-mounting auxiliary locks. The price is about $15 from Builders Hardware, 61 Brightside Avenue, East Northport, N. Y. 11731.

The shrouded lock. This padlock, which sells for under $10, contains a cavity in its top, into which the shackle fits on locking. The shackle is thus protected from bolt cutter, hacksaw, and acetylene torch.

Hasp hardiness. If your hasp is of poor quality, if it is not anchored deeply into solid wood, or if the heads of its screws are exposed, the finest padlock in the world will not deter a break-in.

Hasps made of good-quality steel will cost up to $15 a set, but are necessary in order to give you the maximum amount of protection.

The secure home. A booklet cleverly entitled *Surelocked Homes* gives some useful advice on out-thinking the potential house thief. Locks, latches, keys, and alarms are all covered in an entertaining and informative manner. The publication is available free from State Farm Fire and Casualty Company, Public Relations Department, 112 East Washington Street, Bloomington, Ill. 61701.

DOORS, WINDOWS, AND FENCES

Hinges. If your exterior doors open outward, your hinge pins are, most likely, on the outside rather than on the inside of your door. Are they the type that can be removed easily? If so, the thief will literally be able to walk into your home through an open door.

Replace removable hinge pins on all outward-opening doors with the hidden or nonremovable type, available at your hardware dealer.

Hinge-pin backup. To protect your door from being lifted from its hinges by pulling the hinge pin, follow these simple steps:

Remove two screws, opposite each other, from both leafs of each hinge.

Insert a long screw or concrete nail into the jamb leaf, letting it protrude about ½ inch.

Drill out the opposing screw hole in your door. Do this in the top and bottom hinge of the door. When the door is closed, the hinge pins may be removed, but the protruding screws will hold the door firmly in place.

Hatch latch. Wooden hatch doors, commonly found guarding suburban cellar entrances, offer only slim protection no matter how well locked, since the wood planks can be pried up easily with a crowbar. The enclosed stairwell then hides the burglar, who takes his time entering the basement door.

Replace such doors with steel hatch doors bolted into a concrete base. Then bar the doors from the inside. A contractor can perform such safety surgery at under $200 for the whole operation.

Sliding doors. Sliding glass doors are easily removed by lifting the movable panel, then swinging the bottom clear of the lower track. As silly as it may sound, often this type of door is installed so that it opens and closes on the exterior rather than the interior side of the fixed-glass part. Naturally this allows a housebreaker to simply lift the door out of the way and walk in. Check today to make sure your sliding glass door is properly installed.

Pins for sliding doors. A simple way to secure an inside sliding door is to drill a downward-sloping hole through the top channel into the top portion of the sliding-door frame. Then insert a ¼-inch-thick pin or heavy nail through the frame and into the door.

Such a setup is a minimum security method, capable of keeping out intruders while the house is occupied. The pin protection should be used in connection with other locking devices to secure vulnerable sliding doors during an extended absence.

Door frames. Check your door frames. If they are rotted or poorly constructed, they represent a distinct weakness in your home security. You should call in a carpenter and have him install a new, sturdy frame made of a hardwood such as Douglas fir or oak. Also you'll want him to lag-bolt the frame into place. A professional job will cost in the vicinity of $100, but is well worth it.

Door strength. Doors with glass are obviously vulnerable to housebreakers, but some doors that appear solid and strong are just as vulnerable—thin veneer with a hollow center, quite easy to smash through with a foot or gloved fist. Make sure all your exterior doors are solid wood or metal-clad.

Mail slots. Door slots are the safest way to receive your mail, but these openings can also serve as a hole for housebreakers to work on your door locks or to get a peep at whether your mail is piled up, indicating that you're away. You'll need a flap over the slot with a tight spring keeping it closed and a strong steel basket covering the inside of the slot. The basket should be bottomless. It will keep intruders' wires and tools away from your locks and make your mail drop straight down and out of sight rather than fly out at an angle where a stooping snooper can observe it.

Transom treatment. An apartment dweller may think the transom above his door too small for anyone to crawl through, but it can allow a prowler to reach down and unlock the door from the inside. Your best bet, if you don't need the transom for light or ventilation, is to nail it shut. If it is a glass transom, block the opening with a solid panel nailed into the door frame. To retain airflow or light, install steel bars or heavy wire mesh across the hole to keep out unwanted callers.

Shed security. Toolsheds and greenhouses are often neglected by everyone but the burglar, who knows that lawnmowers, bicycles, and tools make easy loot. Naturally you've clamped case-hardened steel padlocks on the doors of such structures, but the shed's hinges need special attention, too.

If the hinges are exposed, as they often are on back-lot buildings, weld them in place on a metal shed, or insert set screws through the hinges at an unexposed point.

Knockie-talkie. A thug thumping at your door sounds just like the knock-knock of the paperboy or the rap-tap of the old woman passing out religious pamphlets. If you have a solid door—and especially if you live alone—you'll want to think about an indoor-outdoor intercom system to check on that caller while keeping your door deadbolted.

A basic security intercom set is available for $13 from Lafayette Electronics Corporation, 111 Jericho Turnpike, Syosset, N. Y. 11791. A wire is strung connecting a "remote" (small box mounted near your front, back, or garage door) with a "master." At the "master," you can talk or listen to anyone near your door, check strangers' credentials, and see if funny noises are serious prowlers.

Wireless intercoms. Anyone with a knife can silence your wire intercom with one slice. To dodge this puncture in your protection system you'll want to consider the more expensive wireless intercoms for indoor-outdoor use.

Wireless models cost nearly $50 at Lafayette Radio Electronics Corporation. These higher-priced sets operate on radio frequencies and therefore are sometimes subject to outside electronic interference. But they offer constant communication—which is crucial when you're in trouble.

Open-door policy. Automatic garage-door openers can be another crack in your home security scheme. For about $140 you can sit in the safety of your car (warm and dry when raining) and push a button that will open your garage door and turn on the garage light.

The device, called Electronic Power Door at Sears, Roebuck and Co., uses radio signals from a transmitter in your car to activate a motorized lifting arm and light switch. If you return one night and your buttonpushing sheds some garage light on a housebreaker, drive away and get police assistance.

Driveway key. Spend $5 for an outside key-lock switch and your $140 garage-door opener will keep your comings and goings even more secure. Mount this device on a post near your driveway and activate it by reaching out your car window to turn the correct key. Up goes the garage door, on go the lights. Sears, Roebuck and Co. sell this lock-switch. Wire it to your garage-door opener with bell wire (from a hardware store), then throw away the radio receiver that came attached to your electric door opener. The extra investment will prevent accidental openings of your garage doors, as can occur when radio-operated openers are occasionally set off by a passing auto transmitter or airplane.

Window gates. The accordion window gate, securely anchored to a solid window frame, provides excellent protection against entry through a window. One model, called the Invincible, has extra bracing at the upper and lower channels. Another type, the Protect-A-Guard, does not require a padlock to secure it, thus allowing an easy escape by residents in case of fire. Both types are installed on the inside of the window.

These are manufactured by the J. Kaufman Ironworks, 1685 Boone Avenue, Bronx, N. Y. 10462. The gates can be ordered by mail direct from the company or obtained through locksmiths. They cost $80 to $100 each, including installation.

Security bars. Although ornamental iron bars over doors and windows offer the ultimate in home security, they have their faults: they are expensive, they often look terrible, and, unless the bars contain inside release mechanisms, they may trap you and your family inside in the event of fire.

Complete barring of doors and windows (bars over doors are in the form of a gate) in the average five-room house will run about $800. See your Yellow Pages under "Iron Ornamental Works."

Window wisdom. By far the cheapest and easiest way to make certain a window will not be forced open is to drive a heavy nail into each side of the sash, leaving about ½ inch of the nail exposed. Allow for a window opening of about 3 or 4 inches for ventilation if desired.

Window wonder. The cheapest and easiest way to secure a sliding glass door or window is to insert a cut-to-size wooden rod or bar in the lower track after the door or window has been closed. Select the diameter or width to fit into the track.

Beware of louvered windows! These unique windows are to be commended for their attractiveness and convenience. But they're mighty easy prey for the trained burglar. How so? By using a thin screwdriver or piece of metal, a thief can easily slip these slatted windows out of their grooves, thus allowing him to get into your house.

If you must have louvered windows, install protective bars on the outside.

Glass. Because of the noise, a burglar will usually avoid breaking glass in order to gain entry to your home. But, nevertheless, windows do represent a distinct weak link in the security chain of your residence. A strong, wireless safety glass called Secur-Lite, which will withstand the force of a brick tossed against it, is manufactured by Amerada Glass Company, 2001 Greenleaf Avenue, Elk Grove Village, Ill. 60007.

Cellar grill guards. Basement windows in the average home are both the most vulnerable and the least protected passages prowlers use to enter your property. You'll want the protection of window locks, but a better barrier for basement windows is a wire-mesh grate covering the opening.

For inexpensive security, use No. 8 or No. 10 steel wire, welded into a ½-inch round frame. These wire guards are available with various types of burglarproof hinges and closing fasteners from local ironworks.

Shutter-outers. Help secure your windows from the prying tools of housebreakers and the prying eyes of voyeurs by installing wooden, aluminum, or steel shutters on the outside or inside of your home's windows. Louvered shutters allow plenty of light and air while blocking vision.

Buy ready-made pairs of shutters at any lumberyard for about $15. Hang the window covers on pivot hinges attached to the house wall or window frame. A sturdy inside latch will keep shutters shut, and a flat steel bar placed across the inside in retainer brackets will provide additional security.

Glue for louvers. If you're stuck with louver or jalousie windows or doors, you can make the best of a sticky safety situation by applying a bit of paste to these burglars' delights. The most common method prowlers use to gain entry through a louver door is to slip one of the glass panels from its holder, reach inside, and unlock the door.

To keep your doorknob and valuables out of easy reach of housebreakers, glue the window slats into their holders. Epoxy glue will do the job permanently. Other synthetic glues will also be effective and will be easier to remove if a slat is broken and needs to be replaced.

Quick exit. Installing a rope ladder near all second-story bedroom windows makes sense from a fire-safety standpoint and from a personal-safety standpoint, too. If someone unknown is rattling your bedroom door, you'll want to have the ways and means to hit the ground running.

For about $20, Lafayette Radio Electronics (111 Jericho Turnpike, Syosset, N. Y. 11791) will send you a 15-foot chain ladder which can be kept tucked under your bed, ready to attach to your window sill in precious seconds. You'll have a backdoor to safety—which is one of *two* reasons you see so many rabbits around, still.

Plastic protection. A window made of high-strength plastic glazing looks just like ordinary glass, won't mar or scratch, and will resist breakage even when struck full force with a sledgehammer. Manufactured by General Electric under the trade name Lexan, the mar-resistant type costs about $5 per square foot (the ordinary type costs a few cents less) and is available through glass distributors everywhere.

Air conditioners. A poorly installed window air conditioner represents a double treat for the burglar. For if this equipment is screwed or bolted only to the outside of the house, he can not only remove it and haul it away, but in doing so create for himself a commodious opening to the inside of your home.

Make certain your window air conditioner is bolted securely to the interior of your house and that the window sash above it has been nailed or screwed tightly shut.

Chain-link fence. There's no need to go concentration camping in the backyard, but the alleyside of homes and businesses is best protected by a chain-link fence rimmed with barbed wire. Better than walls, hedges, or wood fences, the chainlink is tough to climb. Prices vary with the length of fencing needed. Check your Yellow Pages under "Fence" for sellers and installers.

A thorny issue. Hedges of such plants as barberry, American holly, and multiflora thorned rose can provide a natural barrier between you and a potential housebreaker. Although even tall thorned hedges are not impervious to a determined thief, they will usually discourage the amateur.

Individual plants of multiflora rose planted a foot or two apart will eventually interweave themselves, providing an imposing as well as a decorative barrier. These can be purchased at any nursery for just a few dollars per plant.

ALARMS

Chain lock alarm. This low-cost ($6) battery-operated security device is an effective way to guard against intruders stepping through your doors while you're out working in the yard, next door drinking coffee, or busy in the basement. Available at Radio Shack stores, the Chain Lock Alarm attaches to your door by a couple of screws, much as does a simple chain guard. But if someone attempts to force his way in or to tamper with the chain while the lock is "on," the alarm blurts a warning cry you can hear blocks away! Re-entering your home is easy: Simply open the door slightly, then insert a key in the casing and free the latch.

Protect-it-yourself. Build-it-yourself radio kits have long been the calling card of Heathkit Electronic Centers, but the company is now helping those with a knack for tinkering stay safe, too. The firm offers two books covering construction, installation, and maintenance of virtually every electronic fire and the theft alarm and security system for home and auto. Get the lowdown on how to stop thieves with your own ultimate alarm system by ordering "Building and Installing Elec-

21

tronic Intrusion Alarms" or "Installing and Servicing Electronic Protective Systems" from the Heathkit Electronic Center near you (or the New York City center at 35 West 45th Street, New York, N.Y. 10036). Each costs slightly less than $6.

Flash alarm. The Flashguard Security System is a wireless burglar-alarm setup that works on the same principle as your Instamatic flashcube. Units on doors and windows project a brilliant flash if a prowler tampers with the openings. A light-sensitive cell in the control center picks up the flash and sets off the alarm. Advantages, aside from the wireless feature, include the combination of light and sound to startle intruders. You can get a kit to protect twelve openings for about $450. For a catalog of Flashguard burglar-proofing products, write Flashguard, Inc., 927 Pennsylvania Avenue, Pittsburgh, Pennsylvania 15233.

Modular alarms. A screwdriver and a knife are tools enough to design and install your own burglar-alarm system to fit your home. An installation handbook comes along with your system, and you save money by buying only the parts you need—lengths of wiring, door and window contact switches, alarm bells, and control center. Usually an alarm system can be set up for about $50.

Do-it-yourself warning systems are available from Eico Electronic Instrument Co., Inc., 283 Malta Street, Brooklyn, N.Y. 11207, and from On Guard Corporation of America, Carlstadt, N.J. 07072.

Alarming burglaries. Flip the switch on your $500 burglar alarm system, jump in your station wagon, and you're ready to roll out the driveway and drive away to vacationland . . . right? Well, maybe not.

Unless you've made special arrangements with the neighbors, your burglar alarm could backfire. Housebreakers have been known to go swiftly about their thieving business in a house whose alarm was apparently accidentally triggered, and continues to ring for hours on end. Such alarms advertise the fact that no one's home and no one cares.

Be sure to leave a house key with a neighbor, along with instructions on how to turn off and reset your alarm system.

Bleepers. Let your neighbors know if a creep creeps into your home uninvited! If you live alone, especially in an apartment, and are jittery about prowlers, make friends with your next-door neighbor and then establish an elementary buzzer-bleeper-bell communications system to enlist neighborly aid in emergency situations. Ask your friend whether he prefers a window-to-window or a through-the-wall circuit for wires to your sender-receiver buzzer. Press the distress switch wired near your front door and in your bedroom to signal buzzers in their bedroom and kitchen. Summon help by a prearranged code: one bleep prowler; two bleeps—fire; three bleeps—you're really sick and need help fast.

Whistle stop. A singing doorstop? Yes, and it takes a burglar to name that tune. The Sunbeam Stop Alarm costs about $10, looks like an aerosol can with a rubber stopper, and can be screwed into any door. When the can and stopper are swung down, the stopper keeps the door from opening while the aerosol can emits a piercing whistle if an intruder presses on the door. The can has 40 seconds' worth of whistle, but stops when pressure on the door is released. The Sunbeam Appliance Service Company, 5600 Roosevelt Road, Chicago, Ill. 60650, can tell you more.

Inside-out switch. Candlepower is a good crook deterrent. By now you've no doubt installed outdoor floodlights at entrances, walkways, and driveways. An additional safeguard is an indoor switch—preferably in your bedroom—to unleash your outdoor watt-power.

Hardware stores carry the cable and electric switches you'll need for the hookup, or have a qualified electrician do the job (his bill should be under $100).

Foil foiler. Many businesses border their windows with the electricity-conducting tape sold for a couple bucks a roll at any hardware or electronics shop. A burglar breaking the glass also breaks the tape, which in turn turns on the alarm. While fussy homeowners may find the dull-looking gray tape unappealing for front windows, such favorite points of entry as back and basement windows can well afford the security.

The flexswitch. One type of switch for setting off burglar bells is so unusual and versatile we feel it deserves special mention. Flexswitch, a product of Tapeswitch Corporation of America, is a ribbonlike flexible switch. Merely bending it throws the switch that blows the siren.

Mounted in draperies covering sliding doors, the Flexswitch will uncover anyone ruffling the curtains on his way in. Properly installed, it'll catch housebreakers moving an oil painting, opening a basement window, throwing loot on a bed, opening a dresser drawer, taking a break by sitting in a rigged chair, moving a safe, or even turning a doorknob. Your local security consultant will tell you how to purchase and install Flexswitch.

Pull-trap alarms. Gates, driveways, and garage or house doors are well guarded with a pull-trap burglar alarm available from the Alarm Device Manufacturing Company, 165 Eileen Way, Syosset, L. I., N. Y. 11791. The unsuspecting intruder trips a thin wire stretched across an entrance or attached to a door. This yanks an insulating slab from between two electrical conductors, electricity zings through the circuit, and a piercing screech escapes the open end of a burglar siren.

Panic button. You're scared and you know it. There's no one to hear you scream. Quick, punch the panic button.

The button and wire leading from it you got for small change at an electric-parts store. The inside and outside siren setups on the end of the wires were in the same store for less than $20 total. Maybe you've hooked floodlights and an automatic police dialer to your personal crisis system. But be sure there's real trouble before you flick the switch; don't cry wolf unless you're pretty sure one is there.

Candid camera. In a suburb of San Francisco, a group of 150 homeowners have banded together to form a protective "network." Each home is equipped with a hidden camera and a decal which warns callers that if they knock or ring the doorbell, their picture will be taken automatically and sent to the police. Many people approach the door, read the sign, and walk away, says one user.

If you live in a medium- or high-crime area, you'd be wise to form such a network with your neighbors.

Magnetic alarm. A good cheap portable alarm to protect doors and windows is the Magna-Sentry, made by Hydrometals, Inc., which uses principles of magnetism to detect prowlers. Local security-equipment distributors stock or can order the units.

The battery-powered alarm box adheres to the wall near the opening you're trying to protect. A switch is mounted on the window jamb and a magnet on the window frame. Opening the window separates the two and unleashes a blast heard throughout the house. With each unit comes a smoke detector, to protect you from fire as well as burglars.

A dilemma horn. "Concerned neighbors, may I have your attention please. There are a number of burglarlike noises coming from 418 Ferguson Street and the owner, now speaking to you, is getting kind of worried." This and more frantic distress messages will carry loud and clear the length of a football field if you keep an electronic bullhorn handy. Battery-operated ones are available at any radio-electronics store for under $20. Keep them in your bedroom or carry them on the streets—they're hand-held.

Battery blaster. One of the best portable burglar alarms on the market is a battery-operated model called the Burglar Lock Alarm. These cost only $5 apiece; however, a separate one is required for each window or door requiring protection.

Radar rebuff. One of the most sophisticated alarm systems available for residential use is the Pinkerton Radar Eye Minuteman. This unit utilizes a circular radar beam. When an intruder breaks the beam, the alarm is activated. The system is designed for optional hookup to a local police station.

This system is expensive, costing upwards of $700, depending on the size of the area needing protection.

Door alarm. The P-S-C Apartment Alarm effectively guards against an intruder attempting to gain entry in any way involving a door or its lock. Easy to install, this unit fits over the top of the door and contains an inside and outside part. The alarm may be armed or disarmed from either side of the door. The device operates on one penlite battery and costs $100.

Remote possibility. The Intruder Chaser is a unique remote-controlled alarm, designed specifically to frighten off someone who breaks into your house while you're home. When you push a button on the small, cigarette-pack-sized box, which you can carry with you about the house, a buzzer sounds which can be heard a mile away.

This $150 system can also be set up to work automatically in protecting windows and doors, or it can be made to turn on all the house lights when an intruder enters your home.

Kits. There are several burglar-alarm kits on the market, most of which can be installed by a reasonably handy individual in one day. The On-Guard kit, at $60, is one of the better buys. It includes a large bell mounted in a tamperproof steel box, four sets of magnetic switches, a panic button, and the necessary wire and mounting hardware.

The kit is manufactured by the On-Guard Corporation of America, 350 Gotham Parkway, Carlstadt, N. J. 07072.

Ultrasonic-alarms. For under $300, you can purchase a superior home alarm system that utilizes the latest techniques in ultrasonic sound or radar (both types are available).

25

Alarms utilizing ultrasonic sound send out a pattern of sound waves which are not detectable by the human ear. When this pattern is disturbed by any foreign sound, the alarm is activated. Radar units emit ultrahigh-frequency radio waves, which trigger the alarm when they bounce off a moving object.

Called the Spaceguard Alarm System, the unit is designed for easy do-it-yourself installation. Also, you can purchase a special attachment which will automatically notify the police when an intruder enters your home.

Electric eye. Some types of home alarms utilize a photoelectric cell in conjunction with a beam of light. When the beam is broken, the alarm is tripped. The main disadvantage to this type is that in a dark room the beam can easily be seen by the burglar. He can then walk over it, crawl under it, or go around it.

Three such types are the Photo Electric Relay Burglar Alarm System, the Lafayette Photo Electric Relay Burglar Alarm System, and the Inventronic Eye Safety Alarm. All retail at under $50 per unit. Each unit will protect one window or door.

Invisible beam. A significant improvement over the electric eye with visible beam is the type that utilizes an invisible infrared beam. Cost of equipment and installation of such systems ranges upward from $500, depending on the size and layout of the area requiring protection. Two manufacturers are Ademco (Alarm Device Manufacturing Company), 165 Eileen Way, Syosset, L. I., N. Y. 11791 and Advanced Devices Laboratory, Inc., 848A Stewart Drive, Sunnyvale, Calif. 94086.

Infrared detectors. Less expensive nonpermanent invisible-beam devices are also available. These are small and inconspicuous and can be plugged into any electrical outlet.

Priced at $150, these are manufactured by Optical Controls, Inc., of Burlington, Mass., and by Alarmatronics Engineering, Inc., of Newton, Mass. The latter firm also manufactures a battery-powered type called the Mini-Sentry.

The central-station alarm. The type of alarm known as the central-station system is the most professional for residential use. Upon being triggered, these alarms alert personnel stationed at the alarm company's central office. The company responds by alerting police as well as by dispatching their own security officers to the scene. At the residence, the alarm can be wired for either sound or silence.

Prices, with installation, can run up to $1,000, plus a monthly service charge of $30–$50, depending on the type of system desired. Companies which sell and/or lease and service such systems are: Wells Fargo Alarm Services; Burns International Security Services, Inc., and ADT (American District Telegraph Company) Security Systems. ADT is the leader in the field. Consult your local Yellow Pages under "Burglar Alarms" for locations of local offices.

Window watchman. The Alarmco Watchman is plugged into an electrical wall outlet and wired to a door or window and emits a loud buzzing noise. These cost only $12, but each unit will protect only one window or door.

Dial wiles. A number of alarm systems which utilize the telephone to summon aid (some sound sirens simultaneously) could be lifesavers if you can afford the price—$500 to $700. The major drawback of these systems is that a false alarm brings the police charging to the scene as readily as does a prowler wedging a window, and the cops, understandably annoyed, may be slower to respond in a real emergency.

The phone system with the best record for not turning in false alarms is the Telemergency Automatic Telephone Dialer, DC-98, produced by Scan Security Systems Inc., 310 Willis Avenue, Mineola, L.I., N. Y. 11501. When tripped, the system dials a nearby police station, giving the location and a request for aid.

Switch tips. There are at least as many different types of electrical switches, or sensing devices, as there are alarm systems. The traditional wired alarm consists of strips of foil wiring along a window. If the window is opened or broken, the foil is severed, triggering the alarm. A contact mat is available which can be placed under your carpeting at strategic points. Any pressure on the mat will set off the alarm. Screen contacts can be purchased which are sensitive to the prying off of a window screen. Similar contact switches are available for windows and doors. An inexpensive hand switch for the bedside will, with the push of a button, set off an exterior alarm. Most of these devices can be purchased for under $10.

PROTECTING YOUR VALUABLES

Don't be a show-off. You may be extremely proud of that $250,000 Rembrandt hanging in your study, but for heavens' sake don't point it out to the TV repairman, the plumber, or the grocery delivery boy. And that goes for expensive furniture, jewelry, clothing, or any other possessions that could mark your house as a burglary target.

Even if those you show off to are honest, they may innocently pass on the information to others.

Security closet. A well-built security closet in your home will serve several purposes. With a sturdy door, door frame, and lock, it will provide an additional obstacle between a thief and such items as furs, cameras, and valuable papers. The compartment can also serve as a place to keep potentially dangerous items—drugs and guns—well away from youngsters. If lined with fire-retardant materials, the area will protect your valuables in case of fire.

To obtain free plans for the building of a security closet, write Schlage Lock Company, 2401 Bayshore Boulevard, San Francisco, Calif., 94134.

Home safe. It's possible to buy and install a secure safe in your home for as little as $35. Your best buy here is a shelf safe, which, for maximum protection, should be bolted to the wall, then camouflaged. However, you must be sure that the safe you buy is fire-resistant as well as thief-resistant. Be sure the safe has at least a Class C Underwriters Laboratories rating. This means that the contents are protected for at least one hour against an average temperature of 1700°F. See your Yellow Pages under "Safes and Vaults—Dealers."

Count your blessings. Thousands of dollars' worth of stolen personal possessions could be returned to their rightful owners each year if police could be provided with positive identification of guns, cameras, watches, and other valuables.

Before another day goes by, take inventory of all your valuable possessions, noting make, description, and serial number. Make a duplicate list. Keep one copy at home, the other in your safe-deposit box.

Outta sight! That fine stereo set you recently purchased may be a joy to listen to and a source of pride when you show it to friends, but don't leave it visible through a window when you leave the house. Throw an old blanket over it if necessary, but get it out of sight.

The same goes for sterling-silver dinnerware, jewelry, expensive clothing, musical instruments, firearms, and other tempting items.

Bank it. As unbelievable as it sounds, hundreds of thousands of dollars are lost each year by skeptical souls who, perhaps remembering the crash of 1929, just don't trust the United States banking system. Money is secreted in mattresses, hidden in closets, drains, and garages, and buried in the ground—deposited anywhere but in the bank.

Today, the Federal Deposit Insurance Corporation (FDIC) insures all accounts to $40,000. Therefore, a United States bank is the safest place to keep your money.

Store those valuables! You'd be surprised to discover how many people go on vacation leaving diamond rings, gold necklaces, mink coats, and other valuable items in the home. And how many return to find them gone!

It takes but an hour to collect your valuables and take them down to a safe-deposit box at the bank. And it's surprisingly inexpensive ($20 yearly—in-and-out privileges included) to store a mink coat at a fur-storage firm. Why take chances?

Fur protection. The crook who cops your fur coat will clip labels and linings immediately, thus making it extremely difficult to identify your precious pelts. So that you can identify your fur if it is stolen and recovered, mark the insides of the skins in several places with your initials or social security number.

Invisible I.D. It would take the Bionic Burglar to see your driver's license number marked on your camera or other valuables by a Brink's Security Marker. The identification is invisible in ordinary light, but shows up under the ultraviolet light used by law-enforcement agencies to track stolen goods back to their owners. The pen writes on any surface and comes with window warning stickers and a marking guide.

To protect your prized possessions without marring them with engraving tools, send for the Brink's invisible marker to Montgomery House, Inc., 7614 Carriage Lane, Cincinnati, Ohio 45242. It sells for $2.75.

Crooks cook, too. Be warned—the ranks of the "good help" nobody can get any more are sprinkled with swindlers and underworld tipsters. Of course, you'll conduct elaborate reference checks before hiring such help—enlisting a reputable investigating agency that will make retail-credit checks and ferret out police records in hometowns listed by applicants—but don't forget to check members of their immediate families, too! A maid whose husband sports several burglary convictions or a babysitter whose boyfriend traffics in drugs are better off off your payroll. Checking friends and family before hiring trusted household help will keep your person and property out of jeopardy.

Polygraph tests. Not everybody can afford to hire a housekeeper or other domestic servant, but those who can will no doubt have valuable property worth protecting by investing $40 in lie-detector tests for household help before hiring them. Check "Lie Detectors" in the Yellow Pages for lists of qualified polygraph testers.

You'll need to talk with the person giving the test so he can devise an adequate examination. Discounts are available for giving the same quiz to more than one potential employee. While not foolproof, the polygraph tends to scare off crooks. It's also a strong deterrent to those who pass the test but know they'll be reexamined if they are employed and something turns up missing.

Photograph your valuables. An excellent way to obtain positive identification of your valuables is to take color snapshots of them. Photos of mink coats, diamond rings and necklaces, precious china, valuable antiques, and expensive power tools can help the police immensely in identifying and recovering these goods.

Property form. Police departments throughout the country strongly advise citizens to keep a record of the serial numbers of their autos, bicycles, cameras, and other valuables. The Los Angeles Police Department has published a special form entitled *Valuable Property Record* on which you can keep track of such information. It's free, and available through their Public Affairs Division, 150 North Los Angeles Street, Los Angeles, Calif. 90012.

Your own police force. So you've taken all our advice about security bars, locks and bolts, leaving lights and radios on, notifying neighbors and police—and you're still worried about someone breaking into your home while you're lying on the beach.

Retain a private security agency to guard your premises for you. You can hire patrols either to stand guard outside your home on a part- or full-time basis, or to include your home on their regular rounds. These services cost $20 per week and up, depending on the degree of security desired.

Engrave your goods. An excellent way to provide positive identification for your personal possessions is to engrave them with your name and address. If lost, or recovered by the police after a burglary, they can be returned to you.

An inexpensive electric engraver can be purchased at hardware stores and electronics-supply outlets for under $10.

Computers vs. culprits. Find out if your local police department sponsors a computer identification program. If so, use it. Under this program, you mark your valuable goods with your driver's license number, then file your name, address, and phone number with the police. The information is fed into a computer. Should your stolen goods be recovered, they'll be returned to you.

In addition, you'll be issued decals by the police, to be posted on the doors and windows of your home. These announce to the potential burglar that, as a participant in this program, your goods are marked —an effective deterrent to all but the least cautious burglars.

HIDING PLACES

Closet trick. Who would ever suspect that those small wooden blocks supporting the clothes-hanging pole in your closet are hollow and contain secret treasure? Either hollow out existing blocks or simply install one underneath each end of the pole to look as if they're being used as supports.

Spice-rack back. Before the refinement of modern customs inspection methods, the false-bottomed suitcase was a favorite of smugglers the world over. In our variation, using a few scraps of wood and a few simple tools, you add a false back to your spice rack.

Nail strips of pre-grooved frame onto the back of the spice rack. Slide a piece of plywood paneling into the grooves, and you have a secret receptacle for jewels, stocks and bonds, or those $100 bills you're planning to sock away.

Outlet input. We hope this idea won't be a shocker for you. It involves building a little cubbyhole behind an electrical switch or outlet.

First cut the electricity by throwing the master switch or pulling the necessary fuse. Then simply unscrew the switch or outlet cover plate, wedge or otherwise secure a small wooden shelf behind the wall, and replace the plate. Instant safe deposit!

Baseboard bluff. One of the least obvious places to hide small valuables is behind a baseboard.

First find a short length that looks as though it might be easily removed. Gently pry it away from the wall. You may find a ready-made hiding place just waiting for you. If not, chisel out a small cubbyhole in the wood or plasterboard wall, making sure that your hiding place will be completely covered by the baseboard when re-placed. Then insert your valuables, replace the baseboard, and you're in business.

Cold cash. If you've just made a large bank withdrawal and are going out for the evening, you're probably in a quandry as to whether to keep all that loot in your pocket or stash it at home. After all, either is risky.

Our advice? Slip it into a half-empty package of frozen vegetables in your freezer. Or, if you don't mind the mess, plunge the wad into the middle of a jar full of mayonnaise, mustard, or peanut butter.

Hollow beams. A small compartment in a wooden ceiling beam can be easily constructed by chiseling out an area in an out-of-the-way place, then covering it with a wooden panel stained to the same color as the beam. If you don't have wood beams already, you can purchase the big lightweight foam variety from any building-supply outlet for $2 per foot. These are painted and scarred so realistically that your burglar would practically have to get up on a stepladder and examine them closely in order to determine that they're not the real thing.

Hat-rack camouflage. A wooden hat rack or coat rack can serve as a convincing variation on the old safe-behind-the-portrait ploy. Chisel out a hole in your wall small enough to be covered by your hat or coat rack, using a fire block (the horizontal member between studs) as a shelf if available. Next, insert false screws into the rack, with the heads visible. Then simply hang in place. Double-sided tape will help hold the rack firmly against the wall.

Stair stash. Stairs offer a superb opportunity for the creation of hiding places for medium-sized objects. Simply pry loose one of the kickboards, install a shelf and sides, stash your goods, then replace the kickboard. Naturally, if your stairs are carpeted, you must cut and refasten the carpeting so that the hiding place is not obvious.

False pipe. You've seen those weird-looking pipes that rise up out of a floor, double back in a half-circle, then abruptly stop for no apparent reason.

Buy a piece of such pipe at your local plumbing shop or hardware store. Then chisel out a hole in your floor to barely accommodate the straight end, stash your goodies in the curved end, and cap it. Then simply insert the pipe in its hole.

False-bottomed cages. A burglar is not apt to suspect that your parrot or hamster lives over a vault. Some cages have a slide-out tray for litter, and you can simply put money or papers under the tray. Or construct your own cage with a false floor. If you keep snakes or tarantulas—and both make entertaining pets—so much the better.

LIGHTS

Bright idea. If the electrical power to your home is cut—whether by a burglar or because of a storm—you'll want to be equipped with an auxiliary lighting system. These are battery-operated lights which are normally kept plugged into an electrical outlet. The battery is kept charged by the house current. When power is cut off, the device automatically switches on the light, using battery power.

Check your Yellow Pages for distributors under "Lighting Equipment—Emergency." If such lights are unavailable in your area, write to Lightalarms Electronic Corporation, 288 Scholes Street, Brooklyn, N. Y. 11206. This firm manufactures and sells the lights for $75 and up, depending on the wattage desired.

Floodlights. Next to noise, the burglar's biggest enemy is light. If your street is well lit, chances are a burglar will attempt to enter your home through a side or rear window or door. If these areas are also well lit, there's a good chance he'll go elsewhere.

If you're not handy with electrical wiring, get an electrician or handyman to do the job. Even at the going rate of about $100, it will be money well spent.

Street lamps. If given a choice, a housebreaker will always choose a darkened street over a well-lit one.

If any street lamps are out on your block, report them to the appropriate city agency. If there aren't enough lights, get together with your neighbors and petition the city to erect more or to put high-intensity elements in the existing ones. After all, you pay for these in your taxes. Why not have them?

Master switches. One of the smartest security moves you can make is to have a master light switch for your entire property installed on your bedroom wall close to your bed. Should you hear a noise outside your bedroom window or in another part of your house during the night, a flick of the switch will envelop an intruder with one of his most hated enemies, light, and more than likely send him scurrying off into the darkness.

Electrically, this is a big job. You'll pay an electrician several hundred dollars for the work, but the peace of mind and resultant increased security may be well worth it to you.

Night lights. You don't need anti-aircraft searchlights, and you don't need floodlamps suitable for shooting home movies at midnight. But you *do* need some illumination—around doors and walkways, garages and alleys—to keep you and your family reasonably safe from lurking prowlers.

How much light is enough light? Here's a time-tested answer: Look at your watch. If you can't easily read your watch after dark, or if you have any doubts, add more lighting.

Television lights. Maybe you're one of 100 million Americans who never miss prime time except for funerals which can't be otherwise arranged. Burglars often count on you being riveted to the screen while they make a silent sweep through the rest of the house. Don't get caught watching a cop show while some real-life crook cops your valuables. Leave lights on in scattered rooms other than the television room, and take an occasional stretch during commercials to check other parts of your house.

Porch lights. You probably leave the porch light on when you step out at night. Of course that's okay, but leave that telltale bulb burning while you're home, too. To the burglar studying your home, a porch light which shines only now and then means the coast is clear, the house unattended. Paying your utility company for a few extra watts will be a bright move on your part.

Interior lights. Don't leave the front-room lights on all night when you're away. To the night prowler, it will be clear that you're not home. We're sure you'd pull the front-room drapes, but even a slight crack in the curtains lets outsiders know where the insiders aren't. Hours without shadows on your shades say the same thing.

Alternate which lights you keep turned on during your absences. Go outside at night and check where you can see in your home, then make drapery adjustments to keep roving eyes in the dark.

IN CASE OF CASING

Telephone tricks. The telephone is one of the burglar's most valuable tools. Posing as a survey taker, police official, or utility-company representative, he'll attempt to gain information on where you work, your hours, the location of your bank, and when you're planning your next vacation. These brazen birds have even been known to ask how much money you've saved and inquire about your sex habits! Don't ever give out information like this to a total stranger.

Phone-answering giveaways. Much of our advice on avoiding potential trouble deals with giving out as little information as possible to strangers. Unfortunately, your phone-answering device doesn't distinguish between friends and strangers. If you have an automatic phone-answering device, *don't* divulge the time you expect to return. A determined burglar just might decide to ransack your home or office before you get back. Rather, vaguely state that you'll "be back shortly." This will plug yet another leak in your personal security system.

Obituary giveaways. The obituary column is a veritable storehouse of information for the alert thief. In the past, whole burglary rings have been uncovered which systematically prey on the homes of individuals while they are attending the funeral of a deceased family member.

Protect yourself against this most despicable type of thievery by asking a friend or neighbor to guard your home on such an occasion.

Note giveaways. Occasionally, you may feel the need to tack up a note on the outside of your front door for a deliveryman or friend when going out. Don't. It's a dead giveaway to a burglar that you're not home.

Plan your time. Call that deliveryman or friend on the telephone the day before, and give him the message personally.

Don't be lured. A popular tactic to lure you away from home involves the theft of your purse, wallet, or attaché case while you're out in public. Later, when the thief suspects you're home alone, he calls and arranges to meet you in some public place for return of the item.

You guessed it! After you leave your home, he enters and helps himself to your belongings.

In such a circumstance, have a trusted friend or relative occupy your residence during your absence.

Air-conditioner giveaways. What does an air conditioner have to do with a burglary, you ask? Lots! If you were looking for a house to break into on a sultry summer afternoon, you'd simply listen for a turned-off air conditioner. Nine chances out of ten the owners are out.

It'll cost you more in utility bills to leave your air conditioner running when you leave the house on a hot day, but it's good burglary insurance. If you turn it to circulate only without cooling, it will use considerably less power but make just as much noise.

Golfer's goof. Loading your golfbags in the trunk and driving away can signal the alert housebreaker to strike while the seven-iron is hot. Similarly, your bowling bag tips the intruder that he's got time to spare to strike. If you golf often, avoid revealing your plans to potential prowlers by keeping your clubs in the trunk, loading them in your garage out of a burglar's sight, or loading them in the early morning for an afternoon golf date.

Wedding-bell giveaways. Newlyweds may start off on an unhappy note if a burglar is lifting the gifts while the groom's at church lifting the veil. Wedding announcements in the paper, wedding banns listed at church, or just the sight of a wedding-gowned woman rustling into a church-bound car can tip a burglar to a house that will be empty for an hour or two. Caterers, jewelers, or florists' helpers may also be tipping housebreakers to where they can get loot and a piece of wedding cake.

If there's a wedding in the family, always have a trusted neighbor watch your house during the ceremony, or hire a housesitter. Otherwise you may return to find it all gone but the gown.

Hot-time crime. Fire trucks screeching into your neighborhood to douse a blaze sound a nearly irresistible note to residents. The burglary-minded know that many people will foolishly leave their doors unlocked while they're off seeing what can be seen at the scene.

Before you run out to watch a fire, a car wreck, or other sudden street happening, remember to lock all doors and windows. Apartment dwellers need to be extra-cautious—looters have been known to set fires, pull the alarm, then check for unlocked doors after the building is evacuated.

The flyer track. The house burglar has modified for high-rises, housing projects, and apartment complexes one of his favorite methods of casing single-family dwellings. A burglary team enters one of these multi-family buildings under the guise of passing out advertising flyers, political propaganda, or religious pamphlets. They shove such sheets halfway under every door and return in a few hours to see if the papers are removed. If they are still there, chances are you won't be home, and chances are you will be a burglary victim. The best way to foil the prowler is to strike an agreement with neighbors—anyone seeing anything stuck on or under another's door will kick or flick it all the way inside. Also, lobby your manager to nip flyer-flingers at the main door.

Reference requests. A common casing maneuver used by professional prowlers to spot easy marks is to telephone seeking a reference. They'll call your friends, relatives, or business associates saying you listed them as references and asking questions that might tip them off as to your financial situation, whether you're living alone, and even what hours you are at work. Some such crooks work for employment agencies or personnel departments and misuse their access to your résumé.

To plug this personal-data leak, tell anyone whose name you use as a reference to withhold the information until they've checked with you first. Have them get the firm name, address, and phone number of any person making the inquiry. Call them yourself for verification, checking with police authorities if necessary. Then, if all seems legitimate, call your reference back and instruct him to supply the requested information.

Blame the names. The plaque at your gatepost proclaiming "John Doughboy and Family Dwell Herein" may fill you with pride, but a name on your mailbox could mean a burglar's foot in your door. Housebreakers simply take the name to the nearest phone booth, look it up, and call your phone number, and if no one answers, they do their deed. Even if your phone number is unlisted, a clever con man can use your name as a takeoff point to talk his way in.

Solution: Don't spread your good name around.

Police-call caution. Impersonating a police officer is a crime. It's also a simple technique used to con even the most crime-conscious citizen into volunteering enough information to make housebreaking safe, fun, and profitable to the prowler turned police impostor.

Drop the curtain on this act by asking a telephoner claiming to be a law-enforcement officer to visit you in person so you can check his credentials (unless subpoenaed by a court, you're not required to give out *any* information). Or say, "I can't talk now. Can I call you back?"

Then check the phone directory against the number the supposed police investigator gave you. If it differs, call the directory number and see if your caller works for the police. If not, give the *real* police full details.

Play it safe and use this directory double-check on other telephone solicitors, too.

Car giveaways. Never leave mail, your car registration, old magazines with subscription seals, or anything else bearing your address lying visible and unprotected in your car—*especially* for several hours at a time.

As many as one in ten house burglaries, police estimate, start when a thief runs across such identification. He checks to see if anyone's home at your house, then cleans you out and rips off your car to boot.

Skip tracers. Burglars and confidence schemers often borrow a trick from collection agencies called "skip tracers" to lure you into revealing potentially damaging information about yourself, your business, or your personal affairs. You'll get a letter saying the sender is holding a prepaid package for you which can't be delivered because of error or change of address. There may be no package or one of insignificant value. To get this package, you must print on a "shipping tag" your phone number and address, bank, major credit cards, and working hours. Don't hand burglars these vital statistics! Report skip-tracing attempts to the Postal Service and/or Federal Trade Commission.

Fair snare. The carnival comes to town and everybody shuffles down to the fairgrounds. Caught up in this hoopla spirit, you may be tempted to enter the drawing for a mini-bike, ring, or camera. You may have to pay a nickel per ticket and leave your name, address, and phone number if you won't be there for the drawing. Of course you'll lose your nickels, but that's small change. Your big crunch comes when one of the traveling carnival workers uses your personal information to burglarize your house or work some other con on you or family members. Stay out of lotteries where you must give strangers valuable information. It's too chancy!

CHAPTER 2

In public:
hang onto your hat
(and everything else)

Outside the home, whether on the street, in a public building, or at a private party, the average citizen is confronted with a preponderance of potentially hazardous situations. Muggers, holdup men, pickpockets and pursesnatchers, homosexuals, pimps and prostitutes, and even riots all are potential dangers.

Serious, violent crime in this country's streets and public places was skyrocketing—having risen nearly 40 percent in the first six years of the 1970s. Then, when 1976 FBI crime statistics came in, officials gazed at some startling results. First the good news: Violent crime had dropped by almost 5 percent. Now the bad news: In spite of "lower" totals, every hour of 1976 saw an average of more than 50 aggravated assaults and a like number of robberies. Almost half of the year's nearly 500,000 robbery victims surrendered their cash (totaling about $154 million) at gunpoint! Former Attorney General Edward H. Levi best summed up the hazards of being out and about in public today, saying, "While it's gratifying that violent crimes as a group continue to show an absolute decrease, the basic fact we mustn't forget is that street crime still remains an urgent national problem."

Overshadowing all the tips we give you in this chapter is the crucial advice to think in terms of protecting your life, not your money, when coming face-to-face with a mugger or holdup man. It's counsel we hope you'll never need to use, but the very first thing to say to the crook who has you cornered is, "Tell me what you want. I'll give it to you!" Then let him walk away with your money, your jewelry, your clothes—and be thankful you can walk away, period.

Of course the trick to making your way safely through the streets is to avoid situations where you're an easy victim for roving robbers. Getting "street-wise" is what this chapter is all about. Pickpockets and pursesnatchers, two of the most common street criminals in the city, are given special attention.

Since your survival on the streets may sometime come down to how well you can fight for your life, we suggest you also read the self-defense selections in Chapter 5. Vacationers and traveling salesmen, among others, will also benefit from related ideas in Chapter 9, which details the dangers involved in venturing into the streets of foreign countries.

FOR FURTHER INFORMATION:

Being Safe. Mel Mandel. New York: Saturday Review Press, 1972.

Book of Survival, The. Anthony Greenback. New York: Harper & Row, 1967.

Crime Free. Albert Lee. Baltimore: Penguin, 1974.

How to Protect Yourself on the Streets and in Your Home. Gene Accas and John H. Eckstein. New York: Pocket Books, 1965.

How to Protect Yourself Today. Robert A. Hair and Samm S. Baker. New York: Stein and Day, 1970.

Survival in the City. Gene Accas and John H. Eckstein. New York: Ideal Consultants, 1964.

Survival in the City. Anthony Greenback. New York: Harper & Row, 1974.

Your Money or Your Life. Nora Stirling. New York: Bobbs-Merrill, 1974.

PICKPOCKETS AND PURSESNATCHERS

World's loudest purse. The Radar-Alarm was designed specifically with the pursesnatcher in mind. Powered by two penlight batteries, this cigarette-pack-sized unit serves both as an alarm and as a flashlight. Attached to the device is a looped cord which goes around the wrist. The alarm itself is inserted in the closed purse. With the pursesnatcher's first tug, an alarm is set off which can be heard blocks away. Costs $5.

Handbag howler. The Tucci-Cantalupi Alarm System is a big name for a small (cigarette-pack-sized) pursesnatcher catcher developed by two New York businessmen. The gadget sells for under $20. It is hooked to a purse and buzzes loudly if the purse is opened without the owner's consent. The device is being marketed through Sears, Roebuck. Investing in one could keep your possessions from a pickpurse's prying fingers.

Secret pocket. A woman friend of ours never carries folding money in her purse. Instead, she has ingeniously sewn a small zippered pouch on the inside of each of her outfits and it is here that she secrets her cash.

On skirts and slacks she has access to the pocket through the inside of the garment's waistband. On dresses, the pocket is accessible through a covered slit, just large enough for the hand.

The price-tag ploy. Two women will work as a team in a fashionable ladies' department store. One will distract you by asking you to read a price tag for her, then engage you in small talk, while her accomplice will rapidly make the dip into your purse.

You should train yourself to be alert whenever anyone engages you in conversation anywhere in public, being especially aware of others standing near you.

The easy catch. The "easy catch" is the name given to a type of purse, as well as to a method of pickpocketing. If you're a woman, you're probably familiar with the traditional style of handbag which depends upon one small catch in order to keep it closed. Often this catch will weaken with age, allowing the bag to spring open at the slightest provocation. In fact, one often sees women on the street with purses yawning dangerously open, the clasp having sprung apart.

You'll do well to examine all your handbags, replacing clasps on those which have become weakened with use.

Subway snatcher. Never stand close to the edge of a subway platform. Pursesnatchers have been known to reach a hand out of a train window and grab a purse as the train is leaving the station. They then quickly extract any cash found inside and get off at the next stop, disappearing into the crowd.

The seat tipper. This brazen bird preys on the woman who foolishly leaves her handbag on an empty seat next to her at a movie theater. When the plot gets heavy, the tipper reaches down to the rear of the seat containing the purse and pushes down. This will tilt the seat up, providing just enough space for him to slip his other hand in and pull the handbag through.

Outwit this character by keeping your purse on your lap at all times while at the movies.

The bus-stop trick. One of the most fertile places at which pickpockets can work is a crowded bus stop. Here one of a pair, "the stall," will step on the bus just in front of the victim. Then he'll cause some kind of commotion—he'll drop his fare or have an altercation with the bus driver. With the victim's attention so diverted, and his anxiousness to get aboard the bus at a peak, he's now easy prey for the other pickpocket, "the hook," who can now, unobserved, make his dip from behind.

Public toilets. We can offer you a few valuable tips on how not to get pursesnatched while you're in a most vulnerable position.

Keep your purse on your lap at all times. If you put it on a hook near the top of the door, the thief can stand on a toilet seat in the adjoining stall, reach over the partition, and grab it. Or if you place it on the floor, a thief can swiftly drag it out from under the door or partition.

The elevator trick. Here a team of three men will work together in an elevator to relieve the victim of his wallet. The stall will block the doorway while the second man, called the nudger, will rudely bump the victim in his apparent haste to get off the elevator. With the victim so distracted, the hook, who is stationed on the opposite side and to the rear of the victim, can almost effortlessly make his lift.

The sneezer. This fellow is perhaps the most skilled, as well as the most nervy, operator in all pickpocketdom. He'll attend an opera or ballet, enjoying the performance until the intermission, when his work will begin.

Standing directly in front of his intended victim, he'll pretend to sneeze, spraying mucus and spit all over the front of the poor man's jacket. As he apologizes profusely, one hand is busily wiping off the victim's jacket, while the other hand is hastily, but smoothly, lifting the wallet from the inside coat pocket.

The tote-bag dip. Because the open tote bag is such an easy mark, many neophyte pickpockets will get their first taste of success here. With or without the help of an accomplice, it's an easy matter for a thieving hand to quickly plunge into an open bag, grab a wallet, then beat a retreat.

For this reason, avoid carrying your valuables in any open container.

The flapper. This bird is almost as plentiful as the tote-bag dip. In addition to purses which are obviously open at the top, he'll watch for the type with a loose flap over the top. Actually, this type offers him more protection, as the large flap will hide the movements of his hand from the sight of others.

Make sure, flap or not, that your purse is well secured with a zipper, snaps, or other effective fastening device.

No wallet. Men should never carry cash in their wallets. In fact, one of your authors has never owned a wallet. He keeps his paper money folded up in a front pocket. In the other front pocket he carries a small leather container which holds credit cards, driver's license, etc.

Hip-pocket safeguard. If you must keep your cash in a billfold and feel most comfortable with it in your hip pocket, here's a neat trick. Buy a wallet which is a few inches longer than it is wide. Slip it into your pocket the long way, then turn it 90°. Now, anyone who attempts to pull the wallet out without turning it will have to tug wildly, immediately alerting you.

Dealing from the bottom. The pickpurse must necessarily work from the top down. Therefore, if you must keep a billfold full of currency in your handbag, make sure it is always placed on the very bottom of the purse.

If someone is going to grab something from your purse, far better that he get a comb, ball-point pen, or compact than your hard-earned cash.

Zipper tip. An idea offering even better protection than the foregoing is to carry a purse containing an inside zipper. Then keep your money there.

Obviously, if the pickpurse must first find, then unzipper a special compartment in order to get to your cash, he's very likely not even to bother.

The keyless purse. Never carry your keys in your purse. It's bad enough for a pursesnatcher to get your money and ID cards without getting your house keys as well. Keep these in a pocket of your clothing.

Homeward bound. If you're unfortunate enough to find both your keys and your identification missing, and if no one else is at home, rush home immediately. The crook may already be relieving you of your personal possessions. Naturally, you'll not want a confrontation, so ring your own doorbell before entering, thus giving him a chance to escape. Whether you catch a burglar in the act or not, be sure to call a locksmith and have all your lock cylinders changed.

Don't check. Although we've given you much practical advice in this section, we don't want you to become so paranoid that you develop the habit of feeling for your wallet every few minutes. Pickpockets have sharp eyes. And the man who continually pats his breast pocket or hip pocket might as well give a pickpocket a written invitation to go to work on him. If you're really worried, use the privacy of a phone booth or a men's-room stall to check for your wallet.

Jostling. In a hallway, ramp, or stairway where you're walking through a crowd, be ready to protect your wallet if you're shoved or jostled in any way. Put your hand on the opposite shoulder and press your arm hard against your chest. Refuse to be distracted and keep your arm in place while you move away from the disturbance. This will protect your wallet in an inner jacket pocket without indicating which pocket it is in. It also lets the pickpocket know you're on to his scheme.

Feeling fingers. Line your pockets with flypaper and you still won't catch many pickpockets. They're just too slick-fingered. But if you do feel fingers in your pocket or suspect that someone jostling you is also rifling your coat pockets, holler "What's the big idea?" Pickpockets are cowards and will either run or try an excuse, apology, or I-didn't-do-it look. Shout "Police! Pickpocket!" if your wallet's gone. Others around may find their billfolds missing, too, then help you catch and hold the thief for police.

Calf stash. Taking a tip from Miss Kitty, who was forever lifting her skirts to tuck a buck under her garters, security innovators in Atlanta are marketing a money belt which is strapped around the wearer's calf and hidden beneath his or her pants. Makers claim the Black Belt Protector can protect your wallet, keys, or what-have-you from pickpockets and muggers, and the device is so comfortable you won't know you're wearing it. For about $8 the shin strap is yours. For information, write Black Belt Protector, Suite 1517, William Oliver Building, 32 Peachtree Street, Atlanta, GA. 30303.

Chirp alert. In a bar, at a show, or in a subway crowd, be on guard the instant you hear a chirping, hissing, or faint whistling noise. All are common pickpocket's signals, so check your pockets immediately. Look around accusingly, even if your wallet is still there. Then, if possible (as in a bar or waiting crowd), move away from the area and be suspicious of anyone who drifts over to be near you again. The sounds are meant to draw your attention in one direction while a lifter's accomplice dips into your pockets from the other side.

Purse search. If your purse is snatched, search nearby shrubbery, alleys, trash cans, and public restrooms for it. Such places are favorite dumping grounds for the panicked pursesnatcher, who'll quickly lift all cash, credit cards, and other valuables, then drop the rest. Also call your local post office to find out if any billfolds have turned up in nearby mailboxes. Retrieving driver's licenses, voter registration cards, insurance cards, membership cards, and other identification cards will save you the expense and hassle of getting copies.

Keeping abreast of pickpockets. You can stuff your cash into a silk pouch that snaps onto your bra. The pouch dangles outside your bra and can be adjusted to double as a navel warmer. It's safety of a sort for $6 as Item 1033 in the Catalog of the Unusual from The Liberated Woman, 210 Fifth Avenue, New York, N. Y. 10010.

IN YOUR CAR

Car phones. While a mobile phone allows you to summon assistance on the road, price is a problem. Motorola sells a car phone unit new for $1,959, plus $75 installation, plus charges for Ma Bell, plus FTC license fees, etc. Three-year financing plans can lower the cost to around $60 a month, and used mobile phones are available, starting at $500. However, if your business or travel regularly takes you through rough-and-tumble neighborhoods, the cost may well be a good trade for convenience and safety.

Phony phones. Purchase a telephone receiver with cord from an electronics-supply house or secondhand store. Keep it on the seat next to you in your automobile.

Should a suspicious car begin to follow you, very conspiciously turn your head toward the rear window and glance at the occupants. Then, while they're watching, pick up your dummy receiver and pretend that you're making a call. If it's nighttime, turn on your dome light, in order to be plainly seen by your followers.

They'll most likely surmise that you're a plainclothes policeman calling for assistance and decide to leave the scene pronto.

Phony passenger. Here's a guy you can ride with anytime you're driving night trips alone—a time when all drivers, women especially, are safer if they appear accompanied. He's a real dummy, not much on conversation, but a simple safety ruse.

Make the dummy by propping your spare tire in the front seat, draping a coat around it, and wedging your car jack between tire and seat to serve as a neck. Tie cloth in the shape of a head or use a novelty-store pullover Frankenstein mask with a balloon inside. Add a man's hat if you wish and fasten Jack's seatbelt. From any distance in the dark it seems you have a hulking male figure beside you, making potential attackers think twice.

Repelling boarders. An increasing number of rapes, robberies, and car thefts begin with the attacker strongarming his way into the victims' car as they wait at a stop light or other traffic barrier. The simplest deterrent here is to keep car doors locked at all times, but should an intruder start to get into your car, take off! Run a stoplight to safety!

Mugger's lane. The deserted country road or hilltop with a view is great for mellow talk and romantic interludes. Such places also provide peaceful nooks for thugs, rapists, and sex deviates to await victims.

For your safety while parking, always head your car outward, with doors locked, your key in the ignition, and windows opened only enough to keep your windshield from steaming up. Also, never make a habit of parking at the same secluded spot regularly. Passing perverts will take notice.

Giving the slip. If you just flashed a wad of bills at the corner store or just cashed a check, that car in your rear-view mirror probably *is* following you. Both you and your money are in danger.

To shake the pursuer, turn right, turn left, go around the block—in short, let him know you're aware he's following. If possible, stop at a service station with a phone and call a relative, friend, or policeman to escort you home. Should that be impossible, park and lock your car, then take a taxi home. The cab driver will wait until you're safely inside your door.

Strangers in the night. It happens every night in some American city —a mugger disables a parked car by pulling a few wires under the hood, waits for the driver to return, offers assistance, then zaps his unsuspecting victim. Never accept such a stranger's offer to help. Ask him to call a friend of yours, a relative, or the police if he insists on coming to your aid. If he tries to get you to unlock your car door, blow the horn and keep tooting until he leaves or neighbors investigate the commotion.

Bumper stickers. A certain style bumper sticker will give you a bit of protection from both reckless drivers and grouchy traffic cops. The strip reads "Support Our POLICE." From a distance, the madman freeway tailgater will see only the boldface word "POLICE" and pass you by rather than risk the possibility of tangling with an off-duty policeman. Grumpy highway patrolmen who choose you to hang a ticket on just because you've got an out-of-state license or long hair will be softened by your support for the boys in blue. They'll see your bumper sticker when pulling you over and, if you put on a good yes-sir-no-sir respectful routine, chances are they'll let you go with a warning. Most police community-relations departments and some stores carry such bumper badges.

STREET SAVVY

Pocket alarm. The Mini Gard is an alarm about the size of a small carrot and weighs only a few ounces. But this CO_2–charged whistle emits a shriek that can be heard for a mile. Good for twenty to twenty-five shrieks, this device costs only $4 and is available at hardware stores everywhere.

Cash-dispenser cautions. The automatic cash-dispensing machine is rapidly burgeoning throughout the country. Usually installed just outside a bank, it allows the customer to insert his credit card, punch a code number (which is known only to him) into the machine, and receive up to $200 in cash.

Very convenient, but a mugger may be waiting nearby to relieve you of cash obtained from the device. Always be alert when using such a machine.

Mailbox drop. Here is a clever gimmick commonly employed in the mugging capital of the world, New York City: If you're being followed by what you believe to be a mugger, quickly walk to the nearest mailbox and deposit your wallet or purse therein. You'll have to contact your local postmaster to retrieve it, but you may avoid a large loss in this manner.

Defense sprays. A few well-aimed squirts from a chemical-spray defense weapon into the face of a mugger or rapist coming at you (even if he's wearing glasses) will knock him to the ground or send him reeling, blinded and incapacitated for about five minutes. Many such sprays are on the market, but watch out for cheap, unreliable devices which may prove ineffective in an emergency and provide a dangerous false sense of security. We recommend the Preventor Chemical Defensive Weapon, a mini-version of the spray guns used by thousands of police departments. The product is marketed by Flashguard Security Systems and available at local outlets for under $5. The Preventor shoots a heavy droplet spray from four to eight feet. Practice using it *before* a crisis develops!

Avoiding basement druggers. Most self-service elevators must complete all their up calls or all their down calls in order. That is, if you get in the elevator on the first floor and someone in the basement has called for it before you push the button for your floor, the elevator will first go to the basement—with you inside.

Avoid this potentially hazardous situation by performing the following ritual: When the elevator arrives at the lobby, punch the basement, lobby, and your floor button, in that order. Then, allow the elevator to go to the basement without you. When it returns to the lobby get in and you will be taken directly to your floor.

Take it all. Your first words to a holdup man should be "Take everything." And you should give him everything. For every hero you read about in the paper who resisted or attacked a holdup man, there are quite a few who are not around to talk about it.

Locker-room safeguards. In group showers and dressing areas—at gym class, public swimming pools, and beaches—don't let snatch-and-run bandits steal you dry as you sputter through a shower! A towel with a matching washcloth sewn into the corner to serve as a pocket will let you take your wallet, identification, and valuables with you to the showers instead of leaving them in purse or pocket in a vulnerable locker.

Firecrackers. An effective but often overlooked attention-getter is the firecracker. It will wake up the whole neighborhood, scare any burglar, and draw more than casual attention to the dark corner a molester and you are headed for. In some places firecrackers are illegal, but look at it this way—it's a misdemeanor that could keep you from being a felony victim. If you must, walk in tough neighborhoods fondling a pocketful of cherry bombs and smoking a cigarette to look tough and to light them with.

Police whistle. One of the more psychologically disarming, as well as attention-getting sounds of our society is the shrill blast of a police whistle. Pick one of these up at a sporting goods store for under $2.00, wear it on a chain around your neck, and don't hesitate to use it when in trouble.

The bare minimum. Virtually all law-enforcement agencies advise you to carry as little cash on your person as possible. You should however, carry at least $5, preferably $10, at all times.

The reason? The holdup man is usually an unbalanced individual. If you are able to give him nothing—or next to nothing—he may lose his temper and maim or kill you.

The good samaritan. Don't just stand and watch—but don't endanger yourself either. Not only do you risk personal harm by pouncing in to break up a crime in progress, you also chance becoming the victim of a team of grifters acting out an attack purposely to sucker you in.

We advise this procedure: Don't get personally involved until you or someone else has *sent* for help by calling police or an ambulance. Then, help only if you're sure you're not endangered in doing so.

Counterfeit crackles. Dimly lit lounges, dance halls, and bars are the favorite haunts of forgers and counterfeiters using your battered senses and the lack of illumination to pass off phony bills. Be alert when taking paper currency—*feel* it, don't just count it. Fold the money over your forefinger, and rub the ends of the bill between your thumb and middle finger—it should slide but never crackle. If you suspect you've been handed a bogus bill, notify the management, then the police.

Caught with pants down. Public restrooms pose special safety hazards, as they are frequently sites of robberies—both simple stickups and more complicated group heists. One example in Memphis saw a pair of pilferers station themselves in a public restroom and rob each person who entered. When the crowd of victims reached an unmanageable size, they forced all to undress at gunpoint, then escaped while the victims drew up their drawers and stumbled after help.

Our advice is to avoid public restrooms if possible.

Elevator holdups. If there's something shifty going down the elevator shaft with you—such as a pickpurse, robber, or molester—you should, of course, cooperate if your safety is threatened. But punch the emergency button the minute the robber flees. The clanging of emergency bells under the elevator car and on the ground floor will panic the robber into running, thus making him conspicuous to policemen or security guards answering the elevator alarm.

The flasher. The streaker of a few years back was just a fad, but the flasher is a perennial phenomenon. This strange bird, who wears nothing but a raincoat or overcoat, will hide behind a large bush in a park. When women or young girls walk by, he'll jump out of the bushes and open his raincoat in front of them.

Usually a harmless fellow, the flasher gets his kicks merely from shocking the ladies. Nevertheless, it's best not to antagonize him by making disparaging remarks or by contemptuous behavior. Your best defense is to get away from him as quickly as possible, then report the matter to the police.

The transvestite. These folks—men and women both do it—enjoy dressing up in clothes of the opposite sex. They're usually harmless, but when you're confronted by one, your common sense should tell you not to antagonize him or her. As when dealing with any individual, overt derision can incite violence. If you feel uncomfortable, just leave the scene as quickly as possible.

Some communities have laws against transvestite behavior. If this type of activity is illegal in your town and you feel intimidated by it, by all means report it to the police.

Soliciting. Picking up prostitutes is a tricky business—both for the ladies who turn the trick and for you, who should know a few tricks to avoid robbery and injury. When you pull over to proposition the dame leaning against the streetlight, make sure all the doors are locked and windows rolled most of the way up. That way her accomplice can't jump in and mug you while you and she talk rates and services. Only carry as much money as you want to spend on carnal commodities. Lock the rest, including your wallet, in your trunk before you start carousing. When a woman gets in the front seat to talk business, keep your hand on your door handle, ready to exit stage left. Don't be insulting—prostitutes are often ultrasensitive and should not be provoked.

Know the score. Catering to prostitution sometimes finds you catering to thieves and muggers. The discerning "john" will know the danger signals. Never take up the offer of two girls for the price of one. Instead of turning you on, they may turn on you and rob you at knifepoint. Or one may empty your pockets while you're in the heat of passion with the other. Also, never drive a prostitute to the parking place of her choice. Her pimp and a thug or two may be lurking there to rob you. Return to the quiet site you found before picking the prostitute up and you won't be rolled by hooker or crook.

Blackmail reflections. You may and should become suspicious when you enter the room a pickup enticed you up to and you find most of one wall is covered with a mirror. Is this an extortion plot with a cohort in blackmail stationed behind a two-way mirror with a camera? Find out (and foil their attempt) by suddenly switching off the lights. If those behind the glass have any kind of light on, you'll be able to see it and them the instant your room is dark. Don't tip them off by announcing your switch-flipping intentions. Also, no light will leave the schemers with black pictures, not blackmail pictures.

Subway crowds. Getting caught up in the rush-hour subway swarms or other crowds can be fatal. Move with the crowd if you can't resist —aim not to fall down and be trampled to a pulpy smudge. Hold your elbows by your sides and sticking out, fists clenched in front of your stomach.

If you get nudged to the edge of the subway platform, stand with feet at right angles—your right foot pointing down the track, the left foot pointing at the track—and brace yourself. If pushed in front of an oncoming subway train, throw yourself flat on the tracks. Often there's a trench between tracks and the train will pass safely over you.

Discouraging accosters. Find a man in uniform (*any* uniform— Army, Navy, fire department, TV repairman) and tell him you're being annoyed, followed, or accosted. Uniforms look like authority and will dissuade most annoyers.

Another ploy involves boarding a random subway or bus when you believe you're being followed or hassled, then getting off the instant before the train or bus pulls away. Your harasser will follow you onto the train, only to be whisked away to destinations unknown.

Subway survival. Pursesnatchers, pickpockets, muggers, and thugs of all stripes are attracted to subways, buses, and trains, which offer a steady flow of victims and plentiful places to attack. Keep yourself from becoming a crime statistic by sticking to well-lighted areas and to the safety of numbers when waiting for or riding public transportation.

Avoid "corners" (the last seat or inside seat) where you can't move rapidly. Ride in the car with the conductor or motorman, if possible, especially at night. Schedule public trips to avoid long waiting periods at subway station or bus stop.

SELF-DEFENSE

Judo. Judo is an Oriental method of self-defense which involves using your opponent's own weight and strength against him. Requiring balance, rather than strength, this ancient martial art is ideally suited to women.

Instruction studios proliferate in every large and medium-sized town. Find these in your Yellow Pages under "Judo, Karate and Jiu Jitsu Instruction."

Blade blockers. Faced with a knife-wielding assailant who isn't satisfied with your offer to give him everything (or who doesn't wait long enough to hear it), your self-defense efforts must concentrate on stopping his cutlery. Use a purse, a briefcase, a garbage-can lid, a book, a board, or any other handy object to meet his knife thrusts. A raincoat or jacket is an effective blocker if wrapped around an arm to catch the first blow and give you a chance to disarm your enemy. Your body will probably automatically perform other self-help measures such as screaming, not getting backed against a wall, and running every chance you get.

Female assailants. Violent crime by women is on the rise, so don't be overly shocked if the person mugging you turns out to be female. A man can't afford to be squeamish about applying any of the brutal defense tactics discussed here to a woman assailant—it's better chivalry die than you. The groin kick, of course, loses its disabling effect, though it is still a painful blow. For the distaff attack, grab the woman's breasts, digging in hard with the fingers, and twist. Such painful treatment of a sensitive area will loosen her grip on you and/or her weapon.

Fit to be tied. If you're kidnapped, if you're a bank-robbery hostage, if you're being lashed to a log at the sawmill, to get loose you must be fit to be tied. While being tied up, tense your arm and leg muscles. Try to pump your muscles as big as possible. Breath deeply. Strain at the bonds. When the tyers are gone, relax completely. The half-inch of slack rope you fought for is enough to help you squirm to freedom.

Canes and umbrellas. Elderly citizens, frequent sufferers from strong-arm assaults and robberies, can be better prepared to resist their attackers by carrying a walking cane or umbrella when they venture out in public—even if the sun is shining and they get around just fine without a wooden aid.

Make sure the cane is a hardwood, and "when you hit, go for the attacker's nose, because that's his most vulnerable part," a Los Angeles instructor in self-defense for senior citizens tells his students.

Umbrellas are effective jabbing weapons when thrust into the assailant's eyes or throat.

Stamp out thugs. Mugger, rapist, or grizzly bear—any attacker who grabs you from the rear can be quickly disabled in an easy, one-step method—one step (a hard one) on his foot or ankle. It only takes about 14 pounds of pressure to break someone's foot, so anyone can stomp with enough force to leave a crook with crumpled toes and spirits.

Go for the knee. When Joe Hassle gets just drunk enough to begin picking a fight and singles you out of a bar crowd for the object of his harassment, remember to think "knee" in your time of need. Just about any swift kick to Joe's knee, hitting the front or back, can cause the kneecap to slip out of position, immobilizing Mr. Hassle. If you're knocked to the floor before you can kick his knee, try a slashing chop to the back of his knee. Knee blows work well on muggers and rapists, too.

Dogs. Stray, hungry, mad, and otherwise dangerous dogs are a street hazard in both big and small cities. Your life and health may depend on how well you can fight the bite. Rule one says if a dog is biting, let him chew on your arm—it hurts, sure, but it beats getting your throat munched. Don't pull your arm from a dog's jaws—push it farther into the animal's mouth and it will be forced to let go. Keep pushing the pooch backwards while steering it toward some avenue of escape for you such as a doorway, gate, or car. Yell at the dog forcefully and confidently. If all else fails, punch it in the nose.

CHAPTER 3

Gyps galore:
the costly consumer carousel

Every day of the year a man pulls a $1,000 heist somewhere in this country, using only a rotten, bug-infested board as a weapon. He doesn't club you with the board or threaten to sic the bugs on your dog. He merely crawls around your basement, climbs upstairs to show you the wormy wood, then charges you $1,000 for him to go back downstairs and do nothing.

That may sound like a strange robbery, but it's the favorite method of the unscrupulous termite inspector—one of a horde of swindlers and gyp artists who make their livelihood by bilking the buying public. Such hucksters hawk unneeded services and inferior products with fraudulent claims and dishonest sales tactics to steal millions yearly from the American consumer. Their methods read like a rainbow of rip-offs, including mail-order schemes claiming only a few cents per victim, home-improvement rackets involving thousands of dollars, and everything in between. So widespread are these rackets that experts in the field say most buyers see but the tip of the gyp iceberg. You need all the savvy you can muster in order to outwit these marauders of the marketplace.

The ancient adage "Buyer beware!" has never been more needed than today. Perhaps an act of Congress, similar to the one requiring health warnings on cigarette packages, should make store owners broadcast that two-word warning over every aisle. To that axiom we add one of our own: "Consumer compare!" Check products and services against others to get the lowest price, best quality, and largest quantity. Investigate before you invest your hard-earned money. Keep a note in your purse or wallet, tucked next to your cash where you'll see it before each and every purchase. This note should say, "Am I getting ripped off again?" Think about it before you fork over your funds.

When reading the tips we offer, pay close attention to the seller-stings-buyer theme running throughout. If you develop a consciousness of the underlying subtleties involved, you'll be better equipped to recognize such schemes when you've been marked as the potential victim. Our ideas cover a lot of ground, but though the product may change, the slick sales strategies remain the same. Thus, when you know how to outfox the fast-talking door-to-door salesman, you'll be prepared to ward off the crooked refrigerator repairman using the same basic method.

If you've already suffered from phony huckstering, get a copy of the book *Directory of Consumer Protection and Environmental Agencies,* edited by Thaddeus Trzyna (Orange, N. J.: Academic Media, 1973); or *Consumer Sourcebook,* edited by Paul Wasserman (Detroit: Gale Research, 1974). Both list consumer-service organizations in every state.

FOR FURTHER INFORMATION:

Angry Buyer's Complaint Guide, The. Jack White. New York: Peter H. Wyden, 1974.

Buyer Beware! Fred Trump. New York: Abingdon Press, 1965.

Consumer Survival Kit. John Dorfman. New York: Praeger, 1975.

Consumer Swindlers and How to Avoid Them. John L. Springer. Chicago: Henry Regnery, 1970.

Frauds, Swindles & Rackets, a Red Alert for Consumers. Robert S. Rosefsky. Chicago: Follett, 1973.

Getting Your Money's Worth. Herbert S. Denenberg. Washington, D.C.: Public Affairs Press, 1974.

Great American Food Hoax, The. Sidney Margolius. New York: Walker, 1971.

How I Turn Ordinary Complaints into Thousands of Dollars. Ralph Charell. New York: Stein and Day, 1973.

Innocent Consumer vs. the Exploiters, The. Sidney Margolius. New York: Trident Press, 1967.

RETAIL RIP-OFFS

Artificial robbery. It doesn't hurt right off when you get mugged in the market—some food manufacturers take your money for products laced with artificial additives and preservatives. Many of these fancy foods contain so little nourishment their claim to be food approaches outright fraud.

Avoid giving something for nothing in the supermarket by reading the labels of products you commonly buy. If a number of artificial colorings, flavorings, and additives are listed as ingredients, buy a purer product. For your child's health safety, check the effects of artificial additives in nutrition books at libraries and bookstores.

Bait-and-switch. Here, the consumer is initially snared by the firm's seemingly low prices: a sewing machine with all the accessories for $49.95, a complete aluminum-siding job on an eight-room house for $300.

As the customer is shown the merchandise by the salesman, however, he comes to realize that the product on sale is an inferior one. "Let me show you this one," says the salesman, bringing out a slightly more expensive model. The process is repeated until the customer ends up with a product or service much more expensive than the one in the ad.

More on bait-and-switch. Learn the intricacies of this expensive game by sending for the free publication entitled *Bait and Switch.* Send a self-addressed, stamped, legal-size envelope to the Council of Better Business Bureaus, 1150 17th Street, N.W., Washington, D.C. 20036.

Prescription shopping. Unless it's a medical emergency and you must have the prescribed pills immediately, you'll save as much as 80 percent if you shop around—comparing drug-store prices before filling your medicine order. Chain stores in upper-middle-class suburbs usually have the lowest prescription prices. Ask the pharmacist what your prescription will cost *before* he fills it. Then go to a phone and call three other druggists, asking their prices for the same prescription. You'll be amazed at the price differences! Buy from the pharmacist with the lowest prices and don't drop dollars on overpriced drugs.

Generic medicines. Get the ins and outs on generic drugs, and learn to save at the same time, by sending for the free bulletin *Medicines Can Cost You Less* (Buyers Bulletin no. 15). It's available from the Bureau of Consumer Affairs, City Hall, Room 848, Los Angeles, Calif. 90012.

Hearing aids. Want to know how to avoid falling prey to an unscrupulous hearing aid salesman? You can get some good tips here from the bulletin entitled *Hearing Aids—How to Buy (and Not Buy)* (Buyers Bulletin no. 6), available free by writing to the Bureau of Consumer Affairs, City Hall, Room 848, Los Angeles, Calif. 90012.

More on hearing aids. Types of hearing aids and how to avoid getting ripped-off in their purchase are the subjects covered in the pamphlet entitled *Hearing Aids* (publication no. 311–03250), published by the Better Business Bureau. For your free copy send a self-addressed, stamped legal-size envelope to the Council of Better Business Bureaus, 1150 17th Street, N.W., Washington, D.C. 20036.

Credit cons. Consumers pay out hundreds of thousands of dollars needlessly every year by purchasing cars on credit. There are good contracts and bad ones. Learn the difference by sending for the free pamphlet entitled *Automobiles on the Installment Plan,* available by sending a self-addressed, stamped, legal-size envelope to the Council of Better Business Bureaus, 1150 17th Street, N.W., Washington, D.C. 20036.

Unit pricing. One ploy of food manufacturers to create supermarket confusion and cheat the buyer looking to get the most from his or her food dollar is packaging products in a wide variety of sizes, selling them at an equal variety of prices. Which is the better buy— 28 ounces of Brand X detergent at 88 cents or 36 ounces of Brand Z for $1.19? Few people take the time for long division, and so go about their shopping ignorant of how much their money can buy.

Some state laws require (and some grocery outlets voluntarily institute) a practice called "unit pricing." In this, each product shows both a purchase price and a price per "unit" (such as 10 cents per ounce, 15 cents per quart). Shoppers can then save money by comparing odd-sized brands with others to determine the best buy. If your state mandates unit pricing, use the practice to your advantage. If it doesn't, petition the state government and your local supermarket to adopt unit pricing.

Supermarket safety. Your local supermarket would probably never blatantly cheat you. However, questionable packaging, pricing, labeling and dating methods often work to your obvious disadvantage. To help you cope with such supermarket subtleties, *How to Save in the Supermarket* (Buyers Bulletin no. 3), is available free from the Bureau of Consumer Affairs, City Hall, Room 848, Los Angeles, Calif. 90012.

Weights and measures. We've all heard of the proverbial butcher's thumb on the scale, but how about a crooked scale, a rigged gasoline pump meter, or a 2¾ foot yardstick? These things do exist, and the Los Angeles County Department of Weights and Measures explains all in their free brochure entitled *Full Value.* Get your copy by writing to them at 3200 North Main Street, Los Angeles, Calif. 90031.

Clothing cautions. A free bulletin, available through the Los Angeles Bureau of Consumer Affairs, gives the lowdown on how not to get ripped-off in the purchase of wearing apparel. It's entitled *Ready-to-Wear Clothing: Beware Before Buying* (Buyers Bulletin no. 13), and obtainable by writing to the above agency at City Hall, Room 848, Los Angeles, Calif. 90012.

Beef. Is it wise to join a freezer food plan? What are the various grades of beef? These and other questions are answered in the brochure entitled *Freezer Beef,* available free from the Council of Better Business Bureaus, 1150 17th Street, Washington, D.C. 20036. Send a self-addressed, stamped, legal-size envelope with your request.

Headache hucksters. The following math lesson may hurt the head, but your wallet will love it. The cheapest store-brand aspirin—often as low as 33 cents for 100 tablets—has 10 grains of aspirin per dose as its major active ingredient. "Name brand" pain relievers, costing nearly $1.50 more, contain the exact same ingredients and dosage. Even the "extra strength" remedies selling at $2.25 for 100 pills contain only 15 grains of aspirin per dose. Take three of the store-brand aspirin instead of two and you'll have the same relief power for one-fourth the cost. In short, brand-name aspirins are a rip-off.

Antihistamine antics. A number of over-the-counter drugs combine aspirin with an "antihistamine" such as methapyrilene fumarate and claim the combination delivers relief from the chest cold. Wrong, say medical researchers!

The main use of antihistamines is to dry up secretions in your nose and throat. That's good if you've got hay fever or a nose cold, but twenty years of scientific studies show these medicines do absolutely nothing for a chest cold, regardless of their claims. Avoid antihistamine "cold remedies" unless your cold is mainly in the nose.

Name-brand drugs. Big-name prescription drug manufacturers bilk the medicine-buying public of hundreds of millions of dollars yearly by encouraging doctors to prescribe their expensive brand-name medications rather than cheaper, chemically equivalent brands. You can keep them from collecting an average of $1 per prescription by buying generic equivalent drugs instead of the big brands. Several states have okayed drug product substitution laws. If yours is one, ask your pharmacist to change your physician's prescriptions to the cheapest equivalent brand. If there is no such law in your state, make a point of telling your doctor to prescribe the least expensive generic drug he can recommend.

Complexion confusion. Beauty bars, cleansing creams, and skin moisturizers represent wasted money to smart beauties who know they can reach into their cupboard and come out with common-but-equal complexion aids. Plain old corn meal is a great skin cleanser and refresher. Just lather your hands with a mild soap, sprinkle some corn meal in the suds, and scrub your face gently. The slightly abrasive corn meal will remove dead skin, open your pores, and leave your face feeling fresh. Got a sensitive complexion? Maybe a little sunburn or windburn? Slap on some mayonnaise and forget the expensive store-shelf miracles! The vegetable oil, egg yolk, and vinegar in mayonnaise actually outdo store-bought creams in reconditioning and moisturizing your face. Fresh cream is another excellent skin lubricator.

Hormones. In spite of scientists' findings to the contrary, makeup manufacturers continue to market "wrinkle removers" containing hormones they claim cause "dramatic changes in just two weeks." Tests show, the sellers spout, that dry wrinkly skin looks younger and smoother.

Sure it does. But what the tests *really* showed was that the skin appears "younger" only under a microscope, not to the naked eye. And only on women over seventy years old, and at that, after four weeks the "dramatic changes" fade away.

Making your own makeup. When you buy eye shadow, cold cream, rouge, and other cosmetics, only 30 cents of every dollar you pay goes toward ingredients. The rest of your hard-earned cash goes to pay for all those frilly advertisements and for high profit margins all the way down the distribution chain. Quit paying out "vanity" money and start making your own makeup. If you can follow a simple Betty Crocker cake recipe, you're all set. You can buy ingredients at drug stores and chemical-supply houses. Look for cosmetic recipes in such books as *Cosmetics from the Kitchen,* by Marcia Donnan (New York: Holt, Rinehart and Winston, Inc., 1972).

TV talk. Shopping for a new TV set? You'll have many decisions to make here: brand, model, screen size, type of antenna and, most importantly, the dealer you buy it from. A free booklet entitled *Tips on Television Sets* (Publication no. 225) will help you make the right decisions. You can get a copy from the Council of Better Business Bureaus, 1150 17th Street, N.W., Washington, D.C. 20036. Be sure to enclose a self-addressed, stamped, legal-size envelope with your request.

Appliance alert. Washers, dryers, TV sets—they're all expensive, and even more expensive if the one you purchase doesn't do the right job for you, if the warranty is no good, or if the contract is deceptive. A free 16-page booklet will help you make all the wise decisions on such purchases. Entitled *Home Appliances,* it can be had by sending a self-addressed, stamped, legal-size envelope to the Council of Better Business Bureaus, 1150 17th Street, N.W., Washington, D.C. 20036.

Tape talk. In the last several years, tape recorders and players have developed an increasingly high degree of sophistication—and price. Learn what's what in the selection and purchase of such equipment quickly and painlessly by sending for the Better Business Bureau's free booklet entitled *Tape Recorders and Players* (Publication no. 220). Send a self-addressed, stamped, legal-size envelope to Council of Better Business Bureaus, 1150 17th Street, N.W., Washington, D.C. 20036.

Sound advice. Get the latest information on the various types of audio equipment and accessories on the market today by sending for the free pamphlet *Audio Products* (Publication no. 224). Also discussed are warranties and credit plans. Send a self-addressed, stamped, legal-size envelope to the Council of Better Business Bureaus, 1150 17th Street, N.W., Washington, D.C., 20036.

Slide projectors. A good-quality slide projector can run up into the hundreds of dollars. All the more reason for you to familiarize yourself with how to avoid getting ripped-off. In the booklet *Slide Projectors,* you'll not only learn the pros and cons of the various types, but you'll pick up some good tips on dealer psychology, warranty and service, and other useful items. A free copy is available by sending a self-addressed, stamped, legal-size envelope to the Council of Better Business Bureaus, 1150 17th Street, N.W., Washington, D.C. 20036.

Carpet counsel. Carpeting a home can be an expensive proposition—especially if a dishonest, glib-tongued carpeting salesman prejudices your judgment. Learn how to avoid such a situation by sending for the free booklet entitled *Tips on Carpet and Rugs* (Publication no. 02–230–73). Send a self-addressed, stamped, legal-size envelope to the Council of Better Business Bureaus, 1150 17th Street, N.W., Washington, D.C. 20036.

Free samples. Sending off for a "free trial sample" of an advertised product often means you should brace for a high-pressure sales assault. For instance, we redeemed a coupon for a free vitamin sample, which was followed up by more vitamins in succeeding months. When these unordered pills weren't paid for, the distributing firm sent bills demanding payment, threatening legal action, and worse.

Threats of bodily harm or harm to one's reputation violate postal statutes. How to hold on to your cash and get these peddlers off your back? Don't pay for any unordered items, and report attempts to collect for them to the Postal Service.

Service calls. Before you spend another nickel on repairs, find out what's involved in service calls on appliances, TV sets, swimming pools and other items. It's all covered in a free pamphlet entitled *What About Service Calls?*, which you can get by sending a self-addressed, stamped, legal-size envelope to the Council of Better Business Bureaus, 1150 17th Street, N.W., Washington, D.C. 20036.

Repair rip-offs. The field of appliance repair offers many opportunities for the unscrupulous repairman to collect a dishonest buck. Unless you're aware of the potential hazards involved, you may become a victim. Study up on the matter by ordering the free publication *Consumer Tips on Appliance Service* (Publication no. 245), available from the Council of Better Business Bureaus, 1150 17th Street, N.W., Washington, D.C. 20036.

Major purchases. The sale of houses, automobiles, boats and other big-ticket items provides fertile breeding grounds for all types of unscrupulous hucksters. Learn how to protect your interests in such major transactions by obtaining the free publication entitled *Before You Make a Major Purchase* (Buyers Bulletin no. 9), available from the Bureau of Consumer Affairs, City Hall, Room 848, Los Angeles, Calif. 90012.

Mobile homes. Because the mobile home is a big ticket item, you stand to lose a lot in the purchase of one if you're not cautious. Advantages, disadvantages, facts and figures regarding various types are outlined in the booklet *Buying a Mobile Home* (Publication no. 311–03227). Get your free copy by sending a self-addressed, stamped, legal-size envelope to the Council of Better Business Bureaus, 1150 17th Street, Washington, D.C. 20036.

Taking it back. Many stores cheerfully refund money on returned merchandise, others don't. Get the lowdown on store policies and on what you can or can't do regarding refunds and exchanges by sending for two booklets: *Tips on Refunds and Exchanges* (Publication no. 207) and *I Want My Money Back.* Both are free and can be obtained by sending a self-addressed, stamped, legal-size envelope to the Council of Better Business Bureaus, 1150 17th Street, Washington, D.C. 20036.

Winners lose. You're a winner! Or so says the letter or phone call with appropriate excitement. Maybe you entered the contest or raffle, or maybe they tell you your name was drawn "at random." You're the lucky owner of a new sewing machine—all you have to do now is come down to the store and pick out the cabinet you want.

In this fake-contest fraud, you're about to be all sewn up. You may end up paying more for the cabinet (and whatever accessories the salesman can convince you to buy) than the whole unit is worth. Our moral: Accept all gift horses gladly, but buy your saddles elsewhere. Otherwise you'll get taken for a ride.

Bankruptcy bunco. A recently popular method of double-dealing is the "salvage company" or "liquidators"—front operations which claim to dispose of unsold merchandise of bankrupt companies at rock-bottom prices. These may advertise in the "public notice" columns of newspaper classifieds, or mail out brochures listing wrist watches, radios, electric toothbrushes, and other items they must "sacrifice" at low prices. One "salvage" company sold new cookware, "list price" $200, for $35. An established pots-and-pans dealer said he sells identical sets for $25 and buys them from the manufacturer for $15. What a bilk for bargain-thirsty buyers!

SALESMEN, REPAIRMEN, AND LANDLORDS

Test your own tubes. Eighty percent of all tube-type TV sets that go on the blink do so because of one or more burnt-out tubes. It's a simple matter to unplug the set from the wall outlet, remove its back, then pull the tubes. Next, take them to a local supermarket or drug store, where you can check them on a tester at no charge. After replacing the faulty tubes with new ones, put them back according to the diagram on the interior of set.

Caution: Because of high voltages inside TV sets, do not tamper with other parts of the set.

Repair rip-offs. A friend of ours recently received a TV repair bill which included $21 for new tubes. Checking the inside of the set, she discovered a covey of transistors, but nary a tube. This exact situation may not happen to you, but there are many other cons that the dishonest repairman can devise. Bone up on the subject by ordering the free booklet entitled *Television Service*, available by sending a self-addressed stamped, legal-size envelope to the Council of Better Business Bureaus, 1150 17th Street, N.W., Washington, D.C. 20036.

Car care. How to protect yourself against unscrupulous auto repair shops is the subject of two free publications: *Your Guide to Auto Repair* is available from the California Department of Consumer Affairs, Bureau of Automotive Repair, 3116 Bradshaw Road, Sacramento, California 95827. You can also get *Car Care on the Road* by sending a self-addressed, stamped, legal-size envelope to the Council of Better Business Bureaus, 1150 17th Street, N.W., Washington, D.C. 20036.

Tricks of the trade. Some auto mechanics are in reality highly-skilled magicians. They can make it *appear* as if you need a new fuel pump, starter, or shock absorbers. How to catch them at this profitable prestidigitation? Bone up on their tricks by reading *The Car You Care For!*, a pamphlet published by the California Department of Consumer Affairs. You can get a free copy by requesting it from their Bureau of Automotive Repair, 3116 Bradshaw Road, Sacramento, Calif. 95827.

Ball joint repairs. The ball joints of your car are pivotal parts of its front suspension system. Naturally, if they're worn, you'll want to have them replaced. But how can you tell for sure? By sending for the free pamphlet entitled *Your Car's Ball Joints, How do They Measure Up?*, you'll find out. Available from the California Department of Consumer Repairs, Bureau of Automotive Repair, 3116 Bradshaw Road, Sacramento, Calif. 95827.

Cool off and cancel. Are you a sucker for a door-to-door sales pitch? If so, there is a way to back out of blowing your cash on things you don't really need. On almost all door-to-door purchases (business supplies, insurance, real estate, and securities excepted) you now get a three-day "cooling-off period" courtesy of a 1974 Federal Trade Commission ruling.

During this period you can cancel the deal for any reason or for no reason. Merely notify the company *in writing* that you've changed your mind and want to cancel. We suggest you send your notice by certified mail. It's relatively inexpensive, and you'll get a receipt to prove that you've mailed cancellation papers.

Encyclopedias. Although a good set of encyclopedias can serve a noble purpose, many salesmen of this product indeed labor under somewhat less-than-honorable methods. A pamphlet distributed by the Better Business Bureau advises the consumer on the pitfalls inherent in buying this product. Advantages and disadvantages of the various types are also discussed. For your free copy of *Buying Encyclopedias* (Publication no. 311–02293), send a self-addressed, stamped, legal-size envelope to the Council of Better Business Bureaus, 1150 17th Street, N.W., Washington, D.C. 20036.

Referral rackets. In the referral racket, a salesman will tell you that if you buy his product you'll be paid for each new customer you refer to the firm. Trouble is, he's probably jacked up the price of the merchandise so high beforehand that even if you brought in a small army of customers, you'd still be paying more for the product than if you bought it through a legitimate outfit. Get more details by sending for the publication entitled *Referral Schemes.* It's free, and can be obtained by sending a self-addressed, stamped, legal-size envelope to the Council of Better Business Bureaus, 1150 17th Street, N.W., Washington, D.C. 20036.

Escrow accounts. The quickest way to make a point with the landlord who continues to take your rent money but refuses to fix the faulty plumbing in your apartment is to quit paying rent, putting the cash in an escrow account. An escrow account is simply a holding account. You withhold your rent, the landlord takes you to court for payment or eviction, and you plead that you have the money in escrow and will gladly pay it when the needed repairs to your apartment are completed. If things go well, the court will order the owner to make these repairs and may grant you a rent reduction for having had to put up with the run-down condition. Most landlords won't take these matters to court, but in case yours does, be sure you're up on details of your state's escrow law by contacting a lawyer or legal-aid program before withholding rent.

Damage deposits. Apartment renters know landlords can bilk them of damage deposits when they decide to move on and the landlord decides to deduct every penny possible, using trumped-up damages as an excuse. The time to secure your damage deposit is when you move in and pay it. Make sure you won't be charged for past damages by carefully going over your new apartment, listing marked walls, torn curtains, and anything else that could cost you in the future. Have your landlord sign this list of pre-existing conditions. Also, exact from the owner a statement saying what constitutes "damage" and that he will not deduct for normal wear and tear. If possible, make sure your rent contract includes a date for your refund—preferably within a week of turning in your keys.

Percent sense. Here comes the salesman. He's about to legalize a rip-off by getting you to sign his contract to purchase a vacuum cleaner, encyclopedia set, or swimming pool. "Only thirty-six payments of $25.50, due the first of each month, and that's at a 21.09 APR. Sign here, please," he says.

Wait a minute! What's an APR? Good question, since an APR is the "annual percentage rate" of the company's finance charge. Unless you're up on the lingo, you won't know he's casually telling you you'll pay $1 interest for every $4 you pay on your purchase! If the APR for your purchase is more than 10 percent, you'll do better arranging a bank or credit-union loan to finance your buying.

On the dotted line. A free pamphlet entitled *Tips on Sales Contracts* (Publication no. 311–02208) tells the consumer much of what he must know about contracts in order to avoid getting severely stung. You can get a copy by sending a self-addressed, stamped, legal-size envelope to the Council of Better Business Bureaus, 1150 17th Street, N.W., Washington, D.C. 20036.

Spell it out! When we were negotiating to buy a used car recently, the salesman promised us that a new set of steel-belted radial tires would be included in the price on the car's window. We bought the car, signed the papers, and got only cheaper, nylon-ply tires with the car. On protesting, we were told that adding whitewalls was all we would get.

Our lesson learned: Insist that all promises be *written* into the contract for any major purchase or time-payment plan. A salesman's oral promises *are* binding, but unless you have a witness who will testify for you (or a tape recording of his sales pitch), you'll never win in court.

Holder-in-due-course cop-out. Reject any sales contract with a clause stating, "No transfer, renewal, or assignment of this contract, nor any loss, damage to, or destruction of said property shall release Buyer from his obligations hereunder."

That bit of legal garble means the seller can turn your contract over to a third party, such as a finance company or collection agency, and you must still make payments whether the merchandise works right or not! If anything goes wrong with a freezer purchased under such a contract, for instance, you have to gripe to the seller. But he won't care about your problems since he's already got his money— from the third party. Signing under such a "holder-in-due-course" clause is service-call suicide.

Service-call stall. Dirt-cheap service calls often mean dirty business from the TV or appliance repairman who uses such a gimmick to open your door and your pocketbook to his operation. Typically, the fix-it flim-flam man arrives to diagnose the trouble with your appliance. Then he regrets not having the needed equipment or tools on the truck and claims your appliance must go to the shop. Once your gadget's in his shop, you'll get a big bill for little or no repair work.

Don't fall for this con and let the repairman cart your appliance to his shop. Pay the small service-call fee, but keep the bundle that bogus repair bills could cost you later in your pocket.

Service savvy. Shelling out valuable dollars for the repair of TV sets, stereos, refrigerators, and the like can be an expensive proposition— and it may even be unnecessary. Get some good tips by sending for the pamphlets entitled *Consumer Guide to Repair Services for Electronic Equipment and Appliances* and *Stretch Your TV and Appliance Dollar.* Both are free, and available by writing to the State of California, Department of Consumer Affairs, Bureau of Repair Services, 909 S Street, Sacramento, Calif. 95814.

HOME-IMPROVEMENT SCHEMES

FHA. One way to beat the home-improvement swindlers at their own game is to finance all your home improvements through the FHA (Federal Housing Administration). The FHA keeps close tabs on fly-by-night operators and will only finance loans for work done by reputable firms.

Home improvements. In spite of much recent legislation to stamp it out, the home improvement racket is alive and flourishing in virtually all parts of the country. Learn how to protect yourself against such dupery by sending for the Better Business Bureau's free booklet entitled *Tips on Home Improvements* (Publication no. 205). Mail a self-addressed, stamped, legal-size envelope to The Council of Better Business Bureaus, 1150 17th Street, N.W., Washington, D.C. 20036.

On the string. Often a disreputable home-improvement contractor will work "on the string." That is, he'll use your advance money to pay his past bills, and go out and get new customers in order to pay for materials and labor on your job.

Obviously, this arrangement can work to your distinct disadvantage and should, therefore, be avoided at all costs. Protect yourself by demanding and checking bank references before any advance deposit is given.

Furnace fraud. Invariably, when home-improvement salesmen get together and talk shop, some of their most hilarious tales center around the gullibility of homeowners for furnace-repair schemes.

Sucking in the unsuspecting homeowner with an offer of a free furnace inspection, the "furnace repair specialist" will invariably discover some "trouble" which could result in "a terrible explosion." But in making their "diagnosis," they've almost completely dismantled the poor homeowner's furnace. Now their pitch is that as long as the furnace needs repairs, the customer will save $50–$75 in labor by having it done now, rather than waiting.

Faced with the fearful prospect of explosion, the depressing sight of the components of his furnace strewn across his basement floor, and the incentive to save money, the homeowner will frequently fall victim to the furnace racketeer.

Air conditioning. The booklet entitled *Central Air Conditioning* (Publication no. 311–03201) not only clues you in on the inner workings of the air conditioner, but tells you about installation, costs, finding a contractor, and pitfalls to avoid in your purchase. The free publication can be obtained by sending a self-addressed, stamped, legal-size envelope to the Council of Better Business Bureaus, 1150 17th Street, N.W., Washington, D.C. 20036.

The chimney con. This is a corny grift, but, nevertheless, thousands fall for it every year. A team of two uniformed men appear at your door, claiming to be city chimney inspectors. After getting your permission, they scale a ladder in order to get a close look at your chimney. Surreptitiously, one of them pulls a brick from a coat pocket and lets it drop at your feet. "Oh, oh," they say, "this chimney is a hazard to public health and must be repaired immediately." Naturally, they'll demand payment on the spot for the work.

In this case, before even allowing these men on your property, you should call city hall and verify that they are, indeed, city employees.

The gas-leak game. One morning a team of two uniformed men roll up to your house. At your door, they tell you that a gas leak has been discovered in the neighborhood and that they will have to go into your basement to check for a leak. Unseen by you, one of the men squirts a small amount of lighter fluid on one of the pipes. A lighted match is run along the pipe to "look for a leak." Naturally when the flame comes in contact with the lighter fluid, the fluid bursts into flame. "There's the leak," they say. Now, under the threat of turning off your gas, you gladly pay them the $35 they demand to fix the "leak."

You can avoid such a situation by first demanding that such individuals produce identification. If you're still in doubt, verify their legitimacy with the office of the utility or firm they claim to represent.

Water conditioners. The water conditioner, or softener, is an expensive but often necessary item. You do not want to buy the wrong type or size, or to pay excessively for the item. Get the facts on such equipment by writing for the free booklet entitled *Water Conditioning* (Publication no. 311–02266). Send a self-addressed, stamped, legal-size envelope to the Council of Better Business Bureaus, 1150 17th Street, N.W., Washington, D.C. 20036.

Fire sale. In recent years, the home-fire-alarm business has mushroomed into a multi-billion-dollar industry. Although many firms selling domestic fire-alarm systems are reputable, others use scare tactics and high-pressure sales methods in order to coerce homeowners into buying. Further, these firms will frequently charge as much as ten times the going rate for a system and its installation.

Before being pushed into signing a contract, you'll do well to check the price of the product with a local electronics-supply firm. Then get a quote on installation from an independent contractor. In most cases, the total price will be a lot lower.

Extra charges. Note whether there are any delivery, installation, or other extra charges involved in your contract. If none are stated, demand that the contractor include wording to the effect that there shall be no such extra charges for the job.

Signature setup. One of the best-known home-improvement cons of all time involves getting the customer—before the work is begun—to sign an undated statement that the necessary work has been satisfactorily completed and that the customer waives all further claims against the contractor. This form is slipped inconspicuously between other papers involved in getting the work underway, then dated by the contractor after the work is completed.

Obviously, when contracting for home-improvement work—or any work for that matter—it's of utmost importance to read everything thoroughly before signing it. Even better, let an attorney look the papers over beforehand.

The driveway-repair ripoff. Here, a pair of con men will drive up to your house in what appears to be a truck belonging to a large home-improvement firm. The men will be wearing uniforms. They'll offer to reseal your blacktop driveway for just $30. "At this price," you say to yourself, "I can't go wrong!" They do the job and you pay them off.

The next day, you discover that, instead of sealer, the men used a mixture of kerosene and crude oil, which has now been tracked onto your walkway, lawn, and the interior of your house. You call the number given you by the men and discover that the firm doesn't exist.

Before agreeing to having any such work done, verify the firm's existence—and its good reputation—with your local Better Business Bureau or Chamber of Commerce.

The garage-cleaning racket. In almost every American city and town, there are legitimate men and women who will clean out your garage for you at no charge. Their only demand is that you give them all your throwaways: old lamps, appliances, toys, etc., which they then repair and sell. However, recently the ranks of the legitimate have been infiltrated by crooks who will make such an offer, then go on to help themselves to other valuable garage-stored items as well: washers and dryers, freezers, tools, even an occasional automobile.

To prevent such losses, make sure you get good references from the individual beforehand, then keep a watchful eye on him—and on your belongings—as he goes about his work.

Siding hucksters. Fraudulent sales practices at one time so dominated the aluminum-siding business that the Federal Trade Commission, at the request of legitimate dealers in the Aluminum Siding Association, moved to prohibit exaggerated claims some salesmen were using to hook unsuspecting customers. Claims no longer allowed are: that aluminum siding never needs painting, that its colors will remain unchanged and last a lifetime, that it provides permanent insulation, that it is the best insulator, or that it effects fuel savings. If you hear one of these pitches, close the door.

Roof rap. Lord help the woebegone homeowner who just doled out $600 for a roof repair job and discovers 3 inches of water on his living room carpet after the first rain. Avoid such needless pain and expense by reading up on roof materials before you contract for the work. Get the free booklet entitled *Tips on Roof Coatings* (Publication no. 256) by sending a self-addressed, stamped, legal-size envelope to the Council of Better Business Bureaus, 1150 17th Street, N.W., Washington, D.C. 20036.

Septic skeptic. If someone comes along offering to clean your septic tank at a set price per pound of waste removed, you'd best say no thanks. Itinerant operators will promise to do the job for 25 cents a gallon, which sounds modest enough until multiplied by the 750-gallon tank size. If you can't prove how much material was removed, you may be hard put to dispute that $100-plus bill.

And don't believe their claims that your tank needs yearly cleanings. Normally a septic tank should be cleaned out every five or six years. Be alert to these schemes and septic cleaners won't be able to drain your savings.

Pest-control rip-offs. The only pest in this scheme is the swindler who calls or comes to your door posing as a pest-control-company representative and offering a free inspection of your house. He'll crawl through basement or attic and produce from his pocket a board swarming with termites, roaches, or ants—or even scare you out of your wits with a dead rat. Your happy home is endangered, he's afraid. He'll fix it for a price "depending on how many gallons of poison I have to use."

Never contract for exterminating services from any door-to-door or phone solicitor without comparing with a reputable, established firm. And never contract for work without a written estimate.

Termite talk. The more you know about termites and their prevention and treatment, the less you're likely to get ripped off by either the termites or an unscrupulous exterminator. The free pamphlet *Termite Control* tells you all about it and is available from the Council of Better Business Bureaus, 1150 17th Street, N.W., Washington, D.C. 20036. Send a self-addressed, stamped, legal-size envelope with your request.

Germ gyp. Products poured down toilets and sinks and claiming to contain special bacteria to liquefy household wastes and keep septic systems free-flowing and odorless are a bigger waste than the mess they purport to clean, a Michigan State University agricultural engineer says. The proper bacteria to operate a septic tank are always present in the organic wastes which go into the septic tanks. Save your money by trusting Mother Nature to run its unclogged course.

Contractor contact. The Better Business Bureau of any city in America will tell you that the great majority of home-improvement racketeers make their initial approach by telephone or mail solicitation, or by door-to-door canvassing. Why? Unlike reputable establishments, who rely upon referral by satisfied customers, these firms must depend upon a continuous supply of *new blood* for the continuance of their business.

It's best, then, when you're ready to have work done on your home or yard, for you to make the initial contact, rather than vice versa.

Lightning larceny. Traveling gypsters know they can strike it rich by pushing overpriced lightning rods on unsuspecting homeowners. Sometimes these crooks say they're inspectors from your insurance company, then peddle inferior equipment and do inferior installation work, all at hyped-up prices. While it may be wise to protect your home or barn with lightning rods, it's even wiser to insist on the credentials of the salesman and be sure you know the full price prior to installation. If you have any questions or doubts about fire-safety equipment, contact your local fire chief or marshal.

Deadlines. Make sure any contract you sign authorizing construction or home improvement has a closing date, with strict monetary penalties for failure to meet the date. In this way, you'll avoid paying workers for their own sweet time. It may also be the only way you can be sure the work will be done. A woman we know, for example, contracted to have a swimming pool built "when I can work it in," as the builder told her. After three months there was no pool, and the contractor asked for 10 percent more because of increases in labor and materials costs. She declined, so the builder declined to start work. Six months later she had her pool built by another contractor, but at a 20 percent higher tab. Had she been smart and demanded a closing date in the contract, she'd have had her pool sooner and cheaper.

Overdoing it. Even local, "reputable" contractors who will do a good job on your home improvements can rip you off by using unnecessarily expensive materials or doing more work than is actually needed. You'll save money on any repair project by being advised of price-padding contractor tricks. For the lowdown, write to the Assistant Director for Rulemaking, Bureau of Consumer Protection, Federal Trade Commission, 7th and Pennsylvania Avenue N.W., Washington, D.C. 20580.

The model-home come-on. "Your home has been selected," begins this modern suburban swindle, "as a display house for our wonderful aluminum siding." You're promised a very special price, since the siding work on your house will be good advertising for others in the neighborhood. You'll even be pledged a "liberal commission" from the siding firm for other contracts they sell in your area.

But promised commissions seldom arrive, and if you bite this something-for-nothing bait you could end up with large bills for inferior materials and workmanship. Avoid all "model-home" profit schemes unless you can get the names of more than a dozen nearby homeowners who profited by the arrangement and check with them before signing a contract.

MAIL-ORDER MADNESS

Stopping mailbox stuffers. Advertising mail can become obnoxious in a hurry. It can contain misleading or downright fraudulent sales schemes and high-pressure tactics. Now a New York-based association claims it can stop most postal sales pitches from making your mailbox.

Write the Direct Mail/Marketing Association, 6 East 43rd Street, New York, N. Y. 10017 and request a "name removal form." DMMA member companies, who conduct most large-scale mail ad campaigns, will heed your wishes, they promise. DMMA will also add your name to everybody's mailing list if you request an "add-on" form.

Mail fraud. Even with the combined efforts of the Federal Trade Commission and the U.S. Postal Service to curtail mail fraud, trusting citizens lose millions each year through a surprisingly wide variety of mail fraud schemes. These are outlined in the booklet *Mail Fraud Laws* (stock no. 3900–0231) published by the Postal Service. You can get a copy by sending 20 cents to the Superintendent of Documents, U.S. Government Printing Office, Washington, D.C. 20402.

Signed, smashed, and delivered. Unpack and check that electric backscratcher to make sure it's in itching order before signing the deliveryman's clipboard. Though he'll say it's only an agreement that you received the goods, signing such receipts often indicates you got your order "in good condition." The receipt, which carries the legal weight of a binding contract, can be used against you when you find your gadget with three claws broken and try to get the dealer to make good on the damaged merchandise.

Save ads. Save copies of mail-order advertisements you reply to. They will be essential in pleading your case, should you experience a postal swindle at close range. If complaints to mail-order dealers don't get results, outline the facts in a short letter to Director, Bureau of Consumer Protection, Federal Trade Commission, Washington, D.C. 20580. Include a copy of that ad you saved.

Postal prudence. Through the Better Business Bureau, you can get a free bulletin which will help you to avoid getting ripped off by mail order swindlers. Entitled *Buying by Mail* (Publication no. 211), the information can be obtained by sending a self-addressed, stamped, legal-size envelope to the Council of Better Business Bureaus, 1150 17th Street, N.W., Washington, D.C. 20036.

Mail-order merchandise. Did you know that, under certain conditions, you can legally cancel goods ordered by mail? This and other federal regulations are spelled out for you in the pamphlet entitled *Shopping by Mail? You're Protected!*, available free from the Bureau of Consumer Protection, Federal Trade Commission, Washington, D.C. 20580.

Sample example. Unscrupulous mail-order companies may try to get a foot in your mailbox by mailing unsolicited free samples of products, first installments of book or record clubs, or first issues of newly published magazines. You don't have to pay for any unordered merchandise that finds its way to your mailbox, federal law states, nor must you pay return postage for it if you choose not to.

Consider anything you get in the mail without ordering it a gift! Dealers pressuring you to pay for goods you didn't ask for are breaking the law. Report them to the Postal Service.

Catalogs. Send $2 for our 200-page catalog listing hundreds of brand-name products at prices up to 70 percent below manufacturer's suggested retail prices! Savings, savings, savings!"

Look closely at this kind of spiel, found in ads in the back of magazines and newspapers, and make sure a money-back guarantee is offered before you mail a few bucks for the supposed "discount" catalog. Too often these catalog firms have no connection with the manufacturer of products and they may not even sell any of the goods. All you're likely to get for your dollars is a cheaply printed catalog listing merchandise and prices.

Mailings. You have every darn right in the world to know when the knitting needles you ordered by mail will arrive, a recent Federal Trade Commission ruling states, and manufacturers must live up to their promised delivery dates. If no date is stated by the seller, you should get your goods within thirty days. Otherwise, you can cancel your order and legally demand a refund within seven business days. Exceptions to this safeguard include film, magazine subscriptions, seeds, growing plants, and C.O.D. shipments.

Lonely hearts. Replying to those magazine ads offering to match you with an equally "lonely" or "single" pen pal can leave you with a broken heart and fractured bank account! These mail-order marauders will keep your "fee" (usually $5) and send you a fictitious address or that of one earlier respondent who already has fifteen "lonely" pen pals.

Or they may hook you up with confidence schemers who'll play you along with romantic writings and get you to send them airplane tickets so they can visit. They'll cash in the ticket, leaving you a doubly duped Don Juan.

Mail-order investment schemes. "You can make money in mail order!" scream the advertisements in national magazines. And they're right—you can, but not by paying someone else to get you into the business. Read all about mail order investment grifters and how to avoid them by sending for the free pamphlet entitled *Mail Order Profit Mirages* (Publication no. 219). Available by sending a self-addressed, stamped, legal-size envelope to the Council of Better Business Bureaus, 1150 17th Street, N.W., Washington, D.C. 20036.

FUNERALS

Memorial societies. Learn about alternatives to conventional funeral arrangements and qualify for discount services by joining a "memorial society." These nonprofit organizations dispense literature and have standing negotiated arrangements with many local funeral homes. Membership fees run from $3.50 to $15, paid once. For the name of a memorial society near you write to the Continental Association of Funeral and Memorial Societies, 59 East Van Buren Street, Chicago, Ill. 60605.

Science wants you! Not everyone is dying to give his money to a funeral director. Some spare their survivors a great deal of expense by donating their bodies to science. Many medical schools will pick up donated bodies free of charge and, after using them for instruction, will pay for cremation. Survivors can claim the remains. The high price of dying plummets to zero when you decide to donate your body to help the living. Get information about bequeathing your corpse to science by calling or writing a medical school near you.

Memorial services. One alternative to paying thousands of dollars for a full-blown funeral is a combination burial and memorial service. Bury the body as soon as practical (or, less expensive, have it cremated) and instead of the visitation-style funeral service at a funeral home, hold a memorial service in your home. A memorial service, since no body is present, can be arranged to meet family traveling schedules. Pay your last respects by fondly recalling the contributions the deceased made to the lives of those who loved him. It beats paying for your respects through a commercial funeral service.

Cremation. Unless you've got money to burn, you and your older relatives should consider cremation (burning your corpse) as an alternative to the inflated cost of funerals and burials. Cremation cuts cemetery costs. There's no expense for a plot or for opening and closing the grave or for a vault. Your remains are later scattered, placed in an urn kept by a friend or relative, or put in a columbarium niche costing about $50. A fairly quick cremation, with no showing of the body, can also save embalming costs. To avoid the whole funeral-fraud mess, preplan your cremation.

Caskets. Caskets shown funeral customers range in cost from the wood-and-wool model for $300 to the top-of-the-line copper casket at nearly $3,000. While it doesn't make one bit of difference to the dead person, relatives are often goaded into buying expensive models as a sort of "tribute." Here are two ways to beat the high cost of dying. Try making your own casket—it's elementary carpentry and, since the casket will be buried in a vault anyway, quality construction isn't important. Or order a simple pine box, handmade by two skilled carpenters, from Rocky Mountain Casket Company, White Fish, Mont.

It sells for about $200 and doubles as a wine rack until time for its underground assignment.

Embalming. Arranging a funeral for a friend or family member is no time to pinch pennies, or so the funeral directors who take advantage of your grief seem to think. They often routinely charge several hundred dollars for embalming—whether it is needed or not.

Such unscrupulous cemetery stewards will imply that embalming is required by law. It's not in all but a few states! If cremation is scheduled within a day or two or if there will be no visitation and a prompt burial, embalming is an unnecessary expense. If you can dispose of the deceased without it, avoid funeral directors who pad their standard rates with this cost.

HELP AND WHERE TO FIND IT

Correspondence courses. If you learned the hard way about bogus learn-at-home schemes, there are several government agencies to help you regain your losses. The Postal Service will investigate any complaints against correspondence schools that misrepresent through the mails. Or write your State Education Department and/or the Bureau of Higher Education, United States Office of Education, Washington, D.C. 20202. The latter two can also warn you about disreputable study-by-mail schools if you consult them *before* signing that correspondence-course contract.

Product fact sheets. A monthly magazine called *Consumer Reports* delivers laboratory-tested rundowns on a variety of products which shoppers must buy to get along in today's world. It's a good way to get the facts on the goods you're likely to purchase in the near future. A subscription to *Consumer Reports,* Post Office Box 3000, Orangeburg, N.Y. 10962, costs just $14 a year.

Changing Times. A magazine long noted as a straightforward consumer educator, *Changing Times* contains cautions for both businessmen and consumers in each issue. Recent examples are articles on where an investor should put his money, how TV repairmen may gyp you, and how to knock down the sticker price on the new car you're buying. Check your library or send for a subscription ($9 for 12 issues) to *Changing Times,* Editors Park, Md. 20782.

Getting your Moneysworth. A new way to cheat you hatches every minute. You'll need the latest information on how to avoid getting ripped off, and we suggest a consumer-oriented magazine called *Moneysworth.* The fortnightly publication details which cars are lemons, how to get home loans, and much more. Check a few back issues at your local library, then get your moneysworth by sending $5 for a year's subscription to *Moneysworth,* 251 West 57th Street, New York, N.Y. 10019.

Consumer's Research. That's the name of a pull-no-punches, no-holds-barred monthly magazine which tests products from the store shelves and tells you which brands are recommended, which are rip-offs, and why. *Consumer's Research* editors claim their testing is "competent, independent and unbiased." The sponsoring group is described as "a nonprofit scientific, technical and educational nongovernmental public service organization dedicated to the consumer." Send $9 for a year's subscription to *Consumer's Research Magazine,* Washington, N. J. 07882 or call your public librarian and see when next month's issue is expected.

Consumer News/Register. Forming food co-ops and doing your own canning will help you beat bulging grocery-store prices. Knowing which bubblebath and which pacifier were recently recalled as "dangerous" by the federal government will protect your children. This information, along with a wide array of consumer topics, is provided in twice-a-month newsletters mailed by the Department of Health, Education and Welfare's Office of Consumer Affairs. Plenty of toll-free numbers to handle your complaints, listings of government services and actions, and chances for input into the bureaucratic policy-making process are yours twenty-four times a year in the *Consumer News/Register.* Send your name, address, and a $4 check payable to the Superintendent of Documents, Government Printing Office, Washington, D. C. 20402.

Discrimination investigation. Did the white landlord hike the rent he's asking for the two-bedroom house when he saw you were black? Does he rent to single men but not single women? If you even suspect someone is keeping you from renting the house or apartment you want at the price generally offered, you can file a sex or race discrimination complaint and federal government agents will check into the matter.

Mail a detailed complaint to the Department of Housing and Urban Development, 451 Seventh Street, Washington, D.C. 20410. Many municipalities also have a bureau to handle rental-discrimination rip-offs.

Government guidance. Although today there are literally hundreds of consumer bureaus scattered across the land, there is one publication which lists all such federal agencies. It's the *Guide to Federal Consumer Services,* Office of Consumer Affairs, Washington, D.C. 20201. Let them tell you who to gripe to for fast results.

Small-claims. A relatively new place to turn to for the average person claiming he's been swindled, chiseled, cheated, or ripped off is the small-claims court existing in most cities. There, for a small fee (often $2 or less), you can recover damages up to $500 and more. No lawyers' fees are necessary. A judge usually hears both sides and decides the issue.

Check the county listings in your telephone directory under "Municipal Courts."

Consumer-action panels. Having problems with a major purchase? If complaints on quality, service, or delivery get nowhere with your dealer, go over his head to the article's manufacturer. But if the maker won't help you, there's still another, industry-wide level which operates consumer panels to investigate buyer complaints and keep the industry honest.

Try to right a rip-off by writing the Major Appliance Consumer Action Panel (20 North Wacker Drive, Chicago, Ill. 60606), the Furniture Industry Consumer Action Panel (Post Office Box 951, High Point, N. C. 27261), or the Carpet and Rug Industry Consumer Action Panel (P. O. Box 1568, Dalton, Ga. 30720).

Misleading advertisements. If you've got gripes with ads that are deliberately misleading, incomplete, not a bona fide offer, or out-and-out fraudulent, go directly to the newspaper, publication, or broadcast station where you saw the advertisement with your complaint. Their consumer/advertiser relations desk can help you get your money's worth.

Deadly dealings. Just as regularly as the moon grows full, Detroit recalls some make of automobile to correct unsafe or defective equipment or auto design. If you recently closed a deal on a new car and now discover dangerous flaws in the machine, speed your complaint to the National Highway Traffic Safety Administration, Department of Transportation, Washington, D.C. 20590. Their job is to follow up such complaints, then force the manufacturer to remedy the defect—which may save your life.

Consumer fraud. False or misleading promises by salesmen or repairmen or any other conduct which constitutes fraud or dishonest dealings can be reported to city and county prosecutors or to the state's attorney general. Many states and municipalities list a Consumer Fraud Unit in their prosecuting agency that will help you recoup funds lost to smoothies in the sales and repair rackets.

Defective products. Literally thousands of everyday items sold in department stores, supermarkets, and elsewhere are unsafe—posing health threats to you, your children, and your neighbors. A hard-hitting report by the National Commission on Product Safety details this scandal of hazard after hazard passed off by manufacturers to unsuspecting consumers. Don't get ripped off by not knowing the dangers of merchandise you buy. Send for a copy of the federal product-safety report to: Superintendent of Documents, U.S. Government Printing Office, Washington, D.C. 20402 ($2).

Cash for coins. Chances are very slim that you'll ever accidently come upon a coin worth more than face value—but what if Aunt Emma one day pulls an old jar loaded with nineteenth-century silver dollars from the closet? How could you get a fair market price for these coins without being taken by some crafty coin collector or dealer? Check coin catalogs at a library or write the American Numismatic Association, 3520 North Seventh Street, Phoenix, Ariz. 85014, for the names of reputable coin companies.

Financial fixers. In a fix on financial matters from interest-rate foul-ups to mixed-up credit billings, the Fed (Federal Reserve Board) has a new Office of Saver and Consumer Affairs, c/o Board of Governors, Federal Reserve System, Washington, D.C. 20551, designed to help people with such questions. For problems involving the Truth in Lending Act, the Fair Credit Billing Act, the Equal Credit Opportunity Act, the Home Mortgage Disclosure Act, or the Fair Credit Reporting Act, these folks promise an answer to your queries within fifteen days.

Consumer information. The Consumer Information Center, a wing of the federal government's General Services Administration, collects and distributes consumer pamphlets gleaned from government research on a rainbow of topics. The Center publishes a quarterly index to the nearly 250 advice-filled booklets, complete with order blanks.

Topics range from "Common Sense in Buying a Used Car" to "Quackery." A good many pamphlets are free—almost all can be had for under $1. To get the money-saving booklets, send your name and address to *Consumer Information Index,* Consumer Information Center, Pueblo, Colo. 81009.

Consumer arbitration. In an attempt to help consumers and business owners settle disputes in an expedient and equitable manner, an arbitration program has been developed in which any disgruntled consumer can participate. The program is explained in three pamphlets: *Arbitration for Business and Customers, Twenty Questions and Answers about Consumer Arbitration,* and *Preparing Your Arbitration Case.* All are free and available by sending a self-addressed, stamped, legal-size envelope to the Council of Better Business Bureaus, 1150 17th Street, N.W., Washington, D.C. 20036.

Better business bureau and chamber of commerce. The Better Business Bureau (BBB) and the Chamber of Commerce (C of C) are two excellent targets for complaints regarding fraudulent business practices. Nearly every city has one or the other. Both have procedures for applying peer pressure to make wayward businessmen toe the line. In addition, both groups distribute consumer-protection information. For investigating investors, these organizations can provide you with information about a company before you do business.

Learn more about what kind of help you can expect from the Better Business Bureau by sending for their free booklet *What is a Better Business Bureau?* Mail a self-addressed, stamped, legal-size envelope to the Council of Better Business Bureaus, 1150 17th Street, N.W., Washington, D.C. 20036.

MISCELLANEOUS GYPS

Franchise schemes. Phony franchise schemes drain investors of thousands of dollars daily. If you're considering buying into a business deal and opening a franchise operation, the following tips will help you dodge the fakes and safeguard your stash of cash.

First, send for Consumer Bulletin No. 4, titled *Advice for Persons Who Are Considering an Investment in a Franchise Business,* available from the Federal Trade Commission (6th Street and Pennsylvania Avenue, N.W., Washington, D.C. 20580). Then check to see if the operation you're thinking of hooking up with is among the legitimate franchisers included in the International Franchise Association Membership Listing (1025 Connecticut Avenue, Suite 906, Washington, D.C. 20036).

In the swim. Next to a house, a swimming pool may represent the largest single investment one will ever make. How much do you know about pools, contracts and warranties, and how to select a reputable contractor? You can pick up some valuable tips from the free Better Business Bureau publication *Swimming Pools,* available by sending a self-addressed, stamped, legal-size envelope to the Council of Better Business Bureaus, 1150 17th Street, N.W., Washington, D.C. 20036.

Bill collectors. While he may not actually mug you, the bill-collector bully makes illegal and indecent invasions of your privacy that are subject to strict penalties, a recent Federal Trade Commission ruling holds. Harassment and abuse such as false threats, late-night calls, obscene language, contacting employers to increase pressure on a debtor, and other actions aimed at intimidating or misleading debtors are among common bill-collector practices now outlawed. The collector trying such seamy tricks can be summarily fired and his employer fined up to $10,000 if you report the offense to your nearest FTC regional office. The phone number will be listed under "United States Government" in the Yellow Pages of the nearest big-city phone directory.

The foxtrot front. It's a real two-step, this classic con in which a dance studio is used as a front to attract and bilk lonely men and women. The first step is an enticing call from a phone solicitor for the studio congratulating you on winning "free" dance lessons. Step two is the high-pressure sales pitch, inducing customers to sign up for costly lessons. The contracts often have no termination date, since the dance "instructor" says you can cancel when you feel you've learned enough to be belle of the ball.

Home study schemes. You'd be surprised, but thousands of people lose a great deal of money each year on home study courses that aren't worth their weight in salt. The booklet *Tips on Home Study Schools* (Publication no. 229) gives some good advice on how to get your dollar's worth in this area. The publication is free and can be obtained by sending a self-addressed, stamped, legal-size envelope to the Council of Better Business Bureaus, 1150 17th Street, N.W., Washington, D.C. 20036.

Training schools. Jet-aircraft maintenance and repair, truck driving, TV servicing, modeling—these are just a few of the hundreds of subjects offered by specialized training schools throughout the land. Are they legitimate? Few offer the in-depth training you'll need in order to obtain a paying job in the field. Worse, many lure prospective students into their fold by promising job placements upon graduation, but these never materialize.

Before plunking down your hard-earned cash to learn a skill, demand a list of graduates from the school in question. Then contact them and ask their opinion of the training and after-training placement services they received.

Computer courses. With the advent of computer technology, computer schools are springing up like wildflowers, and many of them are disreputable. Know what to look for when shopping for such courses by sending for the booklet entitled *Facts on Computer Careers*, available free from the Council of Better Business Bureaus, 1150 17th Street, N.W., Washington, D.C. 20036. Be sure to enclose a self-addressed, stamped, legal-size envelope with your request.

Employment agencies. Although most employment agencies are on the up-and-up, there are a few bad bananas discovered in the bunch from time to time. As might be expected, problems usually revolve around fees. Find out what you're getting into when you register with a private employment agency by requesting the booklet *Facts About Private Employment Agencies*. It's free, and available from the Better Business Bureau of San Francisco, 414 Mason Street, San Francisco, Calif. 94102.

Employment-agency aptitude tests. One of the oldest tricks in the employment-agency gyp books is having a "psychologist" administer a battery of tests to job-hunting customers to determine their "mental aptitude." Today, many of these bogus test forms are run through a "computer" to obtain an impressive "analysis." The only trouble is the tests measure nothing but your gullibility. The results are always flattering so that, once buttered up, you'll use the firm's services extensively (and pay extensively, too!). With very few exceptions (as for high-level executive jobs), psychological testing is not a legitimate employment-agency tool.

Vanity publishers. Ah, the romance and status of being an author. After all, your friends don't have to know that you *paid* to have your book published. But if you're contemplating making money on it, forget it.

The "vanity" publisher (the term is an apt one) will charge you heavily for printing and distributing your book—much more than if you yourself had it printed in a local print shop, paid to have it bound, then distributed it yourself. Even so, rarely do vanity-published or self-published works make money for their authors.

Our advice is to submit your book proposals to reputable publishing houses, as listed in *Writer's Market,* Jane Koester and Rose Adkins, ed. (Cincinnati: Writer's Digest, Annual Publication). Publishers know the market. If your idea is commercially feasible, they'll contract for the book. If not, you're not likely to fare any better by publishing it yourself.

Rebuilt engines. Buying a rebuilt auto engine can be a risky business for those not knowledgeable on the subject. Get some good advice by sending for and reading *Rebuilt Auto Motors,* a pamphlet published by the Better Business Bureau. Obtain a free copy by sending a self-addressed, stamped, legal-size envelope to the Council of Better Business Bureaus, 1150 17th Street, N.W., Washington, D.C. 20036.

Dishonest lawyers. If you feel that you have been bilked out of money or property by a dishonest lawyer, check with your local or state bar association. Some, such as the state bar associations for Pennsylvania and California, have client security funds from which they will reimburse wronged clients. For further information consult *How to Keep Them Honest: Herbert Denenberg on Spotting Professional Phonies,* Howard Shapiro (Emmaus, Pa.: Rodale Press, 1974); or *Can You Be Sure of Your Experts? A Complete Manual on How to Choose and Use Doctors, Lawyers, Brokers—and All the Other Experts in Your Life,* Roger Golde (Toronto: Macmillan Company, 1969).

Buying for less? What are the real implications behind the words "wholesale" and "discount"? Is it possible to buy goods below retail? Get the facts by sending for the booklet *"Wholesale"? "Discount"?,* published by the Better Business Bureau. It's free, and you can get a copy by sending a self-addressed, legal-size envelope to the Council of Better Business Bureaus, 1150 17th Street, N.W., Washington, D.C. 20036.

Baby-photo contest con. Proud parents can be super suckers, as bunco artists prove time and time again with this scheme. At first you are approached by phone or in person by a stranger wanting to enter your infant in a baby contest. Your cutie-pie is sure to win, he says.

You'll be asked to sign what is supposed to be a contest entry blank. It turns out to be a contract binding you to pay for an expensive set of baby photos. In other variations of this con, hustlers lure you with "baby-of-the-month" contests or coupons for one "free" photo, then try to stick you with buying other pictures or expensive photo frames.

Garage-sale steals. The hand-me-down bargains you pick up at local "garage sales" may quite literally be a steal. Law-enforcement agencies everywhere are agreeing with Portland, Oregon, police who claim "fencing" (selling stolen goods) at garage sales, yard sales, and porch sales has increased alarmingly.

If you doubt the legitimacy of such goods, take down a serial number or manufacturer's number and check with your local police before putting your money down.

Duping debtors. Why beef and stew over monthly bills, asks the pitchman for a debt consolidator. You may be cooked if you swallow his tasty offer to "just pay us one easy weekly fee" in return for his combining your many debts.

In many debt-consolidation schemes, the first few checks go to pay off the dishonest consolidator's basic fee instead of being credited to the merchants, who by now are threatening to repossess your car or appliances. You can keep from losing your hard-earned money and losing your possessions by doing your own bill paying or at least by checking debt consolidators' qualifications through the Better Business Bureau.

Patent impostors. Disgruntled inventors recently bombarded Los Angeles authorities with complaints about a "patent club" which issued its members a "notary patent" for their devices after payment of membership and notary fees. A "notary patent" is a stamped, suitable-for-framing, official-looking document that is absolutely worthless—but costs you a pretty penny. There is no legal basis for protection with anything but a patent, which must be researched by a patent attorney. Save your money and safeguard your inventions by consulting one.

Buyer's clubs. You can save money by buying items at factory prices. But paying a $5 or more membership fee to a mail-order "buyer's club" or "supply house" is not the way to get wholesale discounts. Members of four such groups in Vermont and New Jersey were unable to get their orders filled or their membership money back. These outfits bilked more than 100,000 members out of more than $1 million before being convicted of conspiracy to commit mail fraud.

For the elderly. A free U.S. Government brochure outlining phony health claims, extra income schemes, land swindles and other dangers to seniors is entitled *Protection for the Elderly* (FTC Buyer's Guide no. 9) and is available by writing to the Federal Trade Commission, 6th Street and Pennsylvania Avenue, N.W., Washington, D.C. 20580.

Name game. The public's ignorance of the law is no excuse—lawyers are guilty of overcharging their clients for simple services that the clients could manage on their own at a great savings. Trying to change your name is one such rip-off. An attorney will charge you $200 or more to fill out the necessary forms. Handle the paperwork yourself for a fraction of the cost. First check the city library or the law library of a nearby college for books on name changing. For just $5, California residents can learn the legal steps in their state by ordering *How to Change Your Name* from Nolo Press, Box 544, Occidental, Calif. 95465. Got a new name already? Then try your own divorce, land-title search, and other routine legal tangles.

Boxtop heaven. Want to make a glob of money *fast* just by scrounging through garbage cans and imposing on your friends enough to collect boxtops, wrappers, coupons, and labels? Well, then, you're on the sucker list for a growing number of con artists. You'll probably never receive that list of "guaranteed cash buyers" promised for your boxtops. And if you did, current refund rates would force you to collect many hundred labels and wrappers before even making back the $2 you risked in sending for the "guaranteed buyers" list.

Rabbit buy-back fraud. Many farm-belt folks become hopping mad when hucksters promising fabulous profits sell them rabbit "breeding stock" at inflated prices of up to $75. They orally pledge to buy back the offspring at market prices. When the time comes, they may refuse to repurchase the rabbits or grudgingly offer to buy them at meat prices (20 cents a pound), then resell them as breeding stock to new suckers. This buy-back scheme is commonly tried with silver foxes, white mice, guinea pigs, and swine as well as rabbits. It is almost always a rip-off. Legitimate breeding-stock sellers don't use the buy-back plan.

The work-at-home racket. One of the oldest and most lucrative cons around is the work-at-home swindle in which housewives, shut-ins, and the elderly lose untold thousands yearly. An informative booklet alerting consumers to this racket is *Work-at-Home Schemes* (Publication no. 204), published by the Better Business Bureau. A free copy can be had by sending a self-addressed, stamped envelope to the Council of Better Business Bureaus, 1150 17th Street, N.W., Washington, D.C. 20036.

Additional information will be found in a bulletin entitled *Work-at-Home Schemes with All Work and No Pay* (Buyers Bulletin no. 4). For your free copy, write the Bureau of Consumer Affairs, City Hall, Room 848, Los Angeles, Calif. 90012.

Cold cuts. Be ready to turn a cold shoulder to that freezer salesman or wholesale meat advertisement promising you T-bone steaks at the price of hamburger.

Actually, the seemingly low price per pound next to the juicy, tempting steak pictures is based on your buying a "half" or "quarter" of beef, which when cut for home use often costs the same as beef on the grocery shelves. You're paying for pounds and pounds of inedible bone and trim (more than 125 pounds per 600-pound "side"), as well as the electricity to keep your meat frozen.

Mail-order plants. The Better Business Bureau reports that shady dealers lurk in the mail-order bush business. These operators feature one plant each season advertised as an "amazing new discovery" that "produces thousands of exotic blocms in a few weeks."

Grossly exaggerated ad claims are the tip-off. Play it safe by purchasing your plants from local nurseries with established reputations.

CHAPTER 4

Protecting your child: molesters, muggers, and marijuana

Today as never before the world is full of dangers to the helpless little ones who depend on you for their safety and well-being—your children. Accounts of child molestation and kidnappings appear in our newspapers day after day. Additionally, thousands of children are physically and psychologically abused by muggers, babysitters, schoolteachers, and other individuals.

And the hazards range beyond people-related problems. Many children in high schools, junior highs, and even grade schools are involved in drugs, and even hopelessly addicted. The wonders wrought by technology to make our home lives more comfortable and our leisure time more enjoyable also maim and kill thousands of children each year.

It's a lot harder to grow up today, and it's even harder than that to be a modern, conscientious parent. You need to be ever vigilant, always anticipating what your curiosity-powered tyke will turn to next. The penalty for letting down your guard can be a battered, electrocuted, or poisoned child, and emotional wounds and psychological scars that may never heal.

Our most important advice to help you keep up with—and stay one jump ahead of—your youngster is to make yourself a part of her or his world. If, for instance, you've never taken the time to join your kid in a bicycle ride around the neighborhood haunts, how can you possibly warn him of the dangerous blind alley where cars continually zip into the street oblivious to approaching tykes on bikes and trikes? Unless you take the time to listen and talk to your child, will you know when he or she learns from a neighbor kid the "game" of nibbling plants, many of which are extremely toxic? Will you recognize signs that your son or daughter is taking drugs or dating and running around with unsavory characters?

There are two basic ways to keep your youngster safe. The first is *prevention*—keeping dangers at a distance. To that end this chapter suggests ways you can manipulate your child's environment to keep him clear of such hazards as electric shock, drowning, nasty falls, suffocation, poisoning, and the like. A second way is *education*. Some of the following ideas are methods of teaching your child to cope with strangers, to report trouble, to walk and play in groups, and to avoid or deal with other unforeseen dangers. You'll do some learning, too: how to deal with molesters and kidnappers and how to make use of community projects which provide the concerned parent with valuable advice and assistance.

Resolve to read well the following chapter, then lay down some home-safety laws for your household. Remind your children that these measures are for the good of the whole family. Make sure your kids know their address and phone number and teach them how to call police or the operator from a public pay telephone in order to get help if they need it.

Remember, you can't drum too much safety consciousness into your youngsters' heads. What they learn will help safeguard them and they will benefit more from the protective measures you urge on them. And when awareness of the value of self-protection is taught as soon as it can be understood, it becomes a valuable part of the youth's equipment for a good life. As your children grow older and their power to comprehend increases, clue them in on crime-avoidance tactics detailed in our other chapters.

FOR FURTHER INFORMATION:

Mother's Guide to Child Safety, The. Bryson R. Kalt. New York: Grosset & Dunlap, 1971.

Parent's Guide to Child Safety, A. Vincent J. Fontana. New York: Crowell, 1973.

Parent's Guide to the Prevention and Control of Drug Abuse, A. Paul M. Goldhill, M.D. Chicago: Henry Regnery, 1971.

What You Can Do About Drugs and Your Child. Herman W. Land. New York: Hart, 1969.

THE MOLESTER MENACE

The child molester. Statistics have shown that in 60 percent of all cases involving child molestation, the perpetrator is a relative, friend, or acquaintance of the child or his family. For this reason, we recommend that parents *not* use the standard method of prevention, which involves cautioning the child against talking to strangers. Further, this may pose deep psychological problems for the child in later life.

Instead, explain to the child, on his own level, how sometimes people are sick, and may want to touch him all over. Since child molesters usually begin by offering the child a ride or candy, explain to them that they should never get into a stranger's car or take candy from them. Above all, let the child know emphatically that if he is molested, not to feel that he did something "bad"—but to come to you and tell you about it immediately.

Safety in numbers. Law-enforcement officials advise us that a child molester only rarely approaches a *group* of children. Usually, he'll select the lone child as his prey.

Therefore, whenever possible, you'll want your child to walk to school, run errands, and play with other children—the more the better.

Kiddie caution. Never allow a child to answer the door alone, even when an adult is in the house and *especially* when one is not. For children are naturally friendly and unafraid. They may innocently admit a robber, rapist, child molester, or other criminal into your home.

Self-defense. Judo, karate, and other self-defense martial art forms rely on quickness, balance, and surprise, not size and strength. As a result, school-age children can readily learn fundamental fighting skills to ward off attacks from strangers in the street or the classroom bully who takes their lunch money.

Build your child's self-confidence and your peace of mind by enrolling your youngster in a self-defense course. Many schools (listed in your Yellow Pages) offer reduced rates for children and/or family instruction.

Childbeating. Childbeating is perhaps the saddest and most difficult-to-prevent crime against children, because it's almost always the youngster's parents doing the beating. Often the child is threatened with more brutal punishment if he reports his parents' actions. Abusing children is a symptom of a mental disorder in the parent. Counseling is urgently needed, since childbeaters usually repeat their violence, sometimes stepping up their abuse to the point of actually killing the child.

Responsibility for protecting children from abusive parents rests on outsiders: schoolteachers, hospital workers, doctors, neighbors, and relatives. By informing police and a local child-abuse agency that you suspect a child is being beaten by his parents, you may well be saving that young human life.

Help in emergencies. Sexist as it may seem, culture and custom combine to make women somewhat more sensitive than men to the needs of youngsters. Whether the problem is finding a restroom, avoiding a child molester, or keeping a big kid from taking a smaller one's lunch money, maternal instincts run deep. Tell your children that in an emergency they should always go to a woman for help, not a man.

KIDNAPPED AND MISSING KIDS

Regular routes. If your children walk to and from school, it's important for them to walk on main streets, frequented by many people. These can help your child in case of trouble whereas on a deserted side street there will be no help at all. Instruct your children to take the exact same route every day. If the child is missing, you'll at least be able to tell the authorities where to begin a search.

Abduction by the ex-spouse. The child-stealing victim often knows exactly who has the child: the ex-spouse. One way for a divorced or separated parent to find a former partner, and possibly missing children, is to contact the post office in the city where the mate-turned-abductor last lived. For a small fee (generally $1) the Postal Service will tell anyone the latest change of address for a given person. This perfectly legal detective method has helped more than one distraught parent regain court-ordered custody of a missing youngster.

Kidnap trap. Dealing with kidnappers is always touchy. Usually one is ordered to hand over large sums of money for the safe return of the victim. To stand the best chance of recovering both your ransom funds and the hostage, avoid publicizing kidnapper demands. Deliver the ransom under police guidance, making sure marked bills are included. Then, after the money is paid, publicize a much higher amount than actually given. This trick often provokes dissension among kidnap gang members, causing them to make some mistake leading to their capture—and the return of your money.

False kidnappings. A few years back, parents of students at a leading Eastern women's college received demands for the ransom of their "kidnapped" daughters. Although none of the young women were, in reality, kidnapped, some terrified parents paid unquestioningly, dropping a king's ransom on a prankster's phone call.

Demand to speak to your child to be sure he's safe and actually abducted. If the threatening caller refuses, a quick check with school or friends may set your mind at ease and save your money.

Hostage behavior. Kidnap victims and holdup hostages must try to keep calm and cooperate with their captors. If you're in this situation, above all stay calm. Kidnappers will be nervous, perhaps dangerous psychotics, so don't threaten them with physical resistance or abusive language. Cooperate with their demands, but avoid giving out information on your family or on possible rescue efforts. Concentrate on noting features of your abductors that will help police track them after your release.

Kidnappers calling. Nobody wants to answer the phone with a cheery greeting and find out he's saluting a kidnapper, extortion artist, or blackmailer, but phones ring with such calls every day. Be better prepared to deal with such terrorists by keeping a tape recorder in working order near your phone.

Recordings are extremely valuable to investigators, helping them find your threatened loved ones, recover your ransom money, and convict the extortionists once they're captured and hauled into court. Background noises or music, accents in the callers speech, and the exact words and speech patterns are all clues to be gleaned from a taped conversation. If you're caught without a tape recorder, try to note these things yourself.

Signing out. It's 8:32—do you know where your children aren't? Good, because then you no doubt are keeping track of where the kids *are.* Knowing the location, company, and expected time of return of your children at all hours is a basic security precaution every family should take.

If a child is not yet disciplined to keep parents informed of his comings and goings, we suggest a two-step process to establish the habit. First invest $10 in an inexpensive watch so the youngster has no excuse for coming home late. Then nail a notepad and pencil on a string near your front door. Tell your child to sign out, giving destination, playmates, and return time. If the child is very late, you and the police will know where to start looking for him.

Picture protection. Police investigators across the country will tell you the basic pattern for child stealing is all too familiar—one parent grabs the child (or hires someone to do this) from the schoolgrounds and vanishes. Typically the child stealer is the divorced parent who didn't get court-granted custody and is striking at his former marriage partner through the child.

Divorced parents can protect themselves and their children from this common and cruel retaliation by taking a copy of their divorce along with a picture of their ex-mate to teachers and school administrators. Tell them to call police should the former spouse show up on the schoolgrounds.

Finding a missing child. As soon as you're reasonably certain your youngster is missing, notify police. They may already have the child in custody, or be able to find him or her unharmed quickly. Tell them what the kid was wearing, where he was last seen, and where he was going. If you suspect kidnapping or your child has run away, tell police this, too. You'll next want to notify your neighbors, friends, relatives, and the youngster's playmates. If you don't find the lost child there, many of these people will help in the search. To facilitate quick discovery, keep a list of your youngster's usual playmates, together with their addresses and phone numbers, tucked inside your telephone book.

Escorts. If you have reason to fear child-stealing or kidnapping attacks, arrange to have your child accompanied to and from school by a responsible friend. Teachers and the school principal should be told exactly who will pick your child up and instructed to release the child to no one else. Taxis or public buses aren't safe transportation, since an assailant can easily commandeer these vehicles.

DRUG ABUSE

Detection. If you discover or suspect your child is using drugs, here's what you should do. Open the lines of communication with your child. Begin building a trusting relationship if none exists. Don't react in anger by punishing him or not letting him see friends, as this will cause the child to react bitterly and not solve the problem. Instead, express genuine concern for your youngster's health and well-being. Try for a long-term approach—helping alleviate the problems that caused your child to turn to drugs. Seek help from local community agencies listed under "Drug Abuse" in the Yellow Pages. Two good books on the topic, available at your library, are *A Parent's Guide to the Prevention and Control of Drug Abuse,* Paul Goldhill (New York: Henry Regnery, 1971); and *What You Can Do About Drugs and Your Child,* Herman Land (New York: Pocket Books, Inc., 1971).

Dope information. A series of free pamphlets describing and illustrating various types of street drugs, including the devil weed marijuana, are available from the Los Angeles Police Department. Entitled *Help,* they're free and can be obtained by writing to the Los Angeles Police Department, Public Affairs Division, 150 North Los Angeles Street, Los Angeles, Calif. 90012.

Bad trips. One of the most terrifying experiences for the youngster beginning to experiment with drugs is a "bad trip" on LSD or some other high-powered hallucinogen which can distort reality into horrifying forms. "Acid" is a mind-expanding drug usually taken in tiny pills, in sugar cubes, or on blotting paper. Take LSD away from your child if you find him or her with it. Give large dosages (500 mg.) of vitamin C or ascorbic acid (available at drug stores) to calm the frightening "trip" you find your youngster experiencing.

Physical clues. Determining whether your teenager is experimenting with illegal and often dangerous drugs is not difficult if you pay attention to physical changes which such drugs often produce in the child. Notice, for instance, dilated pupils, abnormal appetite (more or less than ordinary), sleeplessness, diarrhea, muscle twitching, vomiting, runny eyes or nose, a drunk-like lethargy, and, naturally, needle "tracks" on arms and elsewhere. Such symptoms aren't always indications of trouble, but if they occur in combinations or regularly they are certainly cause to suspect a drug problem.

Personality clues. One indication that a youngster is using drugs is a sudden marked personality change. Such character shifts often follow a change in the friends your teenager hangs around with. To tell if your child may be on drugs, look for: sudden short-temperedness, high and low moods changing quickly from a beaming smile to frowns, uncharacteristic insecurity or withdrawnness, and a sudden "I don't care" attitude toward family, old friends, school, personal appearance, or hygiene.

COMMUNITY PROJECTS

Parent patrols. As children increasingly fall victim to molestation, mugging, kidnapping, and a deplorable variety of senseless acts of violence, concerned parents everywhere are banding together to form child safety patrols. In New York City, for instance, volunteer parents patrol residential areas in pairs during school hours. Their conspicuous orange blazers not only serve to discourage the potential troublemaker, but are easily recognizable to the child who may be in need of assistance.

For help in initiating such a program in your neighborhood, contact your local police precinct.

Block watchers. In New York, St. Louis, and some other cities, the Block Watcher program has met with phenomenal success in deterring those who would harm and harass children. On each block, one housewife volunteers to keep an eye out for any child in trouble.

Each volunteer house is supplied with a decal denoting participation, which is prominently displayed on the front door or window. In turn, neighborhood children are told to watch for the decals and to go immediately to that particular house if help is needed.

Your local police department will provide you with valuable tips on how to initiate such a program in your community.

Beneficent businessmen. A valuable augmentation to the Block Watcher program is the participation of local business firms. Decals and signs are prominently displayed by stores and offices along the routes traveled by children on their way to and from school. The youngsters are then taught to turn to these firms when help is needed.

This type of program is most effectively implemented through the local Chamber of Commerce, which can rally behind the cause, generating pledges of assistance from its members.

Student security units. High-school and college campuses witnessed a crime increase of more than 300 percent over the last five years, making the hallowed halls somewhat less than safe. Students at some schools are taking steps to protect themselves—forming volunteer units to assist local police and campus security forces in spotting trouble situations.

Does your school boast such a group? If not, form one! Your volunteers can patrol campus grounds and parking lots regularly, or provide nighttime escort services for women heading home from the library or crossing campus after dark.

Poison control centers. If your youngster swallows some form of poison, call your physician immediately, write down his instructions, and follow them to the letter. Or, for expert advice on specific toxins, call your nearby government Poison Control Center—dial long-distance if you must, since the few cents extra could save your child's life.

There are more than 600 Poison Control Centers across the nation. For a complete listing of their addresses and phone numbers, write the Superintendent of Documents, U.S. Government Printing Office, Washington, D.C. 20402 (20 cents). Or call one of these major urban centers: New York, 212–340–4495; Chicago, 312–738–4411; Los Angeles, 213–664–2121; Atlanta, 404–523–4711; or Omaha, 402–553–5400.

Crime in the classroom. Growing children spend more and more time away from parental guidance, meaning their safety depends more and more on the youngsters' own knowledge and wiles. In an innovative program currently underway in thirty-six California school districts, seventh and eighth graders are being taught tactics of crime prevention and personal safety for an hour each week. Help educate and protect your children by urging public school boards in your area to adopt safety and crime prevention courses into their curriculum.

CHAPTER 5

Rape:
the ultimate indignity

Rape occurs with alarming and increasing frequency in American streets and homes today. In terming it an "indignity," we by no means intend to overlook the highly physical, often brutal, aspects. Rather we view rape as an assault on the self-respect of *all* women. Rape is the criminal side of a dominance/submission struggle between the sexes.

But just as any woman on the streets is a potential rape target merely because she is female, we contend that every woman should be physically and mentally prepared to fend off a sexual assault. Unfortunately, the woman who has never been raped or who has never known anyone so abused tends to be uninterested in the subject of rape avoidance. We cannot overstate the importance of learning rape-avoidance techniques *before* one is confronted with such a situation.

Recent trends in this criminal area indicate that rape is a more significant crime than many lawmakers have imagined. While other violent crime in the nation dropped by 5 percent in 1976, FBI figures show the number of rapes in the country remained constant. The year saw more than 56,000 reported cases of forcible rape. If that number rings hollow, consider these breakdowns that bring home the cold, disgusting truth.

Crime reports for 1976 show that a woman was raped every ten minutes in our so-called "civilized" society. Nearly half of these rapes were gang attacks involving two or more sexual assailants. The figures tell us that 51 of every 100,000 women and girls in the country reported being raped in that one year. And, since authorities estimate conservatively that three out of four rape victims *don't* report the crime, the nation's rape problem is quadrupled! Have you met 500 women in your lifetime? Allowing for those who didn't report, you can bet at least one of those 500 was beaten, threatened, or otherwise forced into committing sexual acts against her will in America's bicentennial year.

Now let's look at the rapist. Until recently there was little hard information on these desperados. Common myth conjured up an image of the rapist as a hulking figure lurking in alleyways and bushes, poised to leap on the first defenseless female who happened by. Old boyfriends, casual acquaintances, and other attackers familiar to the rape victim were routinely released by juries convinced that such rapists were mere sheep being "led on" by "some hussy who got what she deserved." Systematic studies of rape and rapists in Philadelphia and by the National Commission on the Causes and Prevention of Violence paint a different picture.

Rapes are *not* random attacks, these studies show. In fact, most of them (71 percent) are planned. More than half of all rapes occur in the victim's or in the rapist's home rather than on the street, and most rapists are known, at least casually, by their victims. A full 61 percent of rapists are under the age of twenty-five, and, according to a seventeen-city survey, 51 percent are white, 47 percent black, and 2 percent of other racial origins. The lesson in these statistics is that today's woman shouldn't completely trust anyone but herself. She alone bears the final responsibility for avoiding rape—and the policies and tactics suggested here will enable her to live up to that responsibility.

As with confrontation by a robber or mugger, the important thing to remember when you're approached by a rapist is survival. If a choice *must* be made between death and submission, only a fool would choose the former. But our object is to show you how to avoid situations in which those are the only choices. Whether this means fighting for your life, trying some psychological trickery, or pretending to go limp with submission depends on the peculiar circumstances of each attack and on your own emotional makeup. You must choose among possible avoidance alternatives and tailor your actions to fit your own personality.

Some self-defense hints follow, and more are included in Chapter 2. With one of the psychological ploys suggested you may be able to influence your assailant, throwing him temporarily off guard and giving you precious seconds in which to escape. Whatever tack you take, the only way to preserve your dignity, and often your life, is to prepare now, before it happens, to deal with the all-too-possible likelihood of a sexual assault.

FOR FURTHER INFORMATION:

Against Rape. Andrea Medea and Kathleen Thompson. New York: Farrar, Straus and Giroux, 1974.

Bait and the Trap, The. Jean MacKellar. New York: Crown, 1975.

Career Girl, Watch Your Step. Max Wylie. New York: Dodd, Mead, 1964.

Coping. Martha Yates. Englewood Cliffs, N. J.: Prentice-Hall, 1976.

Effective Unarmed Combat. Malcolm Harris. New York: Arco, 1972.

How to Say No to a Rapist and Survive. Frederic Storaska. New York: Random House, 1975.

Lady Beware. Peter Arnold. Garden City, N. Y.: Doubleday, 1974.

Personal Defense for Women. S. Margaret Heyden and Allan V. Tarpenning. Belmont, Calif.: Wadsworth, 1970.

Politics of Rape, The. Diana E. H. Russell. New York: Stein and Day, 1975.

Rape. Carol V. Horos. New Canaan, Conn.: Tobey, 1974.

Rape; How to Avoid It and What to Do About It If You Can't. June Csida and Joseph Csida. Chatsworth, Calif.: Books for Better Living, 1974.

Self Defense for Girls. Bruce Tegner and Alice McGrath. Ventura, Calif.: Thor, 1967.

PREVENTIVE POLICIES

Car care. What does auto maintenance have to do with avoiding rape? Everything. Especially if you drive a lot at night.

Keep your car well maintained by having frequent tuneups and regular lubes and oil changes. Never let the level of your gas tank get below one-quarter full. A lone woman running out of gas is just asking for trouble. Install steel-belted radial tires on your car; they're the least likely to have flats and blowouts. Carry flares in your glove compartment. Learn how to change a tire quickly so that you can get moving again fast if you have a flat.

Protection in cars. It's late at night. You're walking alone down a dark street. Suddenly, you hear footsteps behind you. Closer now. You're sure someone's after you. What to do?

Quickly you scan the cars parked along the curb, looking for one with its lock button up. Finding one, you jump into the car, locking the doors behind you. Then you start honking the horn. Your would-be assailant takes off down the street and disappears faster than you can yell "thief."

Pick your route. But even if your car is in top mechanical condition, it's only a machine and, as such, subject to breakdown anytime, anywhere. Therefore never drive through rough neighborhoods, even if you must take lengthy detours in order to avoid them. Try to stay out of secluded areas as well, and stick to business sections if possible. These are highly patrolled and if an emergency occurs you're very likely to find help here.

Mobile molestation. Rapes on public conveyances—whether subway or steamer, train or touring bus—can and do occur frequently. One excellent way to protect yourself from danger on public transportation is to stay near the operator at all times. He may not be able to help you personally, but he may be able to send out a radio alert which will bring help.

The lost-and-found rapist. Many times a rapist will find his victim through the newspaper lost-and-found ads. He'll answer an ad, claiming to have found lost jewelry or a pet, then suggest that he and the victim meet for return of the item.

Be extremely wary of such a situation. The best bet is to meet during the day in a public place such as the post office or bus station, or better yet, inside your local police precinct.

Frottage. Frottage is a term denoting some minor sexual advance, such as when a man rubs up against you or touches you intimately in a crowded subway. Your best defense here is to look him square in the eye and say in a loud voice, "Please keep your hands to yourself!" Naturally you'll want to be absolutely sure that the man indeed imposed himself on you in such a manner before so embarrassing him.

Breakdown bunco. Sometimes a rapist will go to surprising lengths to find a victim. Such is the case of the man who would pull his car over to the edge of a deserted road, raise the hood, and set out flares. If a male stopped to offer help, he politely declined, saying help was on the way. If a woman stopped, however, he would force her into his car, then drive off into a field and rape her.

Offer direct assistance to no one in such a situation. Instead, you can be of help by calling the police or highway patrol and notifying them of the location of the car.

Babysitting lures. Unless you take adequate precautions, babysitting can turn out to be an especially hazardous occupation. Rapists have been known to call an unsuspecting sitter from a phone booth and offer her a job. They'll then give directions to their house, requesting that the sitter meet them there, offering to pick her up at a nearby bus stop. What happens next is obvious.

To circumvent such a possibility, accept the job if you desire, then call the number back unexpectedly a few hours later on some trivial matter. If the man answers or if someone else answers who will verify that he lives there, you at least know you're not blindly walking into a compromising situation.

The protector. Occasionally, rapists will work in pairs. One will act as the aggressor, while the other will come to your "aid." Then they will *both* rape you.

Naturally, you may be in a situation in which your only alternative is to accept help from a strange man. However, be leery of such offers and try your best to get away from both individuals as quickly as possible.

Elevator safety. Before getting into any elevator, take a quick look at its occupants. Be especially wary of an elevator containing one or more men, and no women. If you get in, stand as close as possible to the control panel.

Unfortunately, most elevators contain a stop button, allowing a mugger or rapist to stop the elevator between floors before committing the crime. Your best defense here is the emergency alarm button, which in many cases is hooked up directly to the building's main office. Otherwise, employ any of the various physical or psychological self-defense methods described in the "Self Defense" section of Chapter 2.

Ram rapist. In order to find their victims, rapists have been known to go to such extremes as ramming a woman's car or trying to force her off the road.

If you're driving in an isolated area and a man or group of men runs into your car, forget about stopping to exchange driver's licenses. Instead, get the other car's license number and head for the nearest police station. Even if the collision was truly an accident, by reporting the incident you will not be charged with hit-and-run driving.

Car caper. Let's assume some madman does succeed in forcing your car off the road. Chances are he'll do it by pulling alongside and slightly ahead of you, then turning into you. The path ahead of you is now blocked.

What to do? Again, the last thing you want is a confrontation—no matter how angry you are. Quickly throw your car into reverse, then drive around his car—running him over if you must—and get out of there. Catch his license number if you can and report the incident to the police immediately.

Teddy-bear trick. Here's a way to second-guess the potential car rapist or other individual who may bother you while driving at night. Buy or create a large teddy bear or other stuffed man-sized figure, put a shirt and hat on him, and install him in the passenger seat next to you.

Although some people may recognize it for what it is and think you're a bit daft, if it only scares off one potential rapist it will have served its purpose.

The flight plan. In flying, it's standard procedure to file a flight pattern before taking off so that if the plane doesn't arrive within a reasonable length of time of its stated time of arrival, a search party can be sent out.

If you venture out alone in your car at night—even only to the local supermarket—you'd do well to give a friend or relative your destination, route, and expected time of return. Then, if you're late getting back, authorities can be alerted, who can find you and come to your aid if needed.

Word to the wise. If you are being followed late at night in a residential area, and you think you may be in danger, run to the nearest house and bang on the door as hard as you can. Then yell not "help," but "fire." For the word "fire," when screamed out, is one of the most psychologically agitating words in the English dictionary, and it should serve not only to draw others to your aid, but also to send your potential attacker scurrying off into the dark night.

Ladies last. Now we're not going to admonish you not to hitchhike alone. We presume you know better. In fact, hitchhiking in groups, although somewhat safer, is still dangerous. But if you're hitchhiking with your boyfriend, here's a tip: Always let him get into the car before you.

Many times, when the female gets in the car first, a rapist will suddenly drive off, leaving the man by the side of the road. Then he'll drive to a secluded area and rape the woman.

Back-seat lurkers. At night or in daylight, your car's back seat is a favorite hiding place for criminals of all kinds. Always check for intruders before you get in. When leaving a two-door car, pull the front seats forward for an unobstructed view when you return. When leaving a four-door car at night, carry a pocket flashlight to shine into the rear-seat area before reentering your car.

Nighttime errands. More and more womanpower in the work force means more and more women are doing their shopping, their wash, and their errands at night. Since studies show almost all sexual assaults take place during evening hours, women (and men for that matter) should avoid going to self-service laundries alone at night. Take a friend along or wash during daylight hours before or just after work. Choose well-lighted, popular spots to wash clothes or shop at night. You may have to wait for a dryer, but you'll live to gripe about it.

Police pointers. The brochure entitled *Lady Beware* gives women some good advice on how to avoid potentially dangerous situations on the street, in the car, and at home. It's available free by writing to the Public Affairs Division of the Los Angeles Police Department, 150 North Los Angeles Street, Los Angeles, Calif. 90012.

PSYCHOLOGICAL TRICKS

Dispelling fear. You may not realize it, but often a rapist is just as frightened as his victim. He fears counterattack. He fears getting caught. He is afraid that you'll not give him what he thinks he must have. And at the root of it all, he is afraid of his own actions.

You must first assure this person that he has nothing whatever to fear from you—that you represent neither a physical nor a psychological threat to him. By gaining his confidence in this regard, you'll destroy these fears, which form the very basis of his actions.

The turnoff. Turning a man off sexually by urinating or defecating can serve as an excellent psychological deterrent to rape. Granted, such behavior is gross, but after all, who ever heard of observing rules of etiquette with a rapist?

Disease dodge. If you can engage your antagonist at all in conversation, and can manage to keep the panic out of your voice, calmly and convincingly assure him that you indeed would enjoy sex with him but you've just found out you have syphilis. If your act is good, and if the man has any semblance of sense at all, he'll probably decide not to chance it with you.

Lesbian act. A few years back two female friends of ours were foolishly walking in Central Park late at night when they heard footsteps behind them. Turning, they saw two men following them. The ladies had no weapons. Further, screaming would probably only serve to attract a few more potential rapists from the surrounding bushes. They had to think fast.

Their solution? They started acting like two lesbians. The men following them were so turned off by the pair's actions that they promptly turned on their heels and left the scene in disgust.

The couched compliment. Rapists are as susceptible to compliments as you and I. If you can engage him in conversation, comment on his charm and good looks. Speculate on the idea that he has a lot of girl friends or could get one easily. You must build his ego.

This is a delaying tactic—a method of throwing him off guard until you have the opportunity to either disable him physically or escape.

A crazy idea. Believe it or not, there are documented cases of potential rapists being deterred when the intended victim feigned madness. Such actions as giggling, babbling in gibberish, reciting nursery rhymes, and making strange signs and gestures with the hands many times will so bewilder a would-be rapist that he may just forget why he was there in the first place. Sounds unlikely, but you'll want to try every ploy in the book before giving in.

Faint idea. If you go limp in a feigned faint, the rapist may panic, thinking he's killed you, or he may just not enjoy raping an inert mass.

Husband ploy. Suppose you're walking late at night down a deserted street and suspect that you're about to be waylaid by a stranger. Stop walking, look toward an upstairs window and yell "I'm home, George, can you come down and open the door for me?"

Unless your potential assailant is awfully desperate, he'll keep right on walking.

The stall. If your adversary has had any previous experience with rape, he'll expect your first reaction to be a violent one—a heroic and vigorous display of self-defense. Naturally, he'll be prepared for this. But your best defense lies in catching the rapist off-guard, unawares. So if you can placate him in some way, until you can take some course of action for which he is unprepared, you'll gain an important edge.

Stall him by making him think that you'll accede to his demands, perhaps by telling him that you yourself have been needing sex for a long time. Or by saying calmly and convincingly, "Well, let's take our time and enjoy it." Sooner or later his mind will begin to anticipate the act. He'll relax. Then you'll have the opportunity to either utilize one of the disabling tactics given elsewhere in this book or to make your escape.

Contemptuous familiarity. Face-to-face with a mugger or cornered by a rapist or other assailant, you can often avoid attack by convincing the villain you know him. Yell, "Wait a minute. I *know* you! I'd know that face anywhere!"

Many criminals depend on the difficulty of positive identification to police or in court. If he thinks he's been recognized, the thought "I'll be caught" automatically clicks in a rapist's head. Often he'll flee without attacking. But be sure to use this ruse early, *before* the assault. After the act, the rapist might kill you for his own protection.

FIGHTING BACK

Karate. Karate comes to us from the Orient, from days when peasants were forced to defend themselves, unarmed, against armed bandits. This self-defense technique employs swift strikes and thrusts with the hands and feet.

Used as a self-defense tool, karate is unexcelled, and can be learned at any of the many schools set up to teach it. Find these in your Yellow Pages under "Judo, Karate and Jiu Jitsu Instruction."

The baseball bat. One of the best all-around weapons to keep next to your bed at night is a baseball bat. Although it may not bark or bite, neither does it get fleas or require feeding. Nor can it discharge accidentally. It allows you to keep your distance from an intruder, while using it either as a jabbing instrument or more forcefully as a club.

Pressure points. The area just below the earlobes where the jaw and skull meet contains a large concentration of nerve endings. Consequently, this spot is extremely vulnerable to pressure.

First, calm down your attacker. Let him think that you're going along with him. Then, gently caress the sides of his face with your hands. After you've slowly worked the tips of your index fingers over to this spot, quickly jab them inward. This will send your adversary into sudden shock. It could even kill him.

Groin grab. Calm your attacker down by letting him think you'll go along with his demands. Then start caressing him gently—all over. Slowly work your way down toward his testicles. Gently cup them in one hand. Then suddenly squeeze as hard as you can. The excruciating pain will disable him immediately.

Eye gouge. This tactic involves temporarily playing along with your attacker, making him think that you're just as anxious as he for some passionate lovemaking. After you're a few minutes into the heavy petting stage and you see that he's calmed down, gently place your hands on the sides of his face. Slowly lean forward to kiss him, then quickly and forcefully jam your thumbs into his eye sockets. If he's wearing glasses, go under them.

This will temporarily or permanently blind him; if enough pressure is exerted, his eyes will be pushed back against his cortex, killing him instantly.

The karate chop. Extend your fingers and put them together. Now make your hand as stiff as possible. Here you've got a weapon that can seriously disable, even kill a person twice your size. Use the fleshy part of your hand in a swift and vigorous chop to your attacker's neck, temple, or nose. To further unbalance your adversary and tense your body for the blow, let out a loud scream as your hand comes down to make contact.

Practice. Be prepared to resist a rapist's attacks by practicing self-defense in advance. Even the untrained amateur can practice resistance to frontal assaults, choking attacks, and rear grabs with the help of a friend.

Think in what situations you'd jab your attacker's eyes, stomp his toes, or knee his groin, and imagine yourself mad enough or panicked enough to really do it. Practicing resistance will give you a mental edge to battle your way to safety in a real-life situation.

The bicycle pump. Bicycle riders gain protection from rapists as well as blowouts by snapping a detachable metal tire pump next to their bike frame. When molested while riding, jab this excellent weapon into your attacker's stomach or swing it like a club. Bike shops and department stores sell these devices for about $7.

The ankle jerk. From a darkened doorway or pitch-black alley some lummox leaps on your back, his arms pinned around your body. Free yourself by moving fast. Step aside with one foot, reach down between your ankles, and grab one of the attacker's ankles in both hands. Yank the ankle forward and upward and squat down a bit on his thigh. Your leverage will pull him off his feet, snapping his grip around your waist.

Dirty fighting. Self-defense tactics for close-in struggles with rapists, muggers, or murderers are all vicious and all potential lifesavers. Here are some of the most effective:

Bite ends of fingers, toes, nose; chomp ears, cheeks, and other sensitive spots; if held from behind, smash your head back into the attacker's face; drive your elbow into his ribs, or jaw; rake fingernails across his face; jam thumbs into his neck and press hard to stop breathing and blood to the brain; twist his ears off (try to, anyway); or clap cupped hands over his ears, creating a dizzying, thunderlike sound.

The neck blow. A smash to an assailant's neck, particularly the base of his neck where it joins his back, can cause instant death. Deliver this blow with the side of your hand (fingers rigidly extended) in a chopping motion or with your fist, middle knuckle extended.

Improvised weapons. You don't need chemical sprays or expensive store-bought weapons to stop a rapist. Equally effective are common articles easily stashed in purse or coat pocket. Have a squeeze container of lemon juice or red pepper ready to spray at an attacker's eyes. Or keep a hat pin, corkscrew, fingernail file, pencil, or keys ready to cut, scrape and gouge. Sudden pain will sidetrack the assailant while you escape.

Biting. Children bite by instinct, but adults often overlook their teeth as an important close-quarters weapon. If a rapist has you in a face-to-face hold, sinking your teeth into any available flesh of his may be your quickest way to freedom. The feel of teeth chomping into his throat will shake up even the strongest man, filling him with a primeval fear of death. And a properly placed bite can kill. Go for your attacker's throat, ears, or shoulders—or anywhere else possible—when you have to fight and bite for your life or safety.

Shoes. High-heeled shoes and the newer cork or wooden platform shoes are nothing but hobbles to a woman in a hazardous situation. Take such shoes off and carry them when walking (day or night) through areas where you feel threatened.

Should a rapist or other assailant approach, fling your footwear at him, or kick it at him if it's still on your feet. He will duck, giving you a precious moment to flee, barefoot and screaming.

Blows to the throat. Any number of chops and blows to the throat area will drop your attacker grimacing to his knees. With fingers firmly extended, try to jab your fingertips through your enemy's throat at the base or at the Adam's apple. Or chop at his larynx with a swift side-of-the-hand smash. Any of these measures will cause severe pain and coughing and can cut off the attacker's air supply. An elbow ram or hand chop to the collarbone will bring a wince of pain and maybe crack the bone.

Door stopper. For those of you who read our peephole and chain-guard advice in Chapter 1 but didn't follow it, there are a few tactics you can use to repel the creep who tries to force his way in your door after you've opened it a crack. Start with hand blows to the face and fingers in the eyes, then slam the heel of your palm up under his chin, pushing his face upward and back. That should get him back far enough for you to slam the door between the two of you, especially if you're stomping his foot, kicking his knee, and/or loosening his grip by bending his fingers back.

Blows to the spine. A blast to the spine with the ball of your foot or your knee or elbow can kill or paralyze your assailant. When things get dire, smash him in the back with all your might.

Breaking choking holds. If grabbed from behind, step back in the direction of your attacker and stomp *hard* on his foot; if strangled from in front of you, lock your fingers together and drive this double fist up between the assailant's arms. When your hands pass your face, flip them apart to jolt your forearms against the insides of his elbows to drive his arms apart and snap his stranglehold. To block a choke attempt, cross both arms in front of your face with elbows at shoulder level and palms facing outward.

Waking up strangled. More often than not, it's a nightmare. But if you leave doors unlocked at night it might not be a dream one of these times. Someone will really be choking you when you wake up.

If so, slash down with both your forearms on his elbow joint. Punch or chop the strangler on the tip of his nose and gouge his eyes with your fingers if possible. Keep the jabs going to his eyes, nose, and (if he covers up his face) groin while you maneuver to get up and free.

Breaking hair holds. Be ready to react quickly when an attacker grabs your hair, either from in front or from behind. Clamp your hand on top of your assailant's and press it firmly on your head. Then rotate your body and head in the direction of the attacker's little finger.

You'll break his hold by turning his little finger toward his forearm, causing the outside of his wrist to bend and strain.

Defense against clubs. Your arms can be effective shock absorbers when an attacker is flailing you with a club or kicking you. To parry a blow with a board, step toward your attacker, crossing both wrists and extending your arms in front of you to catch his weapon between your wrists (it will hurt him more than you).

This wrists-crossed method works in stopping kicks, too. If you can, catch his foot and return a kick between his legs.

Kidney punches. Punch, kick, jab, or ram your attacker's kidneys and you can leave him screaming, in shock, or dead. The kidneys are located just to the left and right of the spinal column in the lower back. If you can hit or kick forcefully, this area is very vulnerable.

Down but not out. Once you've been knocked to the ground by a rapist or mugger, kicking is your only effective defense option. Turn on your side and start flailing your feet at his shins, and don't stop! It's not safe for you to attempt to stand until your attacker is hurt or goes away. If the assailant tries to get around your lashing legs to your head, use your arms to pivot your body and keep within kicking range. Be ready to roll and dodge if your adversary dives at you while down.

Gun chops. Never attempt to fight an armed man unless you're positive that he plans to kill you. In this case, first make a distracting move (raising one hand to make him look up or talking to him to get him listening rather than concentrating on you). Then as quickly as you can, chop down hard on the gunman's wrist or elbow joint with the edge of your hand. With luck you'll knock the gun down to where you can recover it or have time to escape. Otherwise you must now punch, kick, knee, and gouge for your life. We repeat, *this is a very dangerous move.* Chances are he'll flick his finger and gun you down. Only when it's a matter of life and death and you'll be shot anyway should you make such a last-ditch effort.

Heart and solar plexus. Make a fist with your thumb pressed atop your index finger and middle knuckle protruding. There you have a deadly weapon if you deliver a sharp, forceful blow to an attacker's heart. Or swing for the solar plexus, that nerve center located between the lower portions of the rib cage and directly above the stomach. A single-knuckle fist crashing into this area can cause severe pain or death.

Breaking wrist holds. What to do if you're being pulled into an alley or car by a menacing stranger? If your adversary has gripped one of your wrists with both his hands, kick vigorously into his knee or shin while you grab your captured hand with your free hand. Then jerk your arms up across your body, pulling against his grip's weakest point—between his thumb and forefingers. Repeat this action, if needed, kicking and jerking until your hand is free.

Breaking double wrist holds. Okay, let's say the mysterious menace has grabbed both your wrists—one in each of his hands—and is dragging you away. Here's a way to shimmy free that you can practice to disco music.

Kick at his knees every chance you get and you'll feel his grip loosen. Try to force your arms out to the side and up. His reaction will be to resist by pushing your arms down and in. When you feel that inward pressure, take advantage of it! Jerk your arms in and then up over your head, breaking his grip at its weakest point. Now *run!*

GETTING HELP

Psychological counseling. If you've been raped and feel that you need psychological counseling, you can call or visit any of hundreds of rape crisis centers scattered across the land. If there is one in your area, you'll find it in the white pages of your telephone book under "rape." Or call the National Organization for the Prevention of Rape and Assault (NOPRA), 777 United Nations Plaza, New York, N. Y. 10017, phone (212) 371–3664. They'll put you in immediate touch with a psychological counselor and also refer you to a doctor or lawyer if desired.

For a free list of rape crisis centers throughout the country, write the Center for Women Policy Studies, 2000 P Street N.W., Suite 508, Washington, D.C. 20036.

Preserve the evidence. After being raped, your first impulse may be to wash or douche. Don't. A sperm test will have to be made at the hospital, the results of which may be valuable in the prosecution of your attacker. Don't change your clothes, as they may contain traces of the man's blood or semen. If furniture was upset or broken during a struggle, let it be. In short, don't touch a thing until after the police depart and you've had your physical examination.

Medical attention. Whether or not you decide to report your rape to the police, we strongly urge you to visit your doctor—fast. Not only will he be able to treat any wounds, but he can also give you a shot of penicillin to prevent V.D. And if you're not already regularly taking birth-control pills, he can give you a "morning after" pill in order to reduce the chances of pregnancy. Lastly, he can provide you with emotional support, help soothe your jangled nerves, and, in general, help put the whole ordeal into a better perspective for you.

The facts. If you decide to call the police after you've been raped, the very next thing you should do is to call a friend or neighbor and tell them what happened. Or put your story on tape. Relate every detail you can think of: the rapist's initial approach, his physical description, the clothes he wore, the sound of his voice. Was he nervous or calm? Any tattoos? And, yes, was he circumsized? You'll need this evidence in court, and if you wait till then to recall these details, you'll more than likely find that they've slipped your mind.

Civil procedures. Aside from pressing criminal charges—which often can't be made to stick—against rapists, you can file civil charges. If the offender is salaried, this can be a worthwhile procedure, since the victim can not only demand payment for her pain and suffering, but can recover court costs.

CHAPTER 6

Con games and bunco schemes

"You can't cheat an honest man," said the immortal comedian W. C. Fields. But confidence schemers do just that daily, taking millions of dollars each year from their gullible victims—honest and dishonest alike. Bunco artists across the country pay more heed to another oft-repeated Fields line: "Never give a sucker an even break!"

Con games are basically simple plots and as old as the hills. History tells us that a hustler in Marco Polo's entourage "sold" the Mediterranean Sea to a Chinese nobleman. Recent newspapers report similar swindles where con men took thousands of dollars in return for bogus deeds to the Brooklyn Bridge, the Eiffel Tower, and even to homestead plots on the moon! It may seem incredible to you that people would exhibit such gullibility, but perhaps you underestimate the artistry of the world's top flim-flam folks. Most plots are more subtle than silly, with grifters gently manipulating your trust so that you rarely know what hit you—until it's too late.

A con game called the "pigeon drop," for instance, along with its numerous variations, has been perpetrated on unsuspecting victims for centuries. Yet any cop on the bunco beat today will tell you that the operators of this enduring racket are still able to fleece their "marks" of thousands of dollars at a time! The same applies to all other confidence schemes mentioned here. These games are still being played everywhere from back alleys to bogus bank fronts and from raunchy hovels to ritzy hotels. Some of these schemes are classics. Besides the pigeon drop, such games as the handkerchief switch, the gold-brick con, the badger game, the boiler-room rackets, and three-card monte have enjoyed virtually unchecked success for centuries.

Others that follow are relatively new—though widespread and lucrative for their operators.

Our first advice to help you dodge the racketeers is simply: Be suspicious. Don't turn over your savings or pocket money to *anyone* regardless of how plausible their story sounds. If you suspect you're being drawn into a bunco plot, feign stupidity by asking a raft of ignorant questions, or make up any excuse to get away from the trickster working on you. Distance between you and the con man is your greatest ally.

A second suggestion is to be informed. To this end we've compiled descriptions and cautionary information on the most common of the financially devastating "games" around. Finish reading the chapter, then be on guard for the swindles we mention as well as new twists and slight variations thereof.

Finally, we urge you to report to the police any incident where you believe you've been bilked. Much to the con man's joy, many marks are too embarrassed and feel too foolish to admit they fell for some bunco artist's slick line. Unless you turn in a detailed description of any hustle played at your expense, you stand no chance of recovering your losses. And what's more, a con man who knows his mark isn't squealing to the police will return again and again to take you for all you're worth and freely tell his fellow grifters that you rank high on his sucker list.

FOR FURTHER INFORMATION:

Compleat Swindler, The. Ralph Hancock and Henry Chafetz. New York: Macmillan, 1968.

Hustlers and Con Men. Jay Robert Nash. New York: M. Evans & Co., 1976.

CLASSIC CONS

The pigeon drop. This scheme is the most popular con game of all time. It originated in China over a thousand years ago and was introduced to our shores by immigrating Chinese around the time of the Gold Rush.

The ploy most commonly involves a pair of crooks, working in cahoots to flim-flam you, the "pigeon," out of your hard-earned money. One of the perpetrators approaches you with a purse or envelope containing several thousand dollars but with no identification, which he claims to have found. The accomplice will then "happen by" and the three of you will ultimately decide that you should hold the money for safekeeping for a month in case someone comes forth to claim it. If the money is not claimed, the three of you will split it up evenly. "Easy money," you say to yourself.

Here's the rub: In order to "show faith," you must put up some of your *own* money. You may even be bamboozled (as many others have) into drawing your life savings out of the bank and turning it over to the con men. In return, you'll get the purse or envelope containing the found money, but you'll discover that, instead of bona fide currency, it now contains only play money or bundled-up scraps of paper, having been skillfully switched before your very eyes by the now-departed grifters.

The bank con. In order to put this scheme into action, the perpetrator will stand behind you at the bank while you're making a deposit or withdrawal. Looking over your shoulder, he'll commit to memory your account number and the amount of your transaction, as well as your name, address, and phone number.

A few days later you'll get a phone call, ostensibly from a detective at your local police precinct. In order to establish authenticity, he'll verify your account number and the date and amount of your last deposit. "What's the trouble?" you ask. "Well, it seems one of the tellers is embezzling money and we'd like you to help us catch him."

You're instructed to immediately go to your bank and withdraw $2,000, $5,000, $10,000, or more, then return home with it. The "detective" is waiting at your door with a receipt for your money. You turn over the cash to him and that's the last you ever see of it.

The inheritance racket. "Millions of dollars await lost heirs," reads the tempting display ad in your local newspaper. The ad goes on to explain how you may have come into a large inheritance without knowing it. You call the number given in the ad.

A very convincing "inheritance counselor" is dispatched to your home and you ultimately find yourself writing a check for $100–$1,000 for details on how to claim your sudden fortune. Later you discover that the names and addresses given you are completely phony and that your friendly inheritance counselor has departed.

The employment-agency swindle. An advertisement for an employment agency appears in the want ads of your local newspaper, offering several fantastically desirable jobs at unbelievably high pay. You make an appointment at their offices, and arrive in time to find a man apparently locking the door and leaving. "I'm Mr. Jenkins," he says. "Why don't you come down and have a cup of coffee with me while we talk about it?"

Naturally, you join him. As you listen, he describes the various positions available in glowing terms. So excited are you by his hyperbole that you really don't have to think twice about giving him the $50 "agency fee" he's asked for even before you've taken your final gulp of coffee.

Naturally, you've been set up. In reality, he has no office at the address given. You never see him—or your $50—again.

Rare air. Believe it or not, this con game, which originated in the days of patent-medicine sales, still finds victims in our day. Expensive bottles of "200-year-old air" are offered for sale to desperate, but gullible, health sufferers. The hawker typically claims that one whiff of the air contained therein will cure everything from acne to zoster.

Buy your rare air in the Alps, not in a bottle!

The gypsy switch. One day, just for fun, you decide to visit a fortuneteller. The subject of money comes up and the gypsy claims to have supernatural powers over money. To prove it, she asks you to place a $5 bill in a paper sack on the table. The lights go out, she weaves her magic "spell," the lights go on again. Now you're to go home and open the bag. You do so and, to your delight, you find $10 inside.

She asks you to return the following week with a $100 bill, which you obligingly do. The procedure is repeated. When you open the sack at home, you find *two* $100 bills.

Again she asks you to return, this time with your life savings. Again, your money goes into the sack. But this time, when you get home, instead of a fortune you find a sackful of trash. Meanwhile, your gypsy has skipped town.

The Murphy game. In the days of the Wild West, the madam of a house of ill repute was generally referred to as "Mrs. Murphy." She used a pimp to negotiate with clients for her girls.

In the Murphy game, you're set up by a man claiming to be a pimp for a large stable of prostitutes. He'll steer you to a lower-class hotel. Then, in a dimly lit hallway, he'll explain to you that because many of his girls are untrustworthy, you'd best deposit your valuables— cash and jewelry—with him for safekeeping, for which you'll receive a receipt.

After you comply, you're sent up to the girl's room. You knock on the door and whom do you encounter? An angry old man who wants to know what the hell you're doing knocking on his door! Meanwhile, the "pimp" has long disappeared with your valuables—as well as with your self-esteem.

The Murphy switch. A variation on the foregoing involves the pimp that accosts you on the street, then requests that you place your valuables in a large manila envelope, which he supplies. Next, you're to check the envelope with the desk clerk inside a nearby hotel before going up to the girl's room.

You walk into the hotel, make your request, and the desk clerk is bewildered. "Only hotel guests can check their valuables here," he says. An argument ensues. You open the envelope to find nothing but trash inside. The "pimp" had been hiding a second manila envelope inside a newspaper he was carrying and had made a switch during the negotiations.

The shell game. Originating on riverboats plying the Mississippi during the early nineteenth century, the shell game has earned a place in the arena of American chicanery.

Here, a sleight-of-hand artist attracts a crowd by moving a pea or small rubber ball alternately under each of three walnut shells or cups. After his amazingly fast hands come to rest, you'll bet on which of the three containers the object is under. A shill—an individual working in cahoots with the operator—will help convince you to place a large bet. But, alas, the object will always be under the wrong container, and your dollars will disappear like bubbles in a windstorm.

Three-card monte. Here is another bit of dupery coming to us courtesy of the early Mississippi riverboat grifter.

The game is played with three cards, usually two aces and a queen, called the "old lady." First, the faces of the cards are shown to the crowd. Then they are rapidly manipulated by the operator and placed face down. Naturally, you're sure you know which card is the old lady, so, heeding the urging of the operator's accomplice stationed in the crowd, you make your bet. You may even be allowed to win a few hands. Now, with your confidence soaring, you decide to bet everything you've got, and there goes your hard-earned cash.

The badger game. One of the granddaddies of all bunco schemes, this combination con game and extortion racket still takes its marks for thousands upon thousands of dollars. In a typical badger trick turned in Chicago recently, a nineteen-year-old girl claiming to be from the Moody Bible Institute visited an old man several times. On her last visit, her flim-flam partner burst in, said he was the girl's father, and accused the victim of having illicit relations with his daughter. The "father" demanded money to forget his outrage and the eighty-one-year-old victim withdrew his $10,000 life savings to turn over to the team of grifters. Should you be threatened in such a way, go straight to the police!

The boiler room. From respectable-sounding addresses in the New York financial district, stock swindlers play the big con by mounting batteries of telephones manned by high-pressure salesmen who know every trick of fleecing the gullible. They'll try to impress you by calling long-distance. They'll hurry you into deals promising quick profits from worthless stocks. They'll promise you anything, counting on your get-rich-quick lust to prevail over your cautious, investigating side. This classic con got its name because a number of operations were traced to Wall Street basements, where crooks bribed janitors to let them set up phones in the boiler room and use the impressive address. Last year Americans lost more than $200,000,000 to "boiler room" schemes!

Christmas costume con. Once every year, bunco artists across the country pull on their "official" suits and set out door to door to exploit the spirit of the season by cashing in on a charity ruse. Typically they'll wear a baggy blue suit with gold trim, possibly adding a cape and hat. Claiming to represent a well-known charity, they make off with all the Christmas giving a community can muster. These hoaxers may operate on other holidays as well, just changing the name of their fake cause.

C.O.D. robbery. Parcels sent C.O.D. (cash on delivery) to unsuspecting victims often catch them by surprise and net thousands of dollars yearly for crooks. In their confusion, people pay high fees for unordered packages containing worthless trinkets.

Particularly gullible to this rip-off are close relatives after the death of the addressee. Believing the deceased ordered the merchandise prior to death, the C.O.D. package is paid for and opened to reveal nothing valuable. Avoid being bilked by never, never paying for parcels unless certain they were ordered.

Pyramid rackets. Many forms of pyramid schemes exist, but one of the most notorious is the chain distribution racket which concentrates more on bringing new people into the operation than on the sale of the product involved. Get educated on this scam by sending for the Better Business Bureau's free brochure *Multi-Level Selling Plans* (Publication no. 239). Send a self-addressed, stamped, legal-size envelope to the Council of Better Business Bureaus, 1150 17th Street, N.W., Washington, D.C. 20036.

The heartbreaker hustle. In the stereotype of this lonely-hearts scam, a loveless spinster falls for a polished gentleman at a resort. Compliments and flattery spread like peanut butter and a romance soon blossoms. Worse comes to worst and marriage is proposed. The con man suggests a joint bank account with his spinster-victim's life savings, or he may say he is engaged in big business deals and, as a gesture of affection, he'll "let" his fiancée invest $100,000. Then the crook disappears.

The handkerchief switch. A charter member in the Con Game Hall of Fame, the handkerchief switch is a two-man-team sting that strikes victims coming out of banks. One hustler plays the country dude and hails you as you leave the bank. The other swindler, playing a city dweller, "chances" to run into you and his partner. With a well-rehearsed line they get you to go back into the bank and withdraw your savings, just to show the doubting "dude" that banks aren't crooked. Another slick story finds you holding a large amount of cash for the naive hayseed. To show you how to face pickpockets, the "city" con man takes your money and the dude's cash, wraps them in a handkerchief, and puts them in his coat pocket. Then he takes the handkerchief setup from his pocket and puts it in yours. They leave and you wait. And you wait. You've got a handkerchief full of newspaper scraps in your jacket pocket.

The lowball swindle. An incredibly low-priced offer, called a "lowball" in bargain jargon, is the bait in a con worked by hit-and-run hucksters who harbor no intentions of ever delivering advertised goods. They'll take out an alluring ad in newspapers or magazines, open a post-office box just long enough to net a number of cash, check, or money-order customers, then vanish before postal authorities can corner them.

In a typical "lowball," a conman coin dealer offered a rare 1913 nickel for $10. Hundreds of unsuspecting coin collectors rushed to get the $50 value for $10. The crook disappeared with every penny—and with every nickel.

The gold-brick con. One of flim-flam's finest, this confidence scheme draws those bewitched by gleaming yellow things. Maybe you even went with the huckster to see the chunk of gold assayed. What you didn't notice was that the "assay office" was phony—a ruse put together by the sting team. Or maybe the crook switched bricks on you after having a real gold brick checked. The way around this ancient swindle is embarrassingly simple: Never buy gold bricks from strangers and you'll never be stuck with gold-plated paperweights.

Spanish prisoner swindle. This time-honored con, handed from generation to generation of flim-flam operators for 300 years, continues to return illegitimate profits for the price of postage stamps.

Frantic airmail letters are sent from Latin America (formerly from Spain) to a select list of bankers, businessmen, and other moneyed professionals, claiming the sender is an ex-banker unjustly imprisoned in another country. Before his arrest, he'll say he hid $200,000 and some valuables. Just send him some money to bribe his way out of jail and he'll pay you back double when he makes it back home. He may even give a phone number of his "wife" or "employer" who'll corroborate his story.

You may dial the number and chit-chat with a well-rehearsed accomplice, but if you send this hoaxster a red cent, kiss it bon voyage.

Wiley ways. Methods by which con men (and women) can cheat you out of your hard-earned cash are the subject of a leaflet entitled *Be Aware!* To get your free copy, write California Savings and Loan League, 9800 South Sepulveda Boulevard, Suite 500, Los Angeles, Calif. 90045.

BRAND-NEW BUNCO

The stolen-car sting. In the annals of buncodom, this modern-day swindle ranks as one of the classiest and gutsiest of all time.

Your car is stolen. The next day it reappears in your driveway with a regretful note from an apparently distraught mother who discovered that it was her son who stole your car. "Won't you please understand and forgive him?" the note on the front seat reads. Along with the note, as a token of appreciation, are two theater tickets to the top show in town.

The night of the show comes, and you and your spouse make a fine evening of it—until you return home. There you find that your house has been burglarized. Moral: Look such peculiar gift horses carefully in the mouth!

The watch ripoff. Across our land thousands of "fine" watches, purporting to have the brand name of Omega or Patek-Phillippe, are sold on the street as "bargains" to unsuspecting rubes. True, these goods look like the real product. In fact many of them have the actual cases of these fine firms. But, invariably, the insides are just junk, which renders the watch useless after just a few short weeks.

Avoid falling prey to such a racket by purchasing all jewelry from a reputable, established jeweler.

The talent-agency act. "Children needed for TV shows," reads the ad in the entertainment section of your local newspaper. With visions of your child as another Jackie Coogan or Shirley Temple, you reply anxiously to the ad. Soon, a representative of a local talent agency comes to call. He informs you that photos must first be taken in order for your child to be properly "evaluated." However, the fee for this procedure is $100, payable in advance. The pictures are taken . . . but so are you, as you hear no more from the firm in question.

Depository dupery. Here, the con artist plies his trade silently. He'll hang a very official-looking sign on the night depository of a bank which reads "Temporarily out of order—place funds in alternate depository." A few feet away will be a large, slotted, luxurious-looking metal container which, of course, is the con man's "depository."

Believe it or not, bank patrons are regularly victimized by this corny ploy.

The sublet swindle. "To sublet: luxurious three-bedroom apartment, furnished, only $200 per month," the ad reads. Further, the apartment is located in one of the better parts of town. A fantastic bargain. You rush over to check it out. Fortunately, it's still available. You plunk down first and last month's rent plus a $200 security deposit: $600 in all.

Several weeks later, with all your worldly possessions in a rented truck, you go to take possession of the place, only to find that the man who took your money did the same with thirty others—all of whom are there and ready to move in!

Avoid this type of catastrophe by eyeing very suspiciously any such especially attractive sublet arrangement. Before putting up any money, demand to verify the arrangement with the actual owner of the building.

The lost-key con. The professional car thief who specializes in the late-model, expensive variety can easily find out your name from any number of sources. Then by calling your car dealer (whose name is decaled on your trunk or license-plate holder), he can get the serial number of your car "for insurance purposes." Now, he makes a duplicate key to your car in under a minute with a $50 tool that is widely available.

To be really safe, change your car locks immediately after that beautiful new Detroit wonder is delivered to you.

The genealogy grift. "Only $20," the attractive brochure in your mailbox reads, "for a personalized, detailed genealogy of your family name."

Should your curiosity (and poor judgment) get the better of you so that you decide to send the $20, you'll receive a genealogy all right, but one as phony as an Indian-head dime. For not only will this "personalized" information be pure balderdash, but you'll find that every like-named family in town who fell for the offer has received an identical "genealogy."

Before doing business with such a firm, check with the National Genealogical Society, 1921 Sunderland Place N.W., Washington, D.C. 20036.

The diamond-ring dodge. One day you're stopped on the street and offered a genuine six-carat diamond ring for only $100. "Too good to be true," you say to yourself. So off you both trudge to a jeweler, where the ring, sure enough, is verified to be six carats of pure diamond.

You go outside and the transaction is completed. Some time later, you discover, to your dismay, that what you bought is merely costume jewelry that was switched for the real thing after leaving the jeweler's.

The lost-diamond swindle. You're working in a small grocery store when a refined, well-dressed woman comes to the counter in tears. "My God," she screams. "I've just lost my precious diamond ring in your store and I can't find it anywhere." You help her look for it, but to no avail. She shows you $500 from her purse. "Here," she says, "I'll give you this as a reward if you find it." She leaves her phone number and walks out.

Twenty minutes later you notice a customer pick up a small object from the floor and put it in his pocket. You quiz him and he admits to finding the ring, which he shows you. Figuring you can make some money on the deal, you give him $100 for it. Now you call the lady who apparently lost the ring. The number turns out to be as phony as is the ring. The man and woman have successfully worked as a team to mulct you of your $100.

The advance-fee loan fraud. When money is tight the time is right for this scheme, which bilks businessmen and nets millions for its perpetrators. Ads pop up in the financial newspapers saying this bank or that insurance company has $100 million to loan small business-men. The lending institution is typically located overseas and its doctored financial statements indicate millions in assets. In reality, it is a garage with a phone and a phony secretary to answer it. Entrepreneurs answering the ad are required to put up collateral for the "loans"—sometimes up to 10 percent of the amount requested. The con men disappear with the advances, leaving businessmen in arrears.

Rare-coin con. Send us all the plain old common money you have and we'll tell you about the rare money you don't have. So, in effect, say the coin-catalog sales sharpies who tease for $2 by selling coin catalogs with pitches like this: "Old money wanted . . . $15,500 for a 1913 Liberty-head nickel." You'll never find the old nickel, though the thought of pulling one from the change slot of a Pepsi machine may tantalize you enough to buy the $2 catalog. Owners of the 1913 Liberty-heads (there were only five minted) are all well known and are not selling. Save a pretty penny and go to the library for a rare-coin guide.

Dead-kitty con. Almost by definition, a confidence game capitalizes on a human failing, and this swindle earned its name exploiting a trait humans share with a legendary crowd of killed cats: overwhelming curiosity. In one recent example, a so-called "club" in Jamaica sent cards notifying Americans it was holding a valuable package addressed to them!

What was in it? We aren't telling. And neither was the "club" when hundreds of curious letter writers kept asking what happened to the $5 "postage and handling" fees they mailed its president.

False-arrest rackets. Even having a confidence schemer arrested for operating what looks like a confidence racket does have its dangers. The scam itself may be planned to adhere to the letter of the law, just so the grifter can sue you for false arrest. Many's the bunco artist who'll jump at the chance to file false-imprisonment charges—and they *do* collect.

If you realize you've been ripped off, don't fly into a rage and file charges. Have police or consumer-protection agencies see whether the fraud rap will stick. It'll save you embarrassment and money.

The whiz-kid con. The bogus stockbroker sends 1,000 letters to persons recommending the purchase of Company A's stock. He tells 500 of them the stock will go up, and the rest that it will go down. Something's bound to happen in a week—say it goes up—so the swindler forgets the 500 he advised wrong and writes the other 500 that Company B's stock is the one to watch. The routine is repeated, leaving

125 suckers who have been given correct stock predictions three times in a row. They get a high-pressure sales pitch and many readily hand their money to the whiz-kid broker who whizzes away with it, leaving them broker.

Bogus-benefit con. A rural central Florida county recently made a good mark for hucksters pushing tickets to a "Policeman's Disability Pension Fund Concert." What the duped ticketholders expected to be a country-and-western spectacular studded with Nashville's finest turned out to be a handful of hick twangers under a tent.

The method behind this mischief was telephone solicitation—a team of con artists swooped into town and set up a "boiler room" of locally recruited phone salesmen, then advertised, sought local police endorsement, and made plans to skip town the night before the concert fizzled and flopped. A downhome lesson: Be wary of phony promoters.

Cruise ruse. Would you buy your mother-in-law a round-trip luxury cruise on the *Titanic?* Well then, would you treat yourself to a two-week jaunt to Jamaica aboard the ocean liner *S.S. United States?* Both are rip-offs.

A common con that nets sackfuls for swindlers every year involves booking passengers on nonexistent or harborbound luxury liners, demanding half payment in advance "to hold your place," then disappearing into the dawn as the pier fills with suitcases and bermuda shorts.

Dodge this con by booking all your luxury travel with an established, reputable travel agency.

Oil-lease fleece. The "40-acre Lease Merchant" stings the gusher speculator who thinks he's getting a deal and a half when he's only getting taken. He'll acquire oil and gas leases on large areas of government land in Western states. Due to lack of demand, these near-worthless mineral rights sell for 5 to 50 cents an acre. The rogue operators then sell the oil rights through exciting newspaper and mail advertising for about $10 an acre. Their pitch is the possibility that the leases can later be resold to oil companies at enormous profits. Seek advice from responsible investment consultants before buying any such leases. If the mineral rights were as valuable as claimed, they wouldn't be for sale.

The chinchilla con. One well-worn confidence racket starts with the bamboozler representing himself as a fur processor's agent and offering to set you up in the mink or chinchilla breeding business. These double-dealers sell you "breeding stock" and a book or two on raising the furry varmint for about $300. They'll also sell you a list of furriers where you can peddle your pelts. When it comes time to skin and sell, the companies will tell you your pelts are worthless. Your breeders were "culls," a mixed-breed mink or chinchilla with undesirable, therefore valueless, fur. You are the one who's been skinned, and the swindler who did it is by now fur, fur away.

Sucker's luck. "In appreciation for your donation we'll send you a Tibetan Holy Medallion which will allow you to charm the stripes off a zebra. Send us $5 and your zodiac sign, we'll guide your path to happiness and fortune . . ."

Don't help a con artist make a fortune peddling such trinkets. If you want religion, go to church. If you want charm, attend a charm school.

The mining-claim game. Calling themselves "mining claim locators," bunco artists hit an area and sell mining claims to publicly owned land. Buyers of these "mining rights" are lured by stories of possible mineral wealth buried under national forests and think they acquire valid title to the land. According to the United States Bureau of Land Management, however, the public lands are held by the government, and mining rights should be negotiated with Uncle Sam alone.

CHARITY CHEATS

Fund-drive cons. Sometime or other your NOW chapter, band boosters' club, or church group will want to mount a fund-raising drive for a certain project. Be particularly leery of "idea men" who pop up at such times. They'll use your group's good name to get loans from community banks and big shots, or induce club members to put up advance money for their fund-gathering push—say printing a cookbook or staging a carnival. When it comes time to deliver your group's books, the promoter and your money are both gone. It's better and safer to deal with local volunteer help in planning your fund drives.

Vet debts. A confidence outfit in southern Illinois reaped thousands of dollars in an operation that played on people's patriotic "debt" to disabled veterans. These men sold small crucifixes and other religious novelties to Roman Catholics in the area, claiming the proceeds would go "to help crippled war veterans." As it turned out, one of the men was receiving a small monthly government check for a 10 percent war disability. This "crippled" vet helped himself to the proceeds and left with his partner. Play it safe by checking all veterans-aid appeals with the American Legion or Veterans of Foreign Wars for authenticity.

Charitable appeals. As a concerned individual, you're no doubt eager to help others in their hour of need. But how do you know that the charity to which you're about to donate a portion of your hard-earned cash is legitimate? To help yourself develop your "charity-conscious-ness," get the publication entitled *How to Recognize Charitable Appeals* (Buyers Bulletin no. 8). It's free, and available from the Bureau of Consumer Affairs, City Hall, Room 848, Los Angeles, Calif. 90012.

Legitimate charities. One way to avoid handing your charity-motivated donations over to crooks is to give to local agencies only—you can find their names in the phone book and know they'll be around to answer to any charges. The United Fund is a relatively sure way to avoid charity swindlers. Groups applying for a share of United Fund collections are thoroughly screened. Check the location of your nearby United Fund chapter in the phone book and put your money where you're certain it will do some good!

Status stealers. A ruse with anyone else's name would reek the same. One brand of charity chiseler displays a list of names of prominent people, claiming they've donated, so why shouldn't you? Because the people named aren't contributors, that's why. To get your benefit bucks the charity sharpies use a well-known person's name without his permission or even knowledge. When confronted by one of these birds, ask for an address and say you'll mail a check. But before you do, write or call several of the celebrities listed and see whether they support the cause or whether you've just avoided a rip-off.

Wrong numbers. Charitable appeals over the phone are so often phony they prompt this warning: *Never* agree to donate to any cause espoused by a telephone solicitor. Seeking contributions by phone is illegal in many cities and unethical everywhere else. Legitimate charities don't work this way—and that leaves the snooks and swindlers who do. Keep your bucks out of a huckster's Swiss bank account and don't be a donor to phoners.

Check that license! The surest advice we can give to help keep your donations out of the hands of rip-off artists is for you to demand to see a solicitor's license and identification *before* you give. Most cities require such a license and screen applications to weed out charity frauds. If you have any doubts, ask the solicitor to wait while you call your city manager or mayor's office and verify that the appeal is legitimate. Double-check with a call to the charity's headquarters and you won't fall for fake pleas.

Child charity chiselers. Don't give to kids seeking donations just because you see their frightened wide eyes and go all gooey inside. Innocent faces can hide not-so-innocent motives. Con men are adept at using youth appeal to net literally thousands from unsuspecting communities. Children soliciting for established causes will be accompanied by a responsible adult with an identification card. If there's no grown-up along, don't donate. Also, beware of crooked kids working on their own to gather money for fake Boy Scout or church-group projects! Ask for the phone number of the sponsoring group's leader and call to check the charity out.

Postal fleece. A favorite easy-money maker for the clever con man is setting up a phony "cause" and sending "gifts" in the mail along with requests for a donation. Many people, moved or feeling "obligated" by the handmade bookmark enclosed with the appeal from Saint Ringo's Home for Wayward Orphans, will send the swindler a quick $25 contribution. Before authorities catch up to the ruse, the bunco artist has a new post office box and a new name for his "charity." You can beat this con, of course, by never donating to unfamiliar organizations sending unsolicited "gifts" with their appeals.

Charity check-out. *Changing Times* magazine has compiled a sizeable list of charities that did not reply to any of three query letters regarding their fund-raising operations. Although not dishonest by their lack of replies alone, these charities could conceivably be rip-offs. To get the free list, request the pamphlet *New Ways to Check Out Charities* from *Changing Times*, 1729 H Street, N.W., Washington, D.C. 20006.

CHAPTER 7

Phony physicians and counterfeit cures

Billions of dollars, hundreds of lives, and unimaginable suffering and despair—that's what phony physicians reap each year from their elderly, afflicted, poor, and uneducated patient/victims.

Medical confidence men and women today are merely modern versions of the snake-oil medicine-wagon barkers who years ago hawked worthless remedies to unsuspecting sufferers. Only today's medicine man comes equipped with the latest electronic gizmos and gadgets with important-looking dials that measure nothing, cure nothing, and cost plenty. The plots and ploys of these fake healers are as varied as their imaginations and their clients' gullibility allow. They spout about food fads, and medications and treatments to "cure" nonexistent diseases, return youth and sex drive to aging customers, turn tubbies into skinnies. Some of them perform magic "psychic" surgery. If you're now under a quack's so-called "care," you're playing dangerous games with your health while paying expensive fees. The danger comes in postponing proper treatment for your ailment while you're lured into a false security, thinking the faker's treatment will help you.

Furthermore, danger is in the treatments themselves: devices that electrocute users, face creams that burn the skin away, radioactive cancer treatments that expose users to dangerous radiation levels. Thus it's not just your money, but your very health and life which you may unknowingly be risking.

But let's talk about the money. Health quacks make thousands on schemes so improbable that only those driven to desperation by chronic pain would buy them. For example, do you believe that eating nothing but grapes for two solid weeks will cure cancer? If you suffered from this tragic disease, which has frustrated the legitimate medical world, you might. Thousands of cancer victims did, and they paid for it.

Officials don't know exactly how many health-care quack schemes are in operation. Victims often don't realize, or are too ashamed to admit, that they're being taken. And complicating the situation is the fact that the litigation involved in closing down a medical marauder is painfully slow.

Keeping informed is the only alternative left the consumer of medical services. Our chapter is filled with specific medical rip-offs. Become familiar with these and you will recognize many more with similar themes. Then protect your health and wealth by establishing a relationship with a "family" doctor—one licensed and established in your community. Openly ask her or his advice concerning any "miracle" treatment you may be tempted to try.

The complexity of modern life and modern machines give the quack ample opportunity to make his profit. Take the time to think and re-think before risking your well-being. If you need help, some of the following tips tell you where to turn. Take them! Your life may depend on it.

FOR FURTHER INFORMATION:

Billion Dollar Swindle: Frauds Against the Elderly. Amram M. Ducovny. New York: Fleet Press, 1969.

FAKE CANCER CURES

Gerson's gobbledygook. In the early 1960s a book entitled *Has Dr. Max Gerson a True Cancer Cure?* became famous. The answer to the question posed in the title, "No," is still not well known.

Gerson's treatment is basically a diet regulation. No cooking in aluminum pots is allowed. Liver, vitamins, and fresh fruit and vegetable juices are offered—the juices prepared by a special machine costing victims $150. If all that doesn't work, Gerson prescribes a coffee enema. A real perk-up, but a phony cancer cure.

Drown waves. The infamous Ruth Drown, a chiropractor who died in 1965, came up with a battery of quacky test-and-treat equipment still misused today. Drown claimed a sample of a patient's blood on blotting paper could be analyzed by one of her devices. Another gadget transmitted "treatments" through the air to patients—even in another state! Drown waves are said to cure a deluge of afflictions, including cancer, heart trouble, kidney infections, and common colds. No cures came, of course.

Orgones. The "Orgone Energy Accumulator" is what happens when a psychiatrist starts contriving quack gadgets. Dr. Wilhelm Reich's inventions, touted as cancer cures, let the diseased person soak up "orgone energy" in two ways. In one version, the victim sits inside a zinc-lined box. In the other he merely breathes deeply through a funnel-and-tube hookup attached to a closed zinc-paneled box. The good doctor died in prison, but his rip-off tactics live on.

Spike hype. It looks like a sawed-off nail. It fits in the palm of your hand. It contains a penny's worth of barium chloride. It's called a "Vrilium Tube" or "Magic Spike." Cancer and arthritis sufferers paid $300 for this trinket; the fraudulent sales pitch claimed the tube cured these two diseases.

The diamond cure. A real gem among trumped-up treatments is the joke of a cancer cure relying on "diamond-carbon compounds." Supposedly, American-educated doctors working in Bombay, India, developed a remedy which requires the cancer sufferer to take capsules containing crystals of pure diamonds and other substances. Nobody knows how much diamond is in each pill, but the pricetag for a "basic treatment" of eighty capsules is $1,200. Diamonds can't cure cancer. Unless you're proposing marriage to your stomach, don't swallow these semi-precious pills.

Vaccine schemes. Persons terrified of the ravages of incurable cancers make prime victims for quacks claiming various vaccines will immunize the receiver against malignant growths. Popular bogus preventions are the "Livingston Vaccine" (prepared from the patient's urine and injected back into his arm) and the "Hadley Vaccine" (administered in conjunction with blood tests and claimed effective for five to ten years). Prices start at $50.
Be advised: There is no known vaccine for preventing cancer.

Hot baths. Heat will kill 95 percent of all cancer cells, says the unscrupulous salesman hawking a hot-bath treatment to cancer sufferers. Leave your money at the door and this quack will lead you to his special tub. There you'll sit for up to forty-five minutes in water heated to 110 degrees. Treatment often includes a large dose of a special drug. Such warm and moist therapy will get you clean, but won't cure cancer.

Hormone hokum. Straight out of the medicine-wagon barker days comes Samuel's Casual Therapy, supported by "literature" which throws technical gibberish at cancer-plagued readers. Cancer is caused by hormone imbalance in the body, Samuel's says, and an "automatic short-wave apparatus" to soak the pituitary and sex glands with "short-waves" is the cure. Hogwash.

Nichols nonsense. This useless salve is touted by many, including the Savannah Cancer Clinic, as a cancer cure-all. The "Nichols Method" calls for applications of an arsenic and/or zinc compound to the afflicted area. "Complete" treatments run into hundreds of dollars. Watch out for this one! You're not only wasting time and money, but the acid action of these pastes is so disfiguring it often requires plastic surgery to restore mutilated skin tissue.

Sights and sounds. Then there's the "Spectro-Chrome" and the "Sonus Film-O-Sonic." This first gadget supposedly cures diseases by flashing colored light on the patient's body during certain phases of the moon while the patient is in the dark and in the nude with hands pointing northward. Purple and blue are for cancer, red and purple for heart disease.

A $500 Sonus Film-O-Sonic "silently" plays taped music into electrode pads placed on the patient's afflicted areas. "Smoke Gets in Your Eyes" croons away cancer, while "Holiday for Strings" tames the savage arteriosclerosis. If you know of a cancer victim paying for such sensory treatments, think of a nice way to tell him he's crazy.

The grape cure. This questionable cancer treatment is put forth by Johanna Brandt in her book *The Grape Cure*. Brandt's followers eat nothing but grapes, seven times a day, for two weeks. Then comes a special diet of fruit, sour milk, raw vegetables, nuts, and olive oil.

Z-50. Too many cancer victims trip on the spiel of a doubletalk artist named George Zuccala who claims his concoction, called "Anticancergen Z-50," can stop cancer. Cancer cells, Zuccala claims, produce an "unknown" substance called "motivana" which infects other body cells, making them unable to resist advancing cancer growths. As "proof" of this hokey theory, he developed a "Zuccala Lytic Test" which somehow always shows patients they need a dose or two of Z-50 to bolster the body's cancer defenses. What they really need is a shot of common sense to avoid fraudulent cures.

Chiropractic frauds. Of the many so-called "cures" for cancer which involve some kind of chiropractic technique, the Spears Hygienic System, headquartered in a Denver hospital, is most widely known. The system attacks cancer by spinal adjustments, colon irrigation, nerve and reflex techniques, spinal traction, correctional exercises, and a special diet. It costs hundreds of dollars. It builds up patient's hopes. It doesn't work.

FAKE ARTHRITIS REMEDIES

Tri-Wonda. No matter how useless, if a product seems complicated enough, con men can bank on a gullible public believing their phony healing claims. So, before the Food and Drug Administration banned the potion as a fraud, arthritis sufferers were hustled into buying "Tri-Wonda"—a three-part remedy consisting of a vitamin and mineral compound, a herbal preparation, and a laxative. Patients promised "amazing relief" were relieved of an amazing $12.50. Products similar to Tri-Wonda flood the market today.

Copper jewelry. A myth that takes millions of dollars from millions of arthritics is the supposed "curative circuit" formed by wearing copper bracelets which range in price from $5 to $25 each. This fraud has reached the status of folk medicine, having been handed down through generations and capitalized upon by schemers selling everything from plain cheap bands to "Electro-Galvanic Bracelets." As jewelry, a copper bracelet can be beautiful—but it's no arthritis remedy.

Oxydoner. Got arthritis or rheumatism? Got $30? Then why not get an "Oxydoner" and get rid of your affliction? This gadget, supposed to "reverse the death process into the life process," consists of a metal disk strapped to your ankle and then immersed in cold water. Like many other quack cures, Oxydoner is harmless, worthless, and more than somewhat ridiculous.

Z-rays. Among the more bizarre contraptions ever peddled to unsuspecting arthritis victims is Ferguson's Zerret Applicator, which takes advantage of public ignorance of the new field of radioactive medicine. Con men claim the hand-held plastic container encloses "Zerret Water" which produces "Z-Rays" (a new one to science scholars). Z-Rays are said to expand all the atoms in the body to produce perfect health. For the $50 price of a Zerret Applicator you get a plastic vessel filled with tap water. Z-Rays are a rip-off.

Inducto-scope. In spite of government seizure of this freaky and dangerous quack cure, "Inducto-Scopes," and variations thereof, are still pawned as arthritis treatments to pain-wracked victims. Two loops of cloth-covered electric cord are placed over the afflicted area (one over each wrist, for example) and the Inducto-Scope plug is jammed into a wall socket. Users have reported severe electrical shocks. Healing allegedly comes from "magnetic induction," whatever that is.

Radioactive rip-offs. Any gadget emitting radioactivity to affect parts of the body is dangerous, yet bunco artists continue to foist uranium-filled contraptions to arthritis sufferers. One is a "Wonder Glove"—a uranium-lined mitten selling for $100. Another, the Cosmos Radioactive Pad, is placed wherever its "emanation" will do the most good. These and other radiation treatments are worse than worthless—they're dangerous to your health.

Clinics. Bogus "clinics" and "spas" to treat arthritis snag their victims through newspaper and magazine advertisements and high-pressure follow-up letters to those curious enough to reply to the ads. They promise permanent relief through such practices as electrotherapy, saunas, colon therapy, vitamin therapy, and chiropractic adjustments. Arthritic customers are urged to stay for two weeks or more of "treatment," costing $600 and up. But in spite of what these clinics claim, there is no cure for arthritis. You'll leave their so-called care in the same condition you went to them—except minus the cash spent on simpleminded, overpriced, ineffective treatments.

Plasmatic therapy. Properly applied heat treatments will ease arthritis pain, but the "Plasmatic Therapy" dosage dished out by quacks will only leave you feeling silly and broke. Gullible patients crawl inside a 6-foot-long plastic pouch, leaving only the head protruding. A phony physician then fiddles with some dials, and electric heaters imbedded in the plastic will "directly heat the blood," they claim. Treatments cost $35 and thousands of these worthless machines are in use across the country. A $2.50 heating pad, available at drug stores, does the job better and more safely.

Aspirin. Of all arthritis quirks and quackery, the biggest-selling worthless items are "glorified aspirin" products such as Arth-Rite, Ache-Away, and others. Arth-Rite, a compound of alfalfa and vitamins, was shown to be no benefit whatsoever in treating arthritis. In this and similar phony remedies, the main active ingredient is common aspirin, which dulls the pain of arthritis, but fails to curb the disease itself. The fraud here comes in the high-pressure promotions that claim wonderous relief. The rip-off comes in the prices—$6 for a bottle of Arth-Rite, 75 cents for an equal amount of aspirin with an honest label.

Diet deception. What do cod-liver oil and orange juice have in common with honey and vinegar? Both combinations are mainstays of hokey diets to "cure" arthritis, prescribed by the slick for the sick. Both were put forth in books by authors without medical backgrounds who listed a string of fictitious academic degrees to impress their readers. Both were banned by the federal government. The word from reputable physicians is: Nothing a person eats or doesn't eat will cause or cure arthritis. If you're approached about an arthritis-remedy diet, you can bet it's baloney.

Liefcort. For years Dr. Liefman has pawned his worthless brown liquid "Liefcort" as an arthritis cure which "restores the balance of body hormones." Selling the bogus cure from Montreal, Canada, offices since it's banned in the United States, Liefman has achieved fame and fortune. Thousands of misguided arthritis sufferers fly to Canada to get the drug; others manage to keep supplied through the mails at $10 per bottle. Those who bear the pain of this disease are advised: Liefcort is a fake medicine denounced by the Arthritis Foundation, the American Medical Association, and the Federal Drug Administration.

Seawater swindle. One of the classic cons still going strong is the hawking of ocean water at $3 per pint bottle. How do bunco artists pull it off? First they aim at a vulnerable audience—the nearly 19 million arthritis sufferers in the country whose good sense may be affected by the nagging agony of an incurable disease. Then they distribute pamphlets full of hype, claiming that "this miracle of nature delivers relief-giving rejuvenation of pain-ridden bodies." Seawater may be a miracle of nature, but it's worthless as an arthritis remedy.

The Immune Milk nostrum. This fraudulent arthritis remedy, "Immune Milk," allegedly gets its disease-fighting powers from antibodies produced in cows injected with certain vaccines. Makers claim arthritics swear by it, though in truth, more swear *at* it. Federal authorities have seized large quantities of this rip-off remedy, but still Immune Milk is peddled wherever quack cures are sold. At about $2 a quart, Immune Milk cures heavy wallets, nothing else.

Hotfoot therapy. One of the largest-scale health hornswoggles occurred several years ago in Texas. A couple of clever chiselers there managed to convince 250,000 arthritis victims from the East Coast to come to the Lone Star State and sit with their feet in troughs of "radioactive" earth in mines called "uranitoriums." The gullible paid dearly for their "treatment," which turned out to be pure hogwash. The amount of radiation in the "uranitoriums" was found to be about equal to that given off by an illuminated watch dial. Radiation is not known to cure arthritis, and it can be harmful if applied in large amounts by uninformed quack healers.

Vibrators. Every year arthritis sufferers spend millions of dollars buying some type of vibrator which promoters promise will ease their aches and pains. Selling these devices is a cruel hoax and illegal. They are worse than useless, as use of a vibrator on a diseased area can increase pain and cause further damage. Save yourself money and suffering and report the quacks selling these devices to police and health authorities.

QUACKS OF ALL KINDS

The Theronoid Belt. In 1796 a Dr. Elisha Perkins touted a mysterious magnet said to "draw out the disease" when two magnetic rods were passed over the affected body area. One modern application, the "Theronoid Belt," is an electromagnetic loop the size of a barreltop and said to heal any sickness by "magnetizing the iron of the blood." Though it seems impossible to confuse this quack's gadget with any legitimate medical machinery, another identifying clue is a two-speed switch (for a swift or gradual cure) attached to the rip-off ring.

Rupture cures. Many who claim to be "rupture specialists" support themselves by uplifting hopes of hernia victims and relieving them of their cash. "Sensational new rupture development!" they will spiel. "No shots! No surgery! Instant relief!" Make an appointment and you'll instantly be relieved of $75 for the truss your drug store sells for $5.

Blenders. A borderline form of quackery is the selling of "special-process" blenders to prepare the health diets praised and promoted by natural-foods healers. An $18 juicer is sold for $100 with the totally fraudulent guarantee that it mushes out carrot juice in a unique way to bring forth ulcer-healing powers in the drink. That claim is so much dribble. The sellers are ordinary crooks putting an ordinary squeeze-job on your wallet.

Foul ball. Pain-panicked buyers fall for this item said to permanently squelch pain in neurotic and nervous patients. The gimmick is an everyday steel ball bearing, about an inch in diameter, allegedly energized with thousands of volts of electricity. The ball is "grounded," then passed over the user's throbbing body parts. After a treatment you'll still be screaming "Ouch!" and the $10 pricetag for this round rip-off is another pain.

Quack-by-mail. Hokey healers take out newspaper and magazine ads announcing amazing medical discoveries, treatments, and cures for common ailments. Typical are the fleeced sinus sufferers who ordered a two-week course from a health-food faddist claiming he could cure their clogs. These losers paid the mailman $8.40 when he brought the "treatment instructions" C.O.D. They opened the package to find a 40-cent box of gelatin.

Youth jelly gyp. Promoters recently pawned off a phony rejuvenator containing "royal jelly," a special food prepared by worker bees for their queen bee. It is known that queen bees live longer than other bees, so tiny amounts of royal jelly were capsuled and sold to restore youth, beauty, vitality, and even sexual prowess.

Of course for bees, royal jelly is great. For people it isn't worth a buzz. Claims made for it are false, the Food and Drug Administration has declared.

Vitamin E. Faced with wilting sexual powers, many middle-aged victims go along with health-food shamsters' fraudulent claims that Vitamin E will restore prowess. The pill pimp's pitch says rats eat a lot of Vitamin E and rats have a fervent sex life, so . . . In reality, Vitamin E has no proven aphrodisiac effects, and besides, it is widely present in ordinary foods, making supplemental vitamins unnecessary.

The magic jug. Nearly 10,000 Americans were sucked into parting with $300 to purchase this no-account cure-all contraption in the last twenty years. A salesman/swindler may knock on your door tomorrow hawking this "radium-impregnated" wonder water guaranteed to sprout hair on bald heads, revive virility, and undo rheumatic fever and cancer at the same time.

The device is a regular picnic-type jug with a silver-colored bell, supposedly filled with radioactive radon, a gas. The "miracle gas" does nothing more extraordinary than contaminate the water, endangering the health of those who buy this hucksterism.

Ozone generators. Called "God's gift to humanity," various sizes and prices ($30–$300 each) of "Ozone Generators" are touted as super-cures for forty-seven diseases including whooping cough, tuberculosis, and polio. These worthless machines are a hodge-podge of tubes, wires, and dials and produce a form of oxygen which can be dangerous if inhaled in quantity.

Women need be particularly alert to these fraudulent gizmos, also tabbed Vitazone, Purozone, Orozone, Nevozone, and Airozone. A widely employed ploy is a quack diagnosing a nonexistent vaginal tumor, then treating it with "Ozone" followed by an acid suppository. Vaginal walls scorched off by the acid are claimed to be ejected tumors.

Big-eyed bargains. One con game infecting the health-care field is the selling of magnifying reading glasses to oldsters by grifters who are ignorant of optical health. Through ads in magazines and papers they collect $5 for delivery of 25 cents worth of lenses—satisfaction guaranteed. When buyers return the gunky glasses, the "quality optical company" breaks one lens, sends them back to their dissatisfied customer, and claims the guarantee doesn't apply to broken glasses!

Radio-wave rip-off. A San Francisco charlatan's radio-healing machine, the "Oscilloclast," is still used to trick the sick by many of the thousands of good and bad doctors who bought the contraption in its 1920s prime.

Oscilloclasts are claimed to cure anything—diabetes, malaria, cancer, syphilis, or what-have-you—by using a frequency-controlled radio transmitter to send vibrations through the patient. Since all diseases were said to give off "a disharmony of electronic oscillation" (bad vibes, in other words), Oscilloclasts "cancel" the disease and its nasty waves with the correct radio waves.

Do-it-yourself eyeglasses. "Playing Russian roulette with your vision" is how the American Optometric Association describes the tactics of mail-order houses who send a "test-your-own-eyes kit" to respondents along with the promise of accurately ground lenses at low costs. While the prices are low and the lenses are true to the do-it-yourself specifications, the measuring equipment is crude so the lens "prescription" you write yourself may end up hurting your eyesight. Don't chance buying glasses by mail. Instead, walk into the office of an optometrist, oculist, or ophthalmologist and check his license and diploma—even if you have to squint to do it.

Quackery complaints. "Miracle cure" drugs, food fads, and "wonder machine" treatments amount to no more than cruel, often harmful, schemes to bilk the sick and elderly. If you believe you've been the victim of such quackery, get in touch with the Food and Drug Administration, either at its district office nearest you or at headquarters —5600 Fishers Lane, Rockville, Md. 20852. This agency will begin legal steps to put an end to such heartless, fraudulent practices and possibly recover your money.

Cellular therapy. Swiss and German doctors lure elderly Americans with glowing accounts of this type of treatment they claim can give "worn-out" organs a new lease on life. The "cellular therapy" practitioners inject embryonic cells from organs of freshly killed animals into corresponding organs of their patients. These new cells revitalize the aged human tissues, doctors contend.

American doctors disagree, saying that like transplanted hearts which are "rejected" by a recipient's body, organs often react adversely to additions of strange, new tissues. Don't jeopardize your health and savings being a "guinea pig" or you may find yourself sicker.

Aluminum. Aluminum cookware causes cancer! So says the dishonest pots-and-pans salesman pushing stainless-steel cookery. To prove his point, the salesman puts baking soda and water in both aluminum and steel pans and heats them. The solution in the stainless-steel pan remains clear, while the mixture in the aluminum pan foams and becomes cloudy. It's a scary trick meant to close deals, but it amounts to only a harmless chemical reaction.

Hearing-aid hustlers. Consumer-affairs bureaus are reporting more and more complaints that hearing aid salespeople are selling the wrong type of hearing device to patients who haven't had their ears checked by either the family doctor or an ear doctor (otologist or otolaryngologist). Buying a hearing device without qualified medical advice might leave you deaf and duped, too.

Quackery. An FDA Consumer Memo warning the public of quacks and quackery is available free from the U.S. Government. Appropriately entitled *Quackery* (DHEW Publication no. (FDA) 74–1017), the information can be obtained by writing to the U.S. Department of

Health, Education, and Welfare, Public Health Service, Food and Drug Administration, 5600 Fishers Lane, Rockville, Md. 20852.

Quack information. If you hear of a "special" treatment for an affliction you have or are told you have, where can you turn to see if the medical methods may be those of a quack? For help or information on suspected health-care quacks, talk to a licensed physician or write the American Medical Association, 535 North Dearborn Street, Chicago, Ill. 60610.

Health hints. Quacks, food fads, and phony cures are the subjects of the bulletin entitled *Don't Gamble with Your Health* (Buyers Bulletin no. 7), available free by writing to the Bureau of Consumer Affairs, City Hall, Room 848, Los Angeles, Calif. 90012.

CHAPTER 8

Car thieves, garage and showroom cheats, and bike bandits

By the time you finish reading this introduction, eighteen cars will have been stolen from curbsides and parking lots scattered across the United States. If your car wasn't among them, this chapter will help you protect yourself against the wide array of ways car owners can get robbed, cheated, and chiseled. In addition, you'll learn how to steer clear of all crimes relating to the theft of and willful damage to motorcycles, scooters, and bicycles.

America's passion for the piston coupled with the public's all-too-casual attitude toward auto security create both a market and a method for the novice and for professional car stealers. Strong testimony to this offhand approach is evident in the fact that in more than 40 percent of car thefts, the owner leaves the key in the door or ignition. And unlike the horse thieves of the Wild West, today's horse-power rustlers seldom worry about changing the "brand" on their ill-gotten wheels. Surveys show that most car owners fail to take the simple precautions necessary to identify and reclaim the vehicle if and when it is stolen. When stealing remains so simple, is it any wonder that car theft is so common? The FBI reports that nearly 6 million victims lost vehicles to thieves in 1976—and that's more than 700 cars stolen every hour of the year.

Car thieves fall into one of three categories. Some are youngsters out for a joy ride who look for snazzy sports cars and "easy pickin's" —cars with keys carelessly left in the ignition. When they've had their fun, these thieves will abandon your car, often miles and miles away and usually with several hundred dollars' worth of damage to the vehicle. Others, the professionals, swipe with an eye toward reselling,

138

and are often in cahoots with a crooked "used" car dealer. Still others, called "car clouts," concentrate on pilfering parts from parked and stalled autos.

Fortunately for you, at your disposal is a whole arsenal of anti-theft tactics, including special locks, devices, and alarms. Some ideas that follow will alert you to tricks of vehicle identification—how to put your unalterable mark on your car and how to avoid mistakenly buying a stolen car. Subsequent sections deal with protecting your two-wheeled treasures from the bicycle-theft boom that is stepping right on the heels of the bicycle boom of the early 1970s—now seen as a legitimate transportation trend rather than a craze. The hitchhiker, as well as the motorist who picks up a hitchhiker, is shown how to protect himself in a variety of perilous situations. Another section will aid in avoiding those crafty mechanics and service-station swindlers who open your car's hood and, counting on your ignorance, tell you anything in order to sell you something—whether your vehicle really needs repairs or not.

Unless a distributor is otherwise mentioned, most of the auto and other wheeled-vehicle alarms are available through locksmiths, auto-parts stores, and electronics-supply houses. In addition, your local new-car dealers may be able to point you toward a nearby car-security supplier. Many of our most effective safeguards involve common items frequently found around the house.

Of course the best protection device for your car or bicycle is a locked garage, but this safeguard is unavailable to millions of Americans. Those who can't afford a locked enclosure for their wheels must settle for second-best security, as outlined in the following suggestions. And even if you have a garage you will learn to protect yourself from thieves, vandals, and schemers when your travels take you away from home.

USED-CAR CAPERS

The hot box. After a short initial conversation, a car salesman will excuse himself from the booth, leaving, say, you and your wife to speak privately to each other. Unbeknownst to you, the booth is bugged, and your conversation is monitored by the salesman in another room. He then returns armed with the knowledge of how much you're willing to pay for the car, the monthly payment you can afford, and so on.

Obviously, you can protect yourself here by first excusing yourself, then holding your private conversations outside the showroom.

Tinted glass. In their zeal to sell you options which increase the price of your new car and also increase their sales commissions, car dealers often offer tinted windshields at extra cost, claiming the shaded glass will improve visibility. Such claims are false, consumer publications proclaim, and the salesman making them is out to take your cash and increase the likelihood you'll crash.

Far from improving visibility, tinting and windshield angle combine to reduce incoming light by up to 35 percent. In a fog, at dusk, or after dark, this reduction means a big difference in how much you see and therefore how safe you are. Don't waste your money and endanger your health by buying tinted car windows.

Used-car pricelists. You need facts to haggle your best with the used-car salesman. Is the price on that Rambler window a steal or a rip-off? Find out by checking the average price for any year and any model auto listed in the *Blue Book* or the *Red Book,* two used-car price guides. You can find either handbook at your library or order directly from the publishers. The *Blue Book* lists West Coast prices (order from 4005 Long Beach Boulevard, Long Beach, Calif. 90807), while the *Red Book* averages national used-car pricetags (order from National Market Reports, Inc., 900 South Wabash Avenue, Chicago, Ill. 60605). Depending upon condition, the car you're looking at can vary 20 percent in price from the rates given. If there's a greater difference, you're gazing at a lemon or a gyp.

Balloon notes. One method of financing a car, home, or other major purchase, called the "balloon note," is often misused by unscrupulous salesmen to entice buyers with incredibly low payments and then repossess their cars just before the last payment. A balloon note allows for a series of small payments ending with a large final payment—say $60 a month on a car for thirty-five months, ending with an $800 final payment in the last month. Sometimes balloon-note provisions are in fine print and the salesman "forgets" to mention the monster final payment. When customers can't come up with the cash to close their contract, financers repossess. You may not have to pay that last lump sum if a salesman "forgets" to mention it—contact your local public prosecutor about filing Truth in Lending court actions.

The close-and-bump. In this nearly universal auto sales practice, salesman and sales manager combine to squeeze a final $100 or more out of customers who feel too far into the hassle and paperwork to turn back on their new-car deal. Just as you're about to sign the contract at an agreed-upon price, the salesman will leave to check the deal with his sales manager. The manager returns and tells you he doesn't know why the salesman offered the ridiculously low price. The manager would go broke selling cars at such discounts and he'll have to discipline the salesman. But to be a good guy, he'll let you have the car for just $100 more than you had agreed to pay the salesman.

Your defense: Hold firm. Ask to use their phone book to look up the number and address of the Better Business Bureau and then walk out the door. The manager will stop you, no doubt, and drop his close-and-bump demands.

Trial and trade. You hassle and haggle with that auto dealer to get the price on a secondhand auto reduced from $1,000 to $800. The dealer throws in this guarantee: Drive it for a week, and if anything's wrong, bring it back and exchange it.

A week later, the car is falling apart. The dealer is willing to exchange—but today there's no wheelin' and dealin'; prices are firm as marked. You end up with an $800 car you know he'd sell to anybody else for $600.

Recalls. To avoid the nuisance of shipping high-risk buggies—ones that should be recalled for a defect—back to Detroit, harried owners will palm them off on unsuspecting buyers. Circumvent this ploy by calling a toll-free federal-government number, 800-424-9393, and asking if the car in question has been recalled. Or send the National Highway Traffic Safety Administration, Office of Consumer Services, Washington, D.C., the make, model year, and vehicle identification number for the same information.

Mechanical checkups. When you've finally decided on the used car to adopt into your family, take it to a qualified auto mechanic or diagnostic center for a complete going-over before signing the contract. He'll be able to check things (like engine compression) that you can only hope and guess about. Be ready to spend about $20 for the engine evaluation—a worthwhile investment considering what a costly mistake buying a clunker can be.

Switching. A top-notch pit crew at the Indianapolis 500 can change four car tires in a lickety-split 20 seconds, but they're snails compared to the swift switcheroo that happens every time you turn your back on an unscrupulous used-car salesman. After you've signed to buy the car, he'll replace new tires with worn ones and substitute an old battery for the new one. When you return to pick up your new used car you find it minus several hundred dollars' worth of parts, including spare tire, jack, and floor mats. The simplest way to keep the used-car deal you started with is to drive the vehicle away immediately after you pay for it.

Odometer changing. The oldest used-car rip-off is setting back the odometer (the gadget that gauges how many miles the car's been driven). Odometer tampering is illegal under federal law, but it goes on just the same.

The surest guard against such foolery is to call the car's former owner and ask how many miles his vehicle had when the used-car dealer took it in (if the owner's in on the deceit, this tactic fails). Also check the way the digits line up—if the three right-hand numbers don't line up straight, someone's probably been messing with the mileage indicator. If the one-tenth-mile digit (extreme right) vibrates while the car is moving, odometer fraud is a strong probability.

Tire tricks. Be alert to the used-car dealer who makes a big spiel about having added brand-new tires to this one-owner wonder. He knows new tires won't show the uneven wearing on the insides that was too obvious on the car's original tires. Such unbalanced tread wear would have tipped off potential buyers (like you) that the car probably needs front-end alignment and wheel balancing or possibly has a bent frame. Demand to see the car's original tires or get the dealer's written guarantee that there are no alignment problems at time of purchase. Test-drive the car as far as a reputable auto garage and have a mechanic check the alignment before you buy.

The test drive. Loop around the ramp and out onto the freeway. Your prospective used-car purchase should accelerate smoothly from a slow speed. No skips, spits, sputters, or hesitations. Drive 45 miles an hour down a country road and then pump the brakes three times. Brake pedal should stay well above the floor and feel solid—a soft, spongy touch or the car pulling to one side or brakes grabbing and chattering prophesy expensive brake repairs.

Coast down a long hill, foot off the accelerator. Just before you hit the bottom, trample the gas pedal and watch your rear-view mirror. A heavy blue exhaust cloud means an engine overhaul is needed. Black smoke means an over-rich fuel mixture, costing you at least for carburetor adjustments.

Joints and bearings. It costs plenty to repair or replace a used car's suspension joints and wheel bearings. That impending major repair bill is exactly the reason the car's first owner is trying to palm the sedan off on you. Spot bad joints and bearings by shaking each front wheel hard, in and out at the top, while the car is on the ground. If you hear a couple of clunks, if it feels loose or has a lot of free play, the jalopy needs an appointment with the joint doctor.

Shock absorbers. Yeah, it's a beaut—who would expect to find such a semi-precious gem on a used-car lot? But just to be sure you won't get zapped with lemon juice, check shock absorbers before signing dotted lines. Give each corner a good bouncing and let go. The body should bounce once and stop. If the car keeps bouncing up and down, the shock absorbers need replacing.

Rust. Rust damage is quite expensive to repair—much more so than the salesman will let on. Check any used auto for signs of rust, especially in the wheel wells and around the rocker panels under the doors. Rust here can weaken the car's basic structure and cost you hundreds of dollars for repairs.

Tainted and repainted. The shifty salesman may not tell you the used car you're ogling has survived a major accident with the help of cosmetic body work. Such cars often cost their second owners bundles to repair bent frames or other serious damages. Simple checks help you avoid cars that have been wrecked.

In daylight on the used-car lot, look down the sides of the car, noting ripples in the paint or repainted spots—signs that the car may have been in an accident. Check the color of the car frame inside a door and on the firewall (the metal divider between engine and passenger area). If the hue is different than the car body color, it's been repainted, possibly to conceal the effects of a crash.

CAR-REPAIR CHEATS

A watchful eye. The American Automobile Association warns that willful vandalism is a major problem in service stations and garages across the country. Cutting an ignition wire or gas line, wrenching off a critical bolt, or even slashing a tire in order to sell a motorist a repair job or replacement part is common practice.

Therefore, whenever a strange mechanic checks your car for some maladjustment, it's important to watch him carefully, and to let him know he's being watched.

Unneeded oil. It's hard to believe that a service-station owner or attendant would stoop to cheating a motorist out of a paltry ninety cents, but it happens every day. A former service-station attendant we know relates that it was common practice for his former boss and employees alike to manipulate the dipstick so that it indicated that the car needed a quart of oil.

If you're in doubt, get out of the car and ask the attendant to recheck the oil while you look on.

Testing the mechanic. Let's face it, even honest, competent auto mechanics are expensive. The dishonest ones can be murder. Whenever we move into a new area, here's how we find the former: We simply pull a wire off one of the spark plugs, then drive into a garage. We tell the mechanic that the car is sluggish, then ask him to diagnose the trouble and give us an estimate. If he recommends a major overhaul for, say, $350, we know we've got a crook. On the other hand, if he simply replaces the disconnected spark-plug wire and sends us on our way, we'll know who to go to in case of real trouble.

Be a good customer. If your honest mechanic operates out of a service station, buy your gas, oil, and accessories from him as well. As you become a valued customer, he's likely to quote repairs on the low side rather than on the high. You should also be able to count on him to perform minor adjustments for free.

Replacement parts. Many times, when auto parts such as batteries, generators, fuel pumps, and tires are replaced, the mechanic will sell the older parts, thus making even more profit on the repair job—at your expense. Demand to keep these older parts, then sell them yourself to an auto wrecking yard. Or allow the mechanic to keep them provided he gives you a discount on the work performed.

Repair costs. Before giving the go-ahead on any auto repairs involving significant cost, check the flat-rate manual (available at any auto-repair garage or public library) and compare this with the estimate given you. If the two figures are compatible, and you decide to proceed with the work, demand a *written* estimate from the garage. This will bind them to the figure quoted.

Blanket rates. Be especially wary of blanket rates for repairs and services—a rebuilt engine, for instance, for $139.95. This may include only the engine block. Of course, pistons and rings, carburetor, spark plugs, and installation are all "extras," which could add up to twice the price you'd pay at a legitimate garage.

Before agreeing to such an arrangement, demand in writing a complete list of parts and labor included in the price.

Brake jobs. Many consumers believe that a "brake job" consists only of installing new brake linings. Once your car is in the shop, however, it may be discovered that new wheel cylinders and master cylinders and drum regrinding are needed, which can easily triple the cost quoted for linings alone.

Therefore before agreeing to what may look like a bargain price on brake linings, determine whether this extra work is needed and, if so, the cost of parts and labor.

Claims adjusters. If you incur auto damage which is covered by insurance, make sure that the company's adjuster inspects the damage before it's repaired. Once repairs have been made, many insurance companies will balk at paying a claim—many will even refuse.

Gas sales. Before having a service-station attendant put gas in your car, check the dollar figure on the pump. Dishonest employees have been known to purposely dispense gas from a pump on which a certain amount has already been registered, then charge the customer the indicated amount, pocketing the excess.

Wobbling wheels. Any instant now your wheel could go bouncing off down the road—or at least that's what the gyp-minded mechanic tells you. To prove it, he'll jack up the front end of your car (so the pressure is off the front spring) to show you your front wheel wobbles like a bowlegged whooping crane in a hurricane.

But this is only normal loose movement. Dishonest repairmen will try to convince you it's a dangerous ball joint and new ones, with a $65 price tag, are needed. Save your car allowance and don't buy his story or his ball joints.

Complaints. Victims of auto-repair schemes of all stripes can find solace at several state and federal government agencies. Many states have a Bureau of Repair Services or include consumer-aid divisions in their Department of Motor Vehicles. Check the Yellow Pages of your phone book for local offices.

The Federal Trade Commission handles complaints of national significance at its offices in major cities across the country. Or write Federal Trade Commission, Pennsylvania Avenue at 6th Street N.W., Washington, D.C. 20580.

Transmission trickery. Terrible transmission trouble, the grease monkey tells you as he opens his hand to reveal metal filings he's taken from the bottom of your transmission case. Before you know it he's also taken $200 from the bottom of your pocket to pay for a rebuilt transmission.

Most transmissions shed metal pieces—in reasonable amounts it's not a serious problem. Simply changing your transmission fluid will clean out your transmission.

Self-diagnosis. When you splutter into the repair garage, *don't* tell the mechanic what you think is wrong with the car. Let him figure it out. If you say, for instance, that you think the carburetor needs an overhaul, you leave yourself open for a double repair bill if you're wrong. The dishonest repairman will instantly agree with you, charge you for a rebuilt carburetor, and then also fix your fuel pump, which was the only thing causing the problem in the first place. Avoid paying for unneeded auto maintenance by telling your mechanic what the *symptoms* of your problem are, not guessing at the cause of trouble.

Fuel pumps. The average auto fuel pump lasts more than 50,000 miles. Be suspicious of anyone but a trusted repairman claiming it needs replacement before that. By simply squirting raw gasoline on a fuel pump, mechanics can claim pump failure and fool drivers who aren't too auto-wise.

This "trick" is especially cruel, since it leaves car owners worrying about gas fires that might damage the engine or endanger their lives. If foul play is suspected, take your car to a reputable repairman.

Generator gyp. Last week we took our car to the garage for a routine tune-up. Next day we got a call from a shifty mechanic saying he'd spotted trouble—with our generator. As evidence he pointed out oil "leaks," which were squirted from an oil can.

How did we know? Neither a generator nor a starter is lubricated with sufficient oil to leave external evidence of oil leaking. Unless the starter fails to turn over or the generator doesn't charge, don't be talked into a new or rebuilt generator.

Fan-belt fraud. When you're not looking, a crooked service-station attendant can partially cut through your fan belt, then helpfully point out the need for replacement. There's little you can do at this point —the weakened belt must be replaced pronto.

To stop this trick, keep your eyes open. If it happens anyway, examine the old belt for signs of deliberate cutting. If you find them, demand your money back, and notify your state Bureau of Repair Services of the crime.

Towing. Breakdowns on the freeway can be nightmares, especially since the highways are patrolled by tow-truck tricksters. Such operators commonly monitor police and citizens-band radio channels along well-traveled routes in order to reach their helpless victims fast.

Don't get your wallet lifted along with your car's axle. If at all possible, telephone for a towing service. You'll undoubtably get a better price than from the trucker who appears unsummoned on the scene. And never let a strange towman take you to his own garage, or you'll likely get a rip-off repair bill along with his bloated tow charges.

Dipstick trick. Any gas-station attendant who jumps in front of your car hood saying "Check that oil too, mister?" the moment you pull up to the pump is cause for suspicion. He may be a dipstick juggler out to get his greasy palms on your money.

His quickness is the clue. You'll *always* seem short of oil when the dipstick is pulled out only a few seconds after the car is stopped. It takes several minutes for oil trapped in the top of your engine to drain back into the crankcase. Don't check the oil till the engine has been off awhile.

The empty oil can. The oldest gas-station trick still playing features a sly attendant pouring air in your crankcase and charging you for oil. The best actors can do it right before your eyes—you watch them take a can of oil from the rack, punch holes in it, and turn it up into your engine.

What you didn't see was the crafty gas peddler poking holes in the *bottom* of the same can to give an earlier customer oil, then putting the can back on the rack. You get holes in the can tip, but no oil.

Foil this and other oil hustlers by carrying a quart or two in your trunk. When they ask if you want oil, say yes, then hand them one of your cans—you know *it's* full.

Carburetor crooks. Does your carburetor flood as regularly as the Nile? Something's wrong, but maybe not as much as unethical mechanics will claim.

Odds are all it takes to fix an oozing carburetor is a needle valve and seat (about $7) and not the new or rebuilt carburetor ($35 plus) the tricky mechanic will suggest.

Dead batteries. Anytime a conman in mechanic's coveralls can convince you there's no charge in your battery, he can charge you, instead, for the price of a new battery. He'll put the prods of his battery tester on the wrong electrodes and, of course, get a reading of a dead cell. Or he'll use a broken battery tester (some garages keep one handy for this purpose) that wouldn't register if it were struck by lightning.

When you get a voltmeter test, make sure the mechanic pushes the prongs well below the surface of the corrosion usually covering battery contact points (otherwise the reading will be wrong). Also ask him to demonstrate that his tester works properly.

Wiper tricks. If it's been a slow day, the swindling service-station attendant can always pick up a few extra bucks in a pinch—a pinch of your windshield wipers. A quick squeeze between the thumb and two fingers will knock a wiper blade out of line, causing poor contact between blade and glass.

When this sneaky gas pumper then splashes some water on your window and your wipers can't clean it off, he'll sell you new wipers for a cool $8.

Used oil. Slippery service-station men save the dirty oil they drain from cars and sell it to "refiners" who pour the crud-packed fluid into new cans and sell it back to gas-station operators to put in your car.

To make the gyp complete, there is also a machine to reseal used name-brand cans with dirty oil inside. Your only defence is to get out of your car and pick up the can of oil you want yourself. A slightly pinched lid will tip you that it's a refilled rip-off.

Defective tires. Buying "blemished" tires or "seconds" is one way to save money. But some tire dealers make your bargain dangerous by selling "seconds" unfit for the road. Such tires *are* used in racing, but should be permanently marked "unsafe for highway" or "not for highway use" on the sidewall. Consumer watchdogs report such markings are sometimet buffed off and the unfit tires sold as "blemished."

To ensure your safety, reject any tire showing evidence of buffing on its sidewall for highway use.

Shock-absorber scares. Dishonest wrench wielders at auto-repair garages will stoop pretty low to convince you the shock absorbers under your car need replacement. Commonly, the car-fixing crook squirts oil from an oil can on your shock absorbers as evidence of failure, then tells you stories of all sorts of possible consequences.

In fact, shocks usually last 20,000 or more miles; only rarely will a shock absorber fail suddenly, and almost never will all four fail at once. Don't be pushed into immediate shock-absorber replacement. There's time to shop around.

Spark plugs. By far the most frequent auto-repair swindle is un-needed replacement of spark plugs, with a profitable switcheroo thrown in. Often in conjunction with other repairs, crooked operators claim new plugs are needed, slap in someone else's old set, then charge parts plus labor.

You're better off keeping your cash and changing your spark plugs yourself, if they need it. It's a simple process. First, visit your friendly auto-accessory shop for a spark-plug wrench and gapper (under $2 for both). The salesman will look up the correct gap for your car. After setting the gap, it's just a matter of screwing out the old, screwing in the new.

Nonexistent contraptions. We agree a "rotohemivalve compressor" sounds like a complex gadget, and the sharpie mechanic claims your car will suffer a slow sputtering death without a new one. Truth is often far from such appearances.

For example, one car repairman sold a "pulse suppressor" to "level off generator output peaks" for $111 to a man whose car needed only a spark-plug replacement. Judge a mechanic on his work, not his words. Don't blow your dough on fancy contraptions that don't exist.

ANTI-THEFT TOOLS AND TACTICS

CB security. Stop citizens-band bandits with a special lock ($10), made to fit virtually any CB radio, under-dash tape deck, or AM/FM radio mounting bracket. You get two keys and a small, two-piece clamp-style lock which installs in minutes without special tools. Protect your "hardware" ahead of time and you won't have to rely on the "Smok-ies" to retrieve your stolen CB. Radio Shack carries these devices, called Universal CB Locks.

Registration. Always carry your automobile registration on your person, rather than in your car. The reason? Police, when stopping a motorist, invariably ask the driver to produce the car's registration certificate. If the driver of your stolen car happens to be stopped by a law-enforcement officer for some minor infraction and can't produce the registration, an immediate check is made, which will result in the thief's apprehension and the car's early return to you.

If others drive your car, provide a photostatic copy of your registration certificate for each of the other drivers.

Car cautions. Next to a car thief, who is more qualified to advise you on auto anti-theft measures than the police? And the Los Angeles Police Department does just that in their pamphlet entitled *Careless . . . Careless!* For your free copy, write their Public Affairs Division at 150 North Los Angeles Street, Los Angeles, Calif. 90012.

Rotor removal. One of the best (although somewhat troublesome) ways that we know of to protect yourself against auto theft is to raise the hood, pry off the distributor cap, remove the rotor from the distributor, then replace the cap. Unless the thief has the time to diagnose the problem and has the exact rotor to fit your distributor, he'll be unable to start the car.

Parking precautions. Try to park in lots and garages which allow you to lock your car and take your keys with you. If you must leave your ignition key with an attendant, leave only that key. Unscrupulous parking attendants have been known to duplicate house and other keys, later using them to burglarize your home.

Battery locks. A special clamping device is available which allows you to padlock your battery. The unit can be installed in minutes with a few simple hand tools.

The product retails for $6.95 and can be ordered from Pakton Products Co., 20201 Prairie Street, Chatsworth, Calif. 91311.

Removable radios. A simple way to prevent vandals from breaking into your car to swipe a CB radio or a tape player is to take them yourself as you leave your auto. About $10 will buy a two-piece mounting bracket. Install one piece in the car; the other attaches to your stereo or CB. The unit slides out easily when you leave your car, and electrical contacts are automatically reestablished when you click it back in place upon your return. Removable mounting brackets are available in stereo shops, auto-parts shops, and department stores.

Steering-wheel locks. Most modern wheeled wonders come equipped with steering-wheel locks to discourage car thieves. If you drive a used car or older model without this built-in crimestopper you can purchase a specially designed lock for about $15 and profit from the same protection.

The lock sold at most regular distributors of auto accessories is a tough stainless-steel shaft which connects steering wheel to brake pedal. A key locks the device (and your steering wheel) at the shaft's middle. Even with the engine running, the wheel won't turn.

Fuel-line lock. Underwriters Laboratories considers a new, totally different anti-car-theft device recently developed at tiny Safetech, Inc., in Fairfield, N. J., among the most effective. The Safetech system locks off the fuel supply to the motor.

Even if you leave your ignition key in place, the car can't be started without punching a five-digit code on an eighteen-button keyboard mounted under the dash. A thief would have to jump the ignition and replace the carburetor with its special hardened-steel cut-off valve to start your car. That's a forty-minute job, even if he does miraculously have the correct carburetor on hand.

At $160, the Safetch system is a more than adequate car-theft deterrent.

Chains. If you don't mind the look of long chains dangling out in front of your car, you'll get a measure of protection from a length of hardened-steel chain and a case-hardened padlock to fasten your car hood to the grill. This makeshift system will deter the amateur from your '62 Chevy, but won't stop a boltcutter-equipped professional who's after your shiny new Rolls.

Hood locks. You can frustrate the punk trying to steal your engine parts or hot-wire your car with a hood lock, available at almost all auto stores for about $11. Or, if you don't like drilling two holes about ½ inch in diameter in your hood, $50 will get a locking system installed from the inside. Ask for Kar-Lok, made by Chapman Security Products, Bayside, N. Y., and installed near the ignition lock.

Door locks. Thieves who steal tape players and packages from cars gain entry to one in four of their victims' cars by lifting the door-lock latch with a coat hanger twisted through a window. A 50-cent investment will foil these hanger yankers.

Replace your current door-lock latches with rimless interior lock knobs from your auto-supply store. The replacements can easily be grasped from within, but there's no flange for a hanger to hook to.

Station wagons. Station wagons are very vulnerable. Since there's no trunk, there's nowhere to hide luggage, packages, spare tires, clothing, tools, or sports equipment from the passing prowler's sight. If you have a choice, don't buy a station wagon in the first place. If you must drive such an auto, carry a blanket to conceal your goods, or install a false-bottomed seat.

Note trick. Scribble a note on the back of a blank envelope and keep it in your car's glove compartment. Your message should be "Gone for gas" or "Sugar in gas tank" or "Starter motor dead." Then whenever you have to park in a strange neighborhood at night or high-crime area by day, stick the note under your windshield wiper as you lock your car and leave. It seems that you're informing police or traffic wardens, but the car thief will also get your message. Thinking your car won't run, chances are they won't try to steal it.

Deadbolt car locks. Although standard locks on car doors, hoods, and trunks hold under moderate stress, they open readily for the prying prowler with the right know-how. Make these entry points to your vehicle more secure by installing new dead bolt-style locks specially adapted for autos and available at most parts stores for about $20 for a four-door set. Changing locks is particularly advisable on a newly purchased used car—you don't know how many people have keys to it.

Locking gas cap. All auto-parts stores sell them and so do most large department stores. A locking gas cap, at less than $10, may be an inconvenience at the service station but it will keep thieves from siphoning your fuel. Besides those who pilfer gas from cars in parking lots, driveways, and streets, you'll also foil vandals who slide sugar into gas tanks or set cars afire.

Antenna protection. The recent popularity of CB radios provides thieves with two plentiful, marketable targets: the CB transmitter and the "whip" or CB antenna. Since the antenna must attach to the outside of car or truck, it is the easier rip off. Moreover, such antennas advertise that there is a CB transmitter inside.

Most electronics and CB stores stock "quick-disconnect" antenna attachments ($5) which allow you to take your antenna with you when you park.

Wheel locks. It's the gleam of the racy chrome or "mag" wheels that catches a crook's eye. To benefit sports-car buffs, an adroit Detroit locksmith is marketing locking lug nuts—wheel fasteners complete with a key.

The chrome-rim clampers fit most model cars and wheels, are available at any racing-parts store or sizable department store, and cost slightly more than $6 per wheel (set of four locks).

Antenna vandals. Auto vandalism is largely impossible to avoid—even if you park in a locked garage at home, the paint sprayers and window scrapers will get you in the shopping-center parking lot. One common car vandal, the antenna snapper, can be outwitted with a new-style antenna consisting of a small wire embedded in or taped to your windshield. Many new-model cars come equipped with these. Or, if your older make gets its antenna ripped off or snipped off by a passing punk, you can have this vandalproof variety installed for the price of replacing your old one.

Decals. Stoke up your car's engine any way you like, but don't advertise your super-powerful and super-expensive car parts to passing car strippers by window decals proclaiming the products. Racing and parts insignias proclaim your car holds the hopped-up parts thieves find easy to unload. Keep window decals off your car.

Window protection. It doesn't take Houdini and a puff of smoke to break into a locked car, especially if the auto has a vulnerable wing window. To prevent prying car plunderers, wrap a piece of wire (clotheshanger type) around the wing window latch and secure it to the door handle. Such a precaution will stop many amateur thieves.

CB theft alarm. An install-it-yourself gizmo from Radio Shack, called a CB Theft Alarm, lets loose a blare of your car's horn when a punk tries to snare your CB radio transceiver, your tape player, or your car radio. This sensor works independently of other alarm switches, giving you double protection. Just flick a switch to activate the alarm as you leave your auto. Complete with all mounting hardware, the device sells for $5.

Sirens. All auto alarms employ noise—siren, bell, or horn—in attempting to frighten away a potential car thief. The siren, however, because it is psychologically the most startling, is the most effective. You'll pay more for a siren-type alarm system than you would for a bell or horn type, but in our estimation the extra protection is worth the price.

Siren-type auto alarms retail at about $40. If you can't find them at the usual outlets, write the manufacturers: Ademco (Alarm Device Manufacturing Company), 165 Eileen Way, Syosset, L.I., N.Y. 11791; or A.P.I. (Alarm Products International), 24–02 40th Avenue, Long Island City, N.Y. 11101.

Horn alarm. By far the cheapest type of auto alarm (about $10) uses your car horn as a noisemaker. It's called the Anes Model HB, and is available through all the normal outlets.

Delayed-action shutoff. One of the newest and cheapest gadgets on the auto-security market today is the Buss Time-Delay Auto Protector. Retailing for $2.98, this is a special fuse which is hooked up directly to the ignition system. Before leaving your car, you set a switch. Should a thief succeed in starting your car while you're gone, the fuse will cut out after a minute or so, most likely leaving the car stalled in traffic. Rather than waste more time and take a chance on getting caught, the thief will, nine times out of ten, give up and go on to the next victim.

Hidden switch. An easy-to-install switch can offer you nearly as much auto protection as a $200 siren alarm system. Flick this ignition-killer switch when you leave your car and car thieves can't get your auto started unless they find the magic button. Obviously you don't mount it in some easily discoverable place such as your glove compartment or under the ignition switch.

Babaco alarms. If you want the ultimate in car burglar alarms and can afford it, ask your auto-parts dealer about a truck-type Babaco alarm. Be prepared to pay from $100 to $400 (for the Jeweler's Special), or you can rent one for $35 to $100 a year. Your car's horn or siren alarm will be nearly impossible to disable because the battery is enclosed in a locked steel container.

False alarm. Those who can't afford the luxury of auto alarm systems can achieve some measure of security for under $1 with a kit available at most auto-parts specialists. It's a metalized plastic part that adheres to the side of your car and resembles the locks for burglar alarms. A phony warning decal comes in the same kit.

It won't fool the pros, but for $1 you'll persuade rookies and thrill seekers to look elsewhere.

Dummy chain lock. Count on car thieves to avoid those autos sporting security devices with which they're not familiar. Of course they must *see* the newfangled contraption before it can be an effective deterrent. Any huge-linked log chain can fill both bills.

Loop the giant chain through the steering wheel with the ends tucked under the car seat, presumably padlocked there. A car thief will be unable to cope with such heavy-duty hardware with the few tools he usually carries and will pass your car by.

Wheel alarm. This vibration-sensitive alarm switch goes off when the tire thief jacks. Attach it to your car's horn if you don't have a siren or bell car alarm. When the car's frame is jostled, as by a wheel thief cranking your car off the ground to lift your tires or wheels, the switch triggers a warning.

The device is $5 and sold by Lafayette Radio Electronics, 111 Jericho Turnpike, Syosset, N.Y. 11791. This ticklish alarm may also help keep your auto from being towed.

Door alarm. In most cars, opening the driver's door takes pressure off a switch, which then turns the door or dome light on. That same switch can be rigged to set off a burglar alarm, should a car thief take the most frequent entry point—an unlocked front door. If your car doesn't already have such a switch, most auto-parts stores and electronics stores sell them for under $1.

A problem with these switches is that they automatically turn the alarm off when the door is shut—you'll need a backup switch to prevent the car swiper from hopping in, slamming the door, and taking off. But door switches are an effective front line of car defense.

Vehicle numbers identification. There are literally thousands of stolen used cars on today's market. Make certain the car you buy is not "hot" by taking the following precautions: Check the license and tag numbers and vehicle identification number (VIN) against those on the car's ownership certificate. (If you can't find the VIN, the location of which varies with make and year, a call to the service department of your car's dealership will get you the information.)

If there is any evidence of tampering with the numbers on the car or on the ownership certificate, demand that the owner ride with you in the car to the office of your state Motor Vehicle Department, where you'll be able to determine the car's true ownership before buying.

Hidden ID numbers. Shortly after making off with your automobile, the professional car thief will proceed to obliterate or change your engine and body ID numbers. Sabotage his efforts by etching these numbers, preferably with an electric engraving tool, on some obscure part of your car's chassis. For extra safety, etch your driver's license number or social security number in the same area.

Checking on thefts. Most auto-insurance companies are members of the National Auto Theft Bureau, an organization devoted to tracking down all cars involved in thefts and keeping computerized records on them. If your insurance company is a member, ask it to check the car you intend to purchase with the bureau for any record of theft.

Post-dated checks. Crooks hawking stolen jalopies and used-car dealers unloading lemons are typically in a hurry to close the contract. Say you want some time to think it over. But if the seller insists on a speedy transaction and you don't want to miss the deal, give him a post-dated check.

Beware—the bank can go ahead and cash such a check, regardless of date, if the money's in your account. So leave the check uncovered until you've authenticated the car's ID number on the engine. Cancel payment if you suspect a rip-off.

Classified ads. A favorite dumping ground for hustlers of stolen cars is the classified-ad section of newspapers. Here they'll advertise their loot at super-bargain prices, giving only a phone number—usually a public-booth number. Such fences answer the first call, sell the stolen car, and vanish. When the car is determined stolen, the true owner can recover his property, leaving you bilked of hundreds or thousands of dollars.

If you're car shopping via classified ads, don't deal with sellers who advertise only phone numbers and insist on coming to you with the car. If the number is for a pay phone (check with Ma Bell), don't buy. That way you'll get a bargain that's not a real steal.

Marked merchandise. Clouts for car-stealing rings know exactly where to look for your vehicle number stamped on your car frame. They'll disfigure it soon after they swipe your auto. Often, recovering your stolen vehicle will depend on how cleverly you left your mark on the car.

Try slipping an old license plate down the rear seat, chiseling your initials on a concealed part of the car's chassis, dropping a business card inside the door panels, and placing scotch tape across the registration number on your registration. This last idea will keep forgers from erasing your number and inking in a new one for the stolen car. Peeling the tape off leaves a telltale rip on the registration papers.

Identicar kits. A good way to discourage the professional car thief is to etch your vehicle's registration number on each of your car's windows. For this purpose, most auto stores sell "identicar" kits for less than $5. Once on your car windows, the numbers can't be removed or obliterated by scraping or breaking the window. Most thieves won't go to the trouble and expense of changing all windows —including your windshield.

Identicar kits include an etching fluid, stencils for your car's numbers, complete instructions, and a piece of glass to practice on. Numbers don't obstruct vision.

HITCHHIKING

Shakedowns. Recently come to light is an extortion racket involving pre-teenage and teenage hitchhikers—of both sexes—who will solicit a ride with a single man, then threaten to turn him into the authorities for child molesting if he doesn't come across with a few dollars.

If this should happen to you, your best defense is to refuse to pay, then report the matter to the police immediately. If your young passenger decides to follow through with his or her threat, things will look a lot better for you if *you* have made a report on the matter.

Hitchhiker's hideaway. Despite its dangers, more and more people turn to hitching a ride to meet their transportation needs. The first rule of the road is never to carry more than $5 while thumbing for rides.

If you must carry money, a traveler's check, or a credit card, hide them under a patch sewn onto bookbag, backpack, or jeans seat. Stitch a patch on three sides, slide the money or paper between patch and cloth, then sew up the last side.

Fire as a weapon. Ride thumbers and those who pick up hitchhikers can both benefit by being ready to fight fire with fire. You can smoke a cigarette and carry a butane lighter in your pocket when hitching or picking up riders. If your new acquaintance tries to rob or rape you, you can jab the burning end into his cheek. Or if you're a rider and the driver won't slow down to let you out, flick your butane to ignite his clothes or something else in the auto. His natural reaction will be to stop and battle the blaze, giving you time to spring to safety.

Car-door test. Hitchhikers jumping in a jalopy for a free ride can take a simple but sly precaution to give them time to size up the driver and prepare to escape if necessary. Always fail to shut the car door properly when you first get in. If the driver balks at letting you adjust the loose door, assume you're in trouble and get out to thumb-wag another ride. At any rate, you'll have to open the door again to slam it closed. That gives you time to see just how the door opens and whether there is a lock which must be released first. If the driver must push an electric lock-release button, you're not safe and should get out. Also, never take a ride in the back seat if there are no rear car doors.

BIKE AND CYCLE SECURITY

Handlebar hideaway. An excellent way to retain identification of your bicycle is to write your name and address on a piece of paper, roll it up, then slip it into the handlebar under the hand grip. If your bike is stolen, you may just see it around town one day. If so, it's a simple matter to pull off the hand grip and check inside for the paper. If you find it there, call the police immediately.

Custom paint job. Hand junior a paint brush and a bike and let him paint stripes on the fenders, polka-dots on the mudguards, and a mural depicting the rise and fall of Rome on the bike seat. Ugly bikes pedal the same as shiny ones, but they're less desirable to thieves and much simpler to identify if they are stolen.

Strongarm cycle thieves. From New York to St. Louis to Los Angeles, a new breed of bicycle thief is popping out from behind bushes. This thug shoves passing bike riders to the ground, then pirates their wheels. Or two rowdies may ride up beside a biker, knock her or him over, then pedal away with the victim's bicycle held between theirs.

If you see such trouble ahead, reverse your course fast. If other bikers ride too near you, stop suddenly. The strange pedaler's momentum will carry him yards past you, giving you time to turn and ride away. If knocked down, hold on to your bike and keep it between you and your attackers, who might have knives, while you scream or whistle for help.

Overlong chains. If you must leave your bicycle unattended for a couple of hours, keep this in mind—a crook can use the ground as an anvil and in a few slams of a sledge hammer obliterate most locks, chains, or cables. Foil these bikenappers by wrapping your long chain around the bike frame a few times so it can't touch the ground.

Bike alarms. A lightweight bike burglar alarm, which howls for an hour if the bicycle's lock or cable is tampered with, is widely available at bike shops and department stores for little more than $10.

The "Cycolac" is a 1-pound, battery-powered yelp-box which mounts permanently to your bike frame and guarantees no false alarms. Its small (3 by 4 by 2 inches) high-impact plastic case resists acid and weather. A cable stretches from the top of the box, through your wheels, and back to the box. Cutting the cable or trying to remove the alarm without a key lets loose a yahoo you'll hear up to a quarter-mile away.

Chain it to something solid. A youngster we know strung a ¼-inch steel chain through each wheel of his bicycle, snapping the ends together with a hardened-steel lock. A bike thief came along, lifted the shackled bicycle into a pick-up truck, and hauled bike, chain, and lock away to work on at his leisure.

Therefore, it's important to secure your bike to something solid. Loop your bike chain to some immovable object such as a fence, park bench, or bike rack to keep it from getting carried away by bicycle bandits.

Super bike locks. Most bike thieves carry bolt-cutters to snap chains and locks. The best way to protect your bike from these snip-and-steal bandits is investing in one of two specially constructed bike locks known as "The Citadel" and "Kryptonite" at bike shops. The pricetag will be between $20 and $30, but both are heavy-duty locks impossible to cut with boltcutters and are well suited to bike racks and parking meters. If you ride an expensive 10-speed, your wheeled machinery deserves the protection.

Cycle-Gard. The best anti-theft device for a motorcycle, favored by Hell's Angels and Honda Hoppers Clubs, is the Cycle-Gard, made by Alcotronics Corp., Church Road and Roland Avenue, Mount Laurel, N.J. 08057.

The device, rigged behind the rear license plate, emits a loud bleeping noise for forty seconds if the cycle is moved. If the motion continues, it shrieks another alarm forty seconds later, and so on. This is the $33 version.

The $90 Cycle-Gard II does all this, plus transmitting a radio signal to a small receiver worn by the owner or set up near her or his bed.

Helmet holders. Motorcyclists with up to $25 invested in a crash helmet can protect that investment with a $4 helmet lock. The device is operated by a key and attaches to your cycle's handlebars. Loop the latch through your helmet strap and stroll on into the toughest joint in town to belt down a few brews. Return and you're assured your helmet will be handy. Order the helmet lock from J.C. Whitney and Company, 1917–19 Archer Avenue, P.O. Box 8410, Chicago, Ill. 60680.

Chains. A secure lock and chain is still the most widely used anti-theft device, and while it is not foolproof, it is adequate for most daytime bike use in places like shopping centers and schools. "Case-hardened" or "Thru-hardened" will slow down most chain clippers, since crooks seldom walk around in daylight with 3-foot bolt-cutters in their pockets.

Unfortunately, however, thickness, weight, or hardness of the chain makes little or no difference when a bike is locked outside overnight. Seasoned bike thieves chew through any chain in seconds.

Cables. The protection offered by the hardened-steel cable is at least equal to that of a hardened-steel chain. Costing under $10, the cable is lighter and more flexible, thus making it handier. Available at bike dealers everywhere.

CHAPTER 9

Enjoy traveling— but don't get taken for a ride

The affluent American traveler is particularly susceptible to getting severely ripped off at every turn. The crooks come in different costumes. Some dress as ticket agents, some as cab drivers, some as maids and bellboys, others as foreign merchants and yet others as fellow travelers. Whether you're playing in Pawtucket or on business in Brussels, rest assured that pickpockets (see Chapter 2), luggage thieves, strongarm robbers, and hotel-room burglars are common. Staying safe while traveling from place to place requires advance planning. Those who roam the world would be wise to remember to prepare safety precautions as they arrange hotel reservations.

If the goal of this chapter (indeed, the point of this book) can be said in five words, these words would do it: Prevention is better than cure. Thus, by observing some of our simple, basic precautions while traveling, you'll add to your peace of mind without detracting at all from your pleasure. On the contrary, it's when you get careless and are assaulted or lose your possessions that the pleasures of traveling diminish or vanish completely. If you want to return with wits and possessions intact, then constant alertness is your key.

Before taking to the highways and byways, reread the sections of this book on protecting your purse and person in public, on wheeled-vehicle precautions, and on other pertinent topics. Take as little cash along and leave as many of your valuables at home as possible. Learn as much of the language—especially "utility" phrases—of your destination as time allows. Then you must test your prowess as an actor. Keep a skeptic's eye open to the dangers of any encounter on a foreign shore, but make your every action exude confidence. Your apparent self-assurance shouldn't make you seem an "ugly American" to the natives, but should make you appear less vulnerable than the shaky, confused, and obviously disoriented traveler.

A final tip before your next trip: There is safety in numbers! Wives, take your husbands along on business trips. Consider group tours or arrange for reputable guides or experienced travelers to accompany you on your first ventures abroad. Learn the safety ropes and let your travels be rich and rewarding experiences.

HOTEL HAZARDS

Traveling alarm. A super safety siren that's easy on the jetsetter's budget and especially designed to suit the traveler's security needs is the Powerhorn Jr., sold at Radio Shack stores for just over $2. The battery-powered, pocket-size box features adhesive backing for quick installation as you scoot from hotel room to hotel room. It adjusts to protect either doors or windows—any unauthorized opening sets off a squeal loud enough to wake you and to scare off prowlers.

Jewelry. Never, but never, keep expensive jewelry in your hotel room —even when you're there. Keep all such valuables in the hotel safe. Decide in advance what jewelry you'll wear, then pick it up from the desk clerk before going out. Put it on in the lobby or in a nearby ladies' room.

When returning to your hotel, deposit your jewelry at the front desk for safekeeping on the way to your room.

Traveling lock. A dandy security gadget to carry along with you on your travels is the Yale Travelok. This item sells for $5, is small enough to fit in the palm of the hand, and consists of a combination lock and hook. The lock (operated with a key) may be attached to a door or dresser drawer with the hooked part clamped against the door jamb or the inside of the dresser, thus effectively locking shut the door or drawer.

Concealing valuables. Before your drop the quarter into the hotel's coin-op vibrating bed and ripple off to sleep, take time to tape your wallet, traveler's checks, and passport to the underside of a desk or bureau drawer. Don't leave them in plain view or in your pockets or even in a locked drawer. Your cleverness in hiding these absolute travel necessities is your last line of defense against sneak thieves.

Intrusion indicators. You arrive at the convention, check into your hotel room, and head for the night life. You take your wallet and traveler's checks with you, so a burglar breaking into your room could only swipe your toothbrush. But if he waited for you to return he could snatch your cash and smash your head as well.

To tell whether anyone has entered your room while you've been away, use a thin strip of chewing gum or a thread and dab of glue as intrusion indicators. Stick one end to the door and one end to the door jamb as you leave. If the strand is snapped when you return, get police or hotel-management help before entering. Your door has been opened in your absence.

Drawer booby trap. Before you go to bed in your vacation hotel room, take an extra precaution to warn you of nighttime intruders. Balance an empty dresser drawer atop the door molding (so it hangs over the door) or on the doorknob.

The noise of the falling drawer as your door is jostled will wake up all but the soundest sleepers, as well as scaring off the intruder.

Firecracker alarm. One security measure guaranteed to pop your eyes open is to rig a few firecrackers to your door and/or windows.

Use the pull-type "Chinese" firecrackers with strings dangling from each end. Tie one end to the doorknob, the other to the door frame, a chair, or a nearby dresser. When the strings are pulled apart, as by the door opening, a big bang will make the prowler head for the hills.

Purchase a year's supply of these theft deterrents next July 4, when fireworks stands are on every corner.

SUITCASE SECURITY

Baggage bulge. Avoid packing your luggage to the bulging point. The dishonest baggage handler is on the lookout for such overpacked bags. For these will easily open when dropped, allowing him to help himself to your valuables.

Locker thievery. Coin storage lockers in bus stations, train depots, and airline terminals represent a fine opportunity for the thief. His trick is to duplicate the key to one or more of the lockers or have it duplicated by a crooked locksmith. Then he merely opens your locker and helps himself to your luggage.

Prevent any chance of this happening by instead checking your baggage at the baggage counter, where you'll receive a claim check for each piece.

Key switch. A variation on the foregoing is usually perpetrated on females and the elderly. In a busy depot, if any vacant lockers are available, they are usually at or near the top row. As you struggle to get your heavy bags into a top locker, the thief will saunter over and offer to help. After loading your luggage into the locker, he'll close it, hand you the key, cheerily wish you a good day, then walk away.

But when you return for your goods, you'll find that your key does not open the locker. For your "benefactor" made a switch, retaining the real key for himself and giving you a dud. In fact, as you'll soon discover, he's already cleaned out your locker and made his escape.

Baggage claim. In the airport at the baggage-claim area someone moseys over, nonchalantly clamps onto your luggage, and strides for the exit signs. Should you call for police or airport security? How about a flying tackle?

Before testing any of these tactics, try shouting loud enough for everyone to hear. Yell "Hey there!" in indignant (rather than aggressive) tones. It'll be hard for the thief to make a mad dash with a load of luggage, so he'll either drop your bag and run or pretend it was a mistake and apologize. Either way you get your valuables back without getting hurt.

Baggage tags. Help ensure the safe delivery, easy identification, and probable return if stolen of your suitcases by concealing a tag giving your name and destination on the inside of your luggage. Attach rip-proof plastic or leather tags to the handle outside your bag, but also tape an identification card inside the lid or in a shoe pocket. This is a low-cost, speedy way to recover your possessions in a showdown between you, airport police, and a suitcase swiper.

Distinctive luggage. If your suitcase looks like a sore thumb, the average depot bag-snagger will avoid it. Distinguish your luggage by painting or sticking a bright and contrasting band of color around each piece. Or fashion your initials on your baggage in some large, homemade manner. Circles, stars, triangles, and blocks of color will also help you identify a suitcase from any angle when it first comes into view on a baggage conveyor. A thief is much less likely to snatch it because it is so obviously marked.

Baggage handlers. Not all luggage larceny is committed by thieves who mingle in crowds at air, bus, and train terminals. There are also dishonest baggage handlers who use a random, "lucky dip" method of plundering suitcases when the opportunity presents itself.

One way to beat these thieves is to wrap twelve or more loops of any small string or strap both horizontally and vertically around your suitcase. Loaders won't usually be bothered with untangling such fastenings, frail though they are, when there are so many more vulnerable suitcases around. And if your luggage comes around the baggage pickup turntable with clipped strings, you'll know the culprit was a baggage handler.

Baggage snatchers. Teams of suitcase filchers stroll the busy hallways of air terminals and bus depots, counting on the confusion to provide ready victims and an easy getaway. One trick in these teams' repertoire goes like this: A stranger, often a woman team member, asks you to watch her suitcase while she goes to the restroom. Shortly, an accomplice zings by, snags her suitcase, and makes a dash with it. You give chase, and as soon as you're far enough away another teammate picks up your own luggage and heads for parts unknown. Your best defense against this maneuver is to be leery of requests for "help" and remember always to keep your baggage in hand—tie a reminder string from suitcase handle to wrist if necessary.

Trapdoor suitcases. False-bottomed suitcases have a trapdoor bottom and powerful springs in the sides which grip your suitcase as the crook lifts it and walks away. Often a lifter's assistant distracts your attention by starting a fight, falling and acting hurt, or asking directions to the restroom. A simple way to outwit the false-bottoms is to keep your luggage between your legs when not in hand.

Suitcase insurance. Jetsetters and train trekkers who travel a lot would be wise to invest in luggage insurance—it's cheap (under $10 per year) and pays for replacement of lost or stolen suitcases and travel bags. With luggage sets selling for $75 plus, luggage insurance promises the steady traveler many happy returns. Get baggage coverage through your homeowner's-insurance agent or from insurers headquartered in metropolitan air terminals.

TRANSPORTATION TROUBLES

Phony boarding passes. In an official-looking suit and tie or even a uniform, the depot desperado approaches passengers in waiting areas, asks to see their tickets, then gives them a boarding pass.

Where did the ticket thieves get the boarding passes? In a garbage can. Where will they take the tickets? Back to the ticket counter for a cash refund. Moral: Keep a good grip on your tickets until the instant before boarding your plane, train, or bus.

Sleeping on trains. Dozing on a long train ride is fraught with more problems than just lumpy seats. You'll need to keep your handbag safe and secure your cash before snoozing on any sort of public transportation. Sleep in the seat with your purse on your lap—the strap tangled around your wrist if possible. And before you nod off, take a trip to the rest room to safety-proof the cash in your pockets by pushing most of it down the front of your briefs or panty hose.

Car pools. When you arrive at a strange city you may think it cheaper to share a cab from the airport to your hotel with the fellow traveler who struck up a conversation at the baggage-pickup area. He suggested doubling up on the taxi ride and, since he seems to know a bit about the city, it may seem like a safe offer.

Turn down his offer and keep a tight grip on your traveler's checks! Teams of crooks work air and rail terminals to lure trusting tourists into cabs with them. The taxi driver is in on the plot and gets a share of your wealth after you're mugged and dumped out on an unfamiliar street.

The nearest-farther-point principle. Some airport robbery takes place right at the airline ticket windows, with agents selling jet tickets at illegally high rates to customers who don't know they're being taken for a ride. A common tactic is to compute your air fare on a point-to-point basis. Thus, a flight from Baltimore to Chattanooga is charged as a flight from Baltimore to Atlanta ($50) and a flight from Atlanta to Chattanooga ($19). That's the route you'll actually fly, but the $69 ticket price is $15 too much.

The law stipulates that airlines cannot charge more for a two-step flight than for the direct flight to the nearest farther point. In this case, a Baltimore-to-Huntsville, Alabama, flight is the closest direct flight farther than Chattanooga from Baltimore. The direct-to-Huntsville passage costs $54, which is the maximum legal fee for a Baltimore-to-Chattanooga ticket. You have the right to demand that the nearest-farther-point principle be applied to your airline ticket rates, too.

Airline complaints. If your luggage is lost or mishandled on an airline, if you feel you were overcharged, or if you have any other complaint regarding air travel, write the airline involved, airing your gripe in detail and enclosing a photocopy of your flight ticket. Company officials will look at flying foul-ups a lot closer than ticket agents and baggage attendants at air terminals, and they'll make amends if your complaint is justified. If you get no satisfaction from the airlines, write the Office of Consumer Affairs, Civil Aeronautics Board, Washington, D.C. 20428. The CAB will pressure airlines to correct questionable practices.

Security checks. Airport screening systems devised to protect passengers from hijackers unwittingly expose them to thieves. The most common setup requires you to hand your pocketbook or briefcase over to airport inspectors who check it while you walk through a metal-detecting apparatus. Your purse is waiting for you on the other side of the screening device—unless it's been snatched while you waited in line.

Since you can't guard your purse when separated from it, have a friend hold it outside the terminal area while you pass through the metal detector. Then wait for your pocketbook as the friend sends it through the security checkpoint.

Flight-delay pay. Airlines regularly book up to 120 passengers into a 100-seat flight, banking on many travelers not showing up to confirm their reservations. If more than 100 show up, the latecomers are "bumped" or denied the seat they have reserved and paid for.

While the practice of overbooking and "bumping" is coming before court scrutiny, the law now entitles you to certain compensations which you should demand if you're among the bumped. Airlines must make other arrangements to get you to your destination. If they can't do that without a more than two-hour delay in your arrival time, they owe you the cost of your ticket (up to $200) plus your original ticket back. You can trade your original ticket in for cash and have double your ticket price for the inconvenience caused you.

Cabs in strange places. Grabbing a taxi in a strange country among people of unfamiliar customs and language can be more dangerous than you think. Sure, you're suspicious the foreign cabbie will run up your fare by taking the long way twice. What you might not know is that many drivers, sensing your suspicion, become enraged to the point of dumping you out in some deserted street far from your destination. Act friendly but alert! Better yet, take along another tourist for protection, and split the fare.

Depot double-take. Bus stations, train depots, and airline terminals all are prowling grounds for pickpockets—and the billfold grabber knows how to make more money off the wallet he's lifted. He simply hands you the cashless billfold, says he found it but must rush for a train, so would you kindly turn it over to the police. And by the way, why don't the two of you exchange names and addresses in case there is a reward to share, he'll suggest. Expect a break-in at any hotel room or home address you give this stranger.

To stay safe, never be a middleman in lost-and-found exchanges. Point the approacher toward an information desk or ticket window for speedy help.

MEANWHILE, BACK HOME . . .

Keep the lawn mowed. If you're going to be away for more than a few weeks, you'll want to make arrangements to have your lawn periodically mowed, weeds pulled, hedges clipped, and leaves raked. An unkempt yard can easily arouse a burglar's interest.

Try to get a neighbor to tend to these chores. Then, when he's away, you can do the same for him. If that doesn't work, hire a trustworthy high school or college student.

Police protection. You're paying for it—why not use it? Before you leave on your vacation, call your local police precinct. Let them know that you're leaving town and when you'll be back. Also alert your neighbors.

Don't, however, be like the man who went away on vacation with his family, had an argument with his wife, and returned home in the middle of the night to be shot as a burglar by an overzealous neighbor.

Get a house sitter. One of the simplest ways to keep your home secure while you're away is to hire a house sitter. For a few dollars a day you can hire a reliable college student or senior citizen to stay in your home. An added advantage here is that the house sitter can also feed Fido, water the lawn, and bring in the mail.

Naturally, if you hire someone unknown to you, you'll want to check his references beforehand.

Don't advertise! If you're one of your town's more prominent citizens and you happen to be leaving for an extended trip to Europe next week, throw a going-away party if you must. But don't let it get into the newspapers. After all, if you were a burglar, wouldn't you want to know who's going on vacation?

If you need the publicity, a better idea would be to throw a coming-home party.

Trip talk. Your name doesn't have to be in the newspapers for word to spread that you're going away. Telling your barber or hairdresser, butcher, service-station attendant, auto mechanic, and TV repairman about your forthcoming trip is a sure way to get word around fast. It may sound good to hear yourself say that you're flying to the Bahamas next week, but for your own sake, keep it under your hat.

Better to wait a few weeks, then say: "I've just returned from two marvelous weeks in the Bahamas."

House sublets. One excellent way to provide security for a vacation home, creating a small second income for yourself in the bargain, is to rent it out at a nominal fee. You can stipulate here that the tenant perform regular maintenance on the yard such as mowing the lawn and pruning trees, thus keeping the grounds in shape. Naturally, you'll arrange with your tenant to let you have possession of the place whenever you need it.

Phone service. Now, we agree, you'll save a few dollars by calling the phone company and having them put your service on "vacation disconnect" while you're away, but think of it: Anyone who calls your number will be told that your phone is "temporarily disconnected." And believe us, the seasoned burglar knows exactly what this means.

The best bet: Hire an answering service for the duration, or buy yourself a telephone-answering device. Your phone won't be ringing off the hook all the time—a good signal that you're not home to anyone who might be standing outside your door—and as a bonus, you'll have a whole slew of messages waiting for you when you get home.

Bamboozle that burglar! Here's a nifty idea that will help throw potential housebreakers off your trail when you're on vacation: Ask your next-door neighbor to park his car in your driveway while you're away.

When your neighbor goes out of town, you can return the favor.

Toy trick. A child's ball by the bushes, a doll carelessly dropped near the front door, a toy truck parked alongside the walk—these indicate that mom, dad, and kiddies are all home driving each other crazy as usual. Unless, of course, they're off visiting grandma for the weekend

and only toying with the minds of burglars casing the area for unoc-
cupied houses.

A random scattering of toys will polish off the "lived-in look" that
burning lights and blaring radio give your home during a short absence.

Defer deliveries. One of the surest telltale signs that occupants are
on vacation is the existence of reams of old newspapers littering the
walk and mail bulging from the mailbox.

Before leaving on your sojourn, arrange for a neighbor to collect all deliveries while you're away. Next best thing is canceling
the deliveries. When you tell the route man, also ask him not to
spread the word of your absence around. Call the supervising
office, too, and let the delivery man know his boss knows. He'll
think twice about taking advantage of your vacation plans with a
well-timed burglary.

Window shades and lights. Planning a Bahama pajama party? Have
a trusted neighbor periodically change the positions of shades, blinds,
and drapes as well as alternate which lights are left shining. Not only
will this help pull curtains over a possible prowler's eyes by making
your house seem occupied, it also gets an ally inside regularly to make
sure burglars have stayed outside. Return the favor when your neighbor takes a holiday.

Share the trash. Human beings communicate with one another in
myriad ways—talking, sign language, body language, garbage language. That's right, trash talks! Your empty garbage pails clue gar-
bagemen and any other alley onlookers that no one is home.

What good neighbor could refuse to share refuse? Surely not your
neighbor. When you're gone ask him to divide his weekly junk so you
can deceive crooks snooping in your cans.

Gates. Ask your neighbor to simulate your presence (again and again)
by locking your gate at night, unlocking it in the morning. If this is
impossible, leave all gates locked tight—odds are the thief won't haul
his haul over your fence, particularly in broad daylight.

Second cars. Two- and three-car families need to take care not to give
away their plans (and possessions) to burglars by leaving their
"extra" wheels parked in the same spot day after day while they're
away. Lend your second car to a friend for the duration of your
out-of-town venture, or ask your neighbor to move the left-behind

auto every day or so. This little ruse may be the trick that keeps your place robber-free as you motor about the countryside.

ASSORTED TRIP TIPS

Money. A new, modern version of the old-fashioned pouched money belt will almost defy the holdup thug to find your cash. This item is an honest-to-goodness belt, but with a concealed zippered compartment on the inside. It's available at larger men's-apparel stores everywhere.

Portable list. Before you set out for your vacation, make a list of the serial and identification numbers of cameras, binoculars, suitcases, and any other valuables you will be taking along. Keep the list (which should include a description and dollar value of items) in your wallet as you travel. That way you won't find yourself a robbery victim on a foreign shore with your list of identification numbers at home. The accurate descriptions will be helpful in recovering stolen possessions and in reporting your losses to police and to insurance agents.

Frauds abroad. World travelers will be tempted to bring back artwork and antiques from the countries they visit, but this temptation shouldn't lead you into paying more than fair value for items. Art and artifact fakers know how to spot tourists—you are most vulnerable to being cheated when buying in the area where antiques or art originate. Foreign dealers will freely guarantee authenticity—both in words and in writing—knowing you probably won't make the expensive return trip just to exercise the guarantee. Don't pay extra for claimed "famous" or "ancient" works on the spot. Make such purchases from home, when you've more time to study, identify, and seek expert opinion.

Emergency information sheet. Make yourself a personal safety sheet to aid your arrival in any strange foreign city. From travel guides and magazines on your flight or boat, sketch a rough map of your destination city on an envelope. Immediately after arriving, add the police and American Embassy phone numbers to your reminder sheet. Keep this information sheet in an outside pocket. If you need help you'll know where to get it, and if you're lost it won't be for long.

Last-day carelessness. If you're about to check out of your hotel after that restful vacation, you may be tempted to store your belongings in your car during a final day of sightseeing. Don't. Thieves are especially on the lookout for this type of situation. They've been known to watch for parties loading up their cars at the hotel entrance, follow them into town, then simply pry open a window, unlock the front door, and help themselves to the car's contents. Obviously in this instance a crook will not be fooled by a sheet or blanket draped over your luggage. Avoid being ripped off in this manner by checking your belongings in the hotel checkroom until you're ready to leave town.

CHAPTER 10

Investment and insurance precautions

"Under the existing system, a full 55 percent of auto victims killed or seriously injured receive absolutely *nothing*—no medical expenses, no hospital expenses, no lost wages, and certainly no damages for pain and suffering," explained Virginia Knauer, a special assistant to the President for consumer affairs. Since 80 percent of Americans carry some form of health and auto insurance, what reason or combination of reasons accounts for the insurance industry's failure to return a single penny to more than half of the nation's car-crash casualties? Industry spokesmen say they can't help it if policyholders aren't aware of the limits of their insurance contracts and expect more coverage than they're actually paying for. Disgruntled families who thought they were covered for any emergency blame the insurance establishment, accusing it of fraudulent sales practices, claim-dodging, purposely complex and confusing policies, and inclusion of trick clauses in policies filled with "exclusions," "riders," "deductibles," and other loopholes.

Americans are looking to their insurance companies for protection in a modern world filled with hazards to health and property. Though we spend billions upon billions of dollars yearly in premiums, we are finding no such protection from health, life, auto, property, and other insurance offerings.

There are at least two approaches to the problem. One is to sternly discipline those insurance companies that use fraudulent and unethical practices to bilk consumers out of steep premium payments and then refuse to pay legitimate claims. Steps in this direction are now underway through governmental agencies at the state level. You can help by writing your state's insurance commissioner and urging diligent action to protect your rights, health, and property. The other approach is to educate yourself in the trickery and treachery of the "bad apples" among the country's 500,000 salesmen competing for commissions and for your insurance dollars. It is this second alternative—learning what to look for and what to look out for in your insurance shopping—that is the aim of this chapter.

Here is our basic advice: Think of your insurance investments as a last line of defense against the various physical and financial crises which can hit you. With such a strategy you'll want to be sure your defense is a solid one, helping you avoid the consequences of theft, accidents, attacks, and unexpected tragedies.

The way to be sure you'll get the protection you pay premiums for is to take your time. Read every word of a policy yourself before you buy it and have ambiguous wordings explained by your insurance agent. Get the explanations in writing. The typical insurance policy is a long and complicated document. Most people would rather have a salesman explain it to them than read it themselves. But if the salesman misrepresents the policy's coverage in any way, chances are you won't notice the mistake until you make a claim and your insurance company denies coverage. By then it's too late—it's your tough luck and it's your expense.

If you're only now thinking of buying insurance, this chapter will be a guide to the pitfalls. If you already are covered by one or more insurance contracts, reexamine your policies in light of the tips that follow. Odds are you can lower your premiums, increase the effectiveness of your insurance coverage, and avoid the rip-offs routinely written into an overwhelming number of policies. Then take a deep breath and rest assured that you're well insured!

FOR FURTHER INFORMATION:

Antique or Fake? Charles H. Hayward. London: Evans Brothers, Ltd., 1970.

Forgers, The. E. Patrick McGuire. Bernardsville, N. J.: Padrick, 1969.

Gentle Art of Faking Furniture, The. Herbert Cescinsky. New York: Dover, 1967.

Great American Insurance Hoax, The. Richard Guarino and Richard Turbo. Los Angeles: Nash.

Innocent Investor and the Shaky Ground Floor, The. Sidney Margolius. New York: Trident Press, 1971.

Insider's Guide to Antiques, Art and Collectibles, The. Sylvia O'Neill Dorn. Garden City, N. Y.: Doubleday, 1974.

Insurance Trap, The. Herbert S. Denenberg. New York: Western, 1972.

Shopper's Guidebook to Life Insurance, Health Insurance, Auto Insurance, Homeowner's Insurance, Doctors, Dentists, Lawyers, Pensions, etc. Herbert S. Denenberg. Washington, D.C.: Consumer News, 1974.

INVESTMENT SWINDLES

The pyramid scheme. Here, the promoter gets the investor to lay out a certain sum of money on "inventory" which is supposedly secured by warehoused goods. This makes the investor a "distributor." He is then required to recruit subdistributors who, in turn, likewise invest money, of which the investor gets a percentage, with the bulk of its money going to the promoter. But the subdistributor is told that he also must recruit investors, and so on down an endless line.

Typically, the goods do not exist, and the investors rarely make back their investment, since most of the money is funneled back to the promoter of the scheme.

Avoid such a rip-off by demanding to see the goods you're buying, by thoroughly checking bank references (as well as police records), and by making personal contact with previous investors.

The vending-machine racket. Typically, the promoter of this scam will create a very attractive "package" for the investor, consisting of a number of vending machines which may be cheap stamp or gumball dispensers, expensive electronic game or pinball machines, or anything in between. The promoter will also guarantee a suitable location for each unit. Invariably, the machines are overpriced and the locations poor, resulting in little or no profit for the unfortunate investor.

Before investing in such a scheme, determine the actual value of the machine with the manufacturer or with other distributors of like products, and demand to personally visit and analyze each machine location for its potential profit.

Franchises. The purchase of a franchise can make you a millionaire or a pauper overnight. Therefore, if you're considering buying a franchise, you'll want to learn all you can about such things as cost vs. profit, terms and contracts, assignments and operating practices and controls. The free booklet entitled *Investigate Before Investing: Guidance for Prospective Franchisees* will tell you much of what you need to know along these lines. It is available from the Council of Better Business Bureaus, 1150 17th Street, N.W., Washington,

D.C. 20036. Send a self-addressed, stamped, legal-size envelope along with your request.

Prospectus prudency. In order to help eliminate fraud from the stock market, the Security and Exchange Commission (SEC) requires any company making a large public stock offering to provide every potential investor with a prospectus. This contains information on assets and liabilities, sales and profits, the names of the principals involved, and other pertinent facts.

Before investing in any new stock offering, get the prospectus of the company in question and read it thoroughly.

Work-at-home schemes. Many housewives, retired people, and teenagers—as well as moonlighting wage earners—are attracted by the idea of earning money at home in their spare time. Because of this, there is a proliferation of firms hawking products, skills, and information relating to such home-based money-making schemes as addressing envelopes, making neckties, decorating Christmas cards, selling raffle tickets—you name it. The customer is promised goods or information for a "registration fee" or invited to send cash for a "starter kit," which usually turns out to be only the first of many fees required by the company.

Our advice? Don't pay anyone a fee to set you up in business. Use your own creativity in developing extra income. For ideas, get a copy of our book *1001 Ways to Be Your Own Boss* (Englewood Cliffs, N.J.: Prentice-Hall, 1976).

Churning. The compensation of securities account representatives is invariably based on a commission or salary commensurate with their production. Therefore, the more you can be persuaded to sell one stock and buy another, the higher will be the representative's paycheck. When it becomes obvious that this has been done frequently, and with little regard for the customer's welfare, the customer is said to have been "churned."

Avoid this kind of treatment by thoroughly analyzing with a very jaundiced eye each and every move your securities representative suggests you make in the stock market—before you act.

Cleaning smudged credit. We talked to a St. Louis man recently who said he was denied a personal loan at a bank and turned down by two major credit-card corporations before he discovered a certain credit reporting agency had a file on him that was unjustly tainted. A revenge-seeking former landlord, it seems, had given him a false bad-credit reference.

If you're losing money and opportunities because of a bad credit rating, you now have the right to find out why—under the Fair Credit Reporting Act of 1971. To discover how you can challenge and change your credit ratings, write for *FTC Buyer's Guide No. 7: Fair Credit Reporting Act*, Federal Trade Commission, Washington, D.C. 20590.

Investment companies. Before sinking your savings in an investment company, check it out through the United States Securities and Exchange Commission, Washington, D.C. 20549, which keeps full information on all such firms.

Investment information. Do you know the difference between an open-end and a closed-end investment company? You'd better if you're planning on giving either type some of your money. The free booklet entitled *Investment Companies* gives you this information and more, and is available by sending a self-addressed, stamped, legal-size envelope to the Council of Better Business Bureaus, 1150 17th Street, N.W., Washington, D.C. 20036.

Canadian securities swindle. A favorite of brokers and bilkers in the states along the Canadian border is selling shares in nonexistent or worthless Canadian companies, oil wells, and gold or uranium mines. The bogus and illegal offers arrive in mailed brochures and telephone calls from Toronto. They give their phony "tips" the air of inside information by claiming big-time investors concentrate on Wall Street and ignore the potentials of our huge northern neighbor. Never invest with brokers from another country unless they are licensed in the state where you live or submit to a thorough investigation by a local broker of your choice.

Phony savings associations. These investment vampires sucker the elderly who have a few bucks to tuck away. Their "savings and loan associations" offer high returns on accounts insured by "The Security Financial Insurance Corporation" or some other hokey name (the *government's* insuring agency is the Federal Savings and Loan Insurance Corporation). After a year of opening new accounts, the association officers vamoose with their pockets full of nest eggs. Spot these front-office frauds through their save-by-mail approach, their promise of high interest rates for one-year no-withdrawal accounts, and their offers of expensive gifts for opening new accounts.

LAND LARCENY

Free vacation? One day, you'll receive an offer in the mail to enter a "drawing" for an "all-expense-paid, free vacation" in some glamorous spot—say, Miami or Hawaii. To qualify, you'll only be required to return the enclosed card to the company. A week later, you'll be notified that you "won" (as have all the entrants).

However, as you belatedly discover, in order to claim your vacation, you'll be required to pay a $20 "registration fee" and your own air fare. Upon arrival at your destination, you'll be met by an aggressive land salesman, who will proceed to subject you to a weekend of high-pressure sales tactics—leaving you little time or inclination for your promised vacation.

Best bet here is to avoid all such offers by land-investment firms. You never get something for nothing!

Worthless land. From time immemorial, unscrupulous land promoters have ravenously extracted untold trillions from those who buy land sight unseen. In recent years, we've seen investors lose millions on "sunny Florida retirement acreage" which was, in reality, nothing but worthless swampland, and "improved desert playgrounds" which consisted of the hottest, driest, most barren land this side of Hades.

Obviously, the rule here is to personally inspect every piece of land you buy—before investing.

Property promotions. Throughout our country, the value of land that once sold for a few cents an acre has increased tremendously. According to some land promoters, anyone can make a bundle just by purchasing today and selling tomorrow. But don't you believe it. It's just as possible to lose your shirt. Get some valuable tips on land promotions be sending for the free booklet *Real Estate Promotions,* available from the Council of Better Business Bureaus, 1150 17th Street, N.W., Washington, D.C. 20036. Send along a self-addressed, stamped, legal-size envelope with your request.

Buy now? The rallying cry of the aggressive (and most of them are!) land promoter is "buy now!" But if you're not ready to build for a while, there are many reasons to wait.

The money you invest in a lot is "dead" money. That is, it collects no interest as it would in a savings account or other yield-type investment. Taxes and assessments can eat away at your funds faster than the property appreciates. Further, zoning regulations may change,

178

making your property undesirable as a residence. And, of course, there's always the possibility that your plans may change and you might decide to live somewhere else.

Soil survey. Before buying land on which you intend to erect a house, have a soil survey taken. Here, the condition of your soil up to 6 or 8 feet below the surface is tested to see whether it will bear up under the weight of the house. The survey will also give you an indication of the location of the water table and the soil's ability to sustain plant life.

You can arrange a soil survey through any soil engineer. Costs about $100.

Advance fees. Thinking of selling your home? Watch out for real-estate brokers who offer to take a lower payment for their work if you agree to an "advance fee" deal. They'll tell you your property will sell in a matter of days and collect $200 or more as an advance against their advertising and "showing" expenses. If not one buyer darkens your door, you'll still never see that "advance" again. Legitimate real-estate dealers will take their cut from your home's sale price, *after* the house is sold.

Free lots. Rascal real-estate promoters commonly mail brochures to hundreds of thousands of people saying: "You've been specially selected from your area to receive an allotment of a full-sized lot, in conjunction with our advertising program." It sounds as if you've been handed a free lot, but not so—just an allotment of a lot. A followup will get you a high-pressure sales pitch. Or, the lot may be "free" if you'll just pay the closing costs. Closing costs, you find out too late, come to a lot more than the land is worth.

Land locators. A number of quick-buck bilkers make their petty cash by "locating and doing all the red-tape work" for persons applying for purchase of public lands from the United States Department of Interior, Bureau of Land Management. Some of these "land locators" charge exorbitant fees, the bureau reports, when actually an individual buying public land can arrange the transaction himself without much hassle. See how simple it is by contacting the bureau in Washington, D.C., or a local field office, before letting land locators land your money, too.

Toilet testing. If you're thinking of buying a house, you'll want to check it over thoroughly for problems before purchasing it. In two ways, a house's toilets can tell you things the real-estate agent may not want known. Salesmen, for instance, may ignore the fact that water pressure in the neighborhood is poor, creating a constant problem for residents. By running the bathroom faucets and flushing the toilet at the same time you can gauge the water pressure. Water will stop completely at one of the fixtures if the pressure is low.

Salesmen may also twist the truth about the age of a house. Check their claims by lifting the toilet-tank lid—most are engraved with a date which will tell you the approximate time the toilet was installed, and the house can't be younger than the toilet.

THE ART AND ANTIQUES GAME

Furniture fakery. Antique chairs, tables, and bureaus can be copied in incredible detail—some bogus-antiques sellers even simulate wormholes to make pieces appear older. These signs give away false antiques: On ornate carvings, fakes sport sharp edges, but cleaning, dusting, and rubbing have smoothed the antique's edges. Phony wormholes are straight and near the surface. Real worms burrow in zig-zag paths, deep into the wood. Old wood will feel heavier than it looks, while the new wood in furniture forgeries is lighter. Also, dark stains on undersides of furniture often disguise new wood.

Fake finders. Your local library is a storehouse of information on artists, both old and modern. Once you know the name of the supposed painter of the masterpiece you're eyeing, look it up in biographical lists and references there to spot inconsistencies in dates, styles, native country, and other points in your art dealer's spiel. While at the library, check out one of several excellent books on art forgery. *Fakes*, by Otto Kurz, and *The Art Game*, by Robert Wraight, are fine for starters.

Art-trade courtesies. When buying expensive paintings or sculpture from an art dealer, don't make snap judgments. Take advantage of courtesies commonly extended throughout the trade. You may ask that a painting be reserved for you while you decide at your leisure. You can also ask to have a piece you're thinking of purchasing delivered to your home for approval. Neither favor obligates you to buy. The short delay period gives you time to seek expert advice. A good man for beginners to consult is the curator of a nearby art museum. Many will act as private consultants, for a fee, as will some art-history professors at your local university or college.

Who done it? The market value of fine artwork depends, to a great extent, on who the artist is. Fly-by-night art dealers will try to make you think a painting is an original Van Gogh without actually *saying* so, thereby avoiding fraud charges. Don't get stuck with "could-be's" at original prices. Watch for catchphrases like "from the workshop of Van Gogh," "attributed to Van Gogh," or "from a Van Gogh protégé." The only acceptable attribution for an original is "by (author's full name)," such as "by Vincent Van Gogh." And get this statement from a leading specialist-scholar and *in writing*.

Markings. Collectors of pottery, fine china, and porcelain know you tell the value of cups, dishes, and pots by tipping them up to look at markings on the bottom. Each maker or factory has its own mark—some worth more than others. Fakers and forgers include marks on their phony pottery, too, but you can avoid buying their junk ceramics by looking for three mark messages.

First, are there scrapes or file marks on the glaze at the pot's bottom? If so, the mark's been tampered with. Second, does a well-known mark have an "X" through it? That notes factory rejects. Finally, don't pay big for the cheap china marked Wedgewood, Wedgwoode, Wedgewoode, Edgwoode, or Hedgwood when the real McCoy is spelled "Wedgwood."

Eskimo art. Eskimo sculpture—carved by northern Indians in gray soapstone, ivory, or whalebone—is booming in popularity both among art and artifact collectors and among chislers who hawk worthless imitations for handsome prices.

If you're thinking of adding Eskimo handiwork to your private gallery, living room, or igloo, there's a foolproof way to tell the genuine from the phony. Each Eskimo carving should have a number and identification tag from its governmental control unit (either Alaska or a Canadian province). A letter or phone call to the proper agency will authenticate the artwork.

Ancient art. Bogus vases and sculpture allegedly from ancient empires flood the auctions and display rooms of dishonest dealers, making dabbling in this collector's field financially dangerous. Stay out of it unless you're ready for serious study.

Know that experts and museums have already snatched up valuable items—especially clay pottery, which is easily faked. Items said to be stolen from King Tut's Tomb, or a similar excavation, are almost always phonies. There are no "bargains" in ancient art—you're safe only when buying (generally at high prices) from established, reputable dealers, or with their advice.

Glass. Collectible glass is difficult to authenticate—antique pieces are easily faked, often by sanding to create false signs of wear and age. Insist, as the experts do, on comparing an item with a proven piece before making an expensive purchase.

Also, beginning glassware collectors should note two common huckster's tricks. One is the grinding off of impressed trademarks and passing the scar off as a "pontil mark," which indicates the piece is an antique. This is doubletalk. In reality, pontil markings don't accurately indicate age. Trick number two is embedding an ancient coin in the glass. While it may be an old coin, the glass could have been made yesterday.

Dust check. A time-tried test to tell whether a desk or bureau is an authentic antique is the drawer-dust check. Pull a drawer all the way out and inspect the back—in particular the ledge where the drawer bottom projects behind the back panel. The passage of decades will leave a gritty, well-settled layer of dust here.

If the dust's there, try to wipe it off. A favorite faker's dodge is to brush a thin coat of glue along drawer backs and sprinkle dust on it to simulate the accumulation of years. If there's no dust or if it won't wipe off onto your finger, it's not true grit and the chest of drawers is not a true antique.

Silver. The handiwork of silversmiths is art to some, and collectors face the same question as other art patrons—how do you spot fakes? Most silver forgers sign their pieces with a hallmark—an identifying design. If the hallmark on the piece you're considering is worn, don't pay top price. They are often altered to confuse the age, making silver appear older. Hallmarks are also often switched, with crooks lifting a spoon's marking, for instance, and soldering it to a teapot which can be sold for more than the spoon. But if you breathe hard on the silver around the hallmark, such solder marks will show. Another common silver fraud involves cutting down worn pieces to make smaller "perfect" pieces with good hallmarks. Sharp, unworn edges are tattletales here.

Crack check. Check that antique china pitcher for repaired holes, cracks, and chips before you buy. Chipped china is inferior to unblemished pieces, but a good restorer will try to pass off his patchwork at "mint condition" prices. Ultraviolet light will show repairs by a difference in color. But check the piece while still in the dealer's shop. A rogue will claim you did the damage. Remember to look under felted bottoms and taped tags and stickers which could be there to conceal a hole or mar. If you suspect a chunk of your china has been replaced, tap the questionable part with a coin. The sound will be different from that of the rest of the piece.

Handicrafts. A high pricetag is all that's needed to convince most novice buyers that cheaply designed, mass-produced junk is indeed handmade, highly crafted Indian jewelry, baskets, rugs, or blankets. Tags can be tips to such rip-offs.

Look for tags saying "Indian Handmade." Labels claiming only "Indian Made" often mean the trinkets come from a factory with one Indian employee. "Navajo" (in quotes) rugs are Navajo-type rugs, and machine-made. If tags say Indian rugs or blankets are imported from Mexico or Guatemala, they're most likely factory-woven. Handmade rugs and blankets often show a missed thread where colors change, and no two are ever exactly alike.

Forged autographs. Autograph collectors beware! The field of signature sellers is fraught with forgers! The importance of dealing with a trusted vendor is paramount. Less than fifty well-known autograph dealers operate full- or part-time in the United States, and *all* guarantee the authenticity of their signatures for sale on an unlimited money-back basis. Don't settle for anything less!

Demand a signed authentication by an expert and an appraisal before buying from a private owner. And remember, the most famous figure's signature may be absolutely worthless if he was a prolific writer. Beginners can avoid gyps by studying library books on autograph collecting, such as Mary A. Benjamin's *Autographs: A Key to Collecting* (New York: Bowker Company, 1946).

Coin certification. Forgers of valuable coins chisel coin collectors out of hundreds of thousands of dollars yearly. Some frauds are newly forged, some are genuine coins with mint marks removed, or with figures altered. Nickels may be gold-plated and passed as $5 gold pieces. To spot these and other highly skilled fakes, the American Numismatic Association now runs a series of intricate tests to pedigree your pennies. On either foreign or U.S. coins they'll use high-powered electron microscopes, X-ray diffraction, specific-gravity scales, and electron probes to confirm that there's been no tampering. Write the American Numismatic Association Certification Service, Box 2366, Colorado Springs, Colo. 80901 before you blow real money on fake money.

183

GENERAL INSURANCE GYPS

Policy check. Inflation alone will rob you of hundreds of dollars when you find your insurance policy is outdated and inadequate and you must pay extra, above and beyond your top coverage amount, to replace stolen or damaged property or finance a medical emergency. You'll need to reconsider your insurance needs periodically and adjust your coverage so that increased replacement prices, current property values, rising medical and hospital charges, and newly acquired valuables are provided for. Designate one day of each year (why not the day after your birthday?) to consider investing a couple extra premium dollars to avoid being stuck with the financial difference between growing going prices and your outdated insurance limits.

Deductions. Buying car, home, or health insurance with a "deductible" stipulation is a good way to save money, but a good way to get gypped if you aren't careful. First of all, make sure the deductible applies for each "benefit period" and not "per illness" or "per accident." Then sign up for the highest deductible you can reasonably afford. By going from full coverage to a $50 deductible on comprehensive auto insurance, for example, you can cut your premium by 45 percent. Paying the first $100 of the crash costs reduces your premium by more than 56 percent.

Claims jumper. One section of your insurance policy that requires your attention during the buying process is the part telling you when and how to file a claim. Some companies require you to file claims within twenty days of the accident, theft, or damage or they won't pay. As you buy your policy, find out from your agent exactly what the procedure is for filing a claim. If you'll need forms filled out, request a copy of each document to see what information you'll need (medical histories, item descriptions, registration numbers) to get a jump on beating those claim-filing deadlines.

Checking the company. If zeroing in on fine-print insurance clauses gives you blurry vision, and using Webster's to make plain talk out of highfalutin lawyers' language makes your brainwaves fuzzy, use the phone to check up on a potential insurer effortlessly instead. Call your state's insurance department to make sure the company you buy from is licensed in your state. (Purchasing coverage from a nonregistered company leaves you with little or no protection, should problems develop with your future claims.) While on the line, ask the insurance bureau whether your company has been mentioned in many consumer

184

complaints. Also dial directory assistance in your state's capital city to make sure the agency has a listed number.

Premium plans. Planning how and when you pay for your insurance policy will keep you from getting tagged with terrible coverage and keep the company from tacking on extra "financing" charges if you decide to quit after a short trial period. No matter what your agent encourages you to do, pay as little as you can get away with when starting a policy. Arrange to split a year's premium into quarterly or monthly payments—then you've less cash loss if you decide to drop the particular policy.

After the first year, when you're *sure* the coverage lives up to the salesman's promises, switch to paying premiums on an annual basis. Once-a-year payments will save you as much as 18 percent by eliminating surcharges.

Payment delays. You can make your insurance company live up to its obligations and pay your legitimate claims promptly. In most states, you have legal recourse for tardy claims settlements. Depending on your particular state's statutes, you can sue if insurance reimbursements don't arrive within thirty to sixty days of filing your claim. You can collect from 25 percent to 100 percent over the claim amount as a penalty for their dilly-dallying, plus your attorney's fees. In addition, the court will order fast payment of your entire claim. See your attorney about exercising this little-used right to prod slow-poke insurers.

Termination tips. To boost policy sales to (and their commissions from) middle-aged and elderly insurance buyers, the slick salesman will promise "no automatic termination age" and "no reduction in benefits because of age." Don't let this lure of secure Golden Years convince you to buy—even if the policy makes the pledge in writing.

Most policies sold in auto, health, and life-insurance fields are renewable solely at the option of the company. Each new premium payment starts a new contract, and by refusing the payment, the company can cancel at its whim. It may trump up another reason than age, or policy fine print may allow them to cancel without stating a reason. When studying your insurance policy before buying, look long and hard at *every* clause allowing for termination or you'll find your company has dumped you when you need it most.

Group policies. Individual policies are insurance at retail prices. Group policies offer the same coverage at wholesale discounts. You can save from 10 to 25 percent of individual policy rates by joining group insurance plans for health, auto, life, and homeowner needs. Your employer, trade union, professional association, church, or newspaper may already offer such a deal. If not, urge them to try it.

Insurance agents. If you get a good insurance agent, your chances of getting a good insurance policy go up substantially. Here's how to collect that rare bird, the astute policy pusher:

Get a full-time agent with experience, not a part-time sideliner. Ask your banker, your lawyer, or a businessman friend to recommend a good agent—they're experienced in dealing with insurance representatives. Look for the initials CLU and CPCU in agents' credentials. These indicate special training as a Chartered Life Underwriter or a Chartered Property and Casualty Underwriter—the equivalent in insurance of CPA status in the accounting field.

Return ratings. A good way to gauge how stingy a prospective insurance company will be about filling your future claims is to ask about the company's "percentage of premium dollar returned in benefits." Buy into a company with a high return rating—they're "easiest" in paying claims and usually consumer-oriented. Some companies return as much as 97 cents on the premium dollar. The bad ones return only 30 cents or less. Even the Illinois State Lottery returns more than 45 cents of each dollar!

How firm the foundation? Want to give your money to the operators who run Mutual Bozo Life Insurance Corporation on a shoestring and file bankruptcy forms from Sweden where they live in all the luxury your purloined premiums can provide? Probably not.

So check to see if your prospective insurance company is financially strong before you invest. Pull *Best's Life Insurance Reports* from your library's reference shelf. Of the 1,200 insurance companies rated financially, only one in four is recommended and just 125 companies receive the strongest recommendations. Buy from one of these companies and rest assured they won't go bankrupt.

Comparison shopping. Many consumers who compare price and quality by visiting every car lot in town before buying an auto will buy a more important commodity, their insurance coverage, from the first salesman they see. The reason is often the overwhelming confusion of tens of thousands of different types of policies and the questionable sales tactics of insurance agents.

You'll save money—both in premium payments and in future payment for uncovered calamities—by shopping around. Before signing any home, health, or car insurance contract, get on the phone and make appointments with a dozen different companies over the span of a month or two. Compare their offerings, ask tough questions, and refuse to buy from any until you've reviewed all.

Do your homework. Insurance today is a mass of confusion, with hundreds of companies, policies, and payment plans. Bewildered buyers left at the mercy of commission-conscious salesmen in planning family insurance protection often end up paying too much for too little.

Besides following other insurance-buying tips in this chapter, we suggest you read at least one book on insurance before making this major investment. *The Shopper's Guidebook to Life Insurance, Health Insurance, Auto Insurance, Homeowner's Insurance, Doctors, Dentists, Lawyers, Pension, etc.*, by Herbert S. Denenberg (Washington, D.C.: Consumer News, 1974), is a good, easily understood one available at most libraries.

The twister. This bird still sells insurance policies with a tactic illegal in many states: He'll spout misleading information to get you to cash in your present policy and buy one offered by his company. If you take him up, you'll soon find yourself paying the twister's big commission, as well as either higher insurance premiums (since you're older than when you started your present policy) or the same premiums with drastically reduced coverage. Protect yourself by getting the salesman's offers on paper or on a tape recording if you decide to deal with him. But first consult the company which now insures you. They may be able to solve your coverage problems without a risky switch.

Fine print vs. promises. It's a dandy idea to save all advertisements, letters, or tape recordings of salesmen's promises and other enticements to buy your insurance policy. That way, if the insuring company rejects your future claim on the basis of some fine-print clause, you may still be able to obtain at least partial benefits by suing under "the doctrine of reasonable expectations." Simply put, this legal provision guarantees that if the major sales pitch promised certain benefits, the fine print cannot void them.

Insurance information. Poor insurance planning can rip you off once for premiums and once again for the personal possessions that burglar makes off with. If you're underinsured, your losses won't be fully compensated for. If you carry too much insurance, excessive premiums will needlessly drain you.

How much insurance is enough for your house or apartment? You'll surely want to cover your belongings at a "replacement price"

—an amount sufficient to buy new models at today's inflated rates. A good guide to liability insurance—worth reading before talking to your insurance agent—can be had from the Insurance Information Institute, 110 William Street, New York, N. Y. 10038.

LIFE INSURANCE

Cash value vs. term. Of the two main types of life insurance, "straight life" and "term" insurance, most Americans buy the first but would be better off buying the second. With term insurance you pay for "pure protection." Straight life adds the cost of a "cash value" which is functionally equal to a savings account. Your cash value builds as the years go by and as that part of your premium gathers interest. But a healthy part of your interest goes to pay the salaries of insurance-company bureaucrats. You'd profit far more if you'd put the difference between straight-life and term-insurance premiums in a bank account and keep all the interest yourself. Your insurance salesman will push his straight-life policies (higher commission for him), but you'll save by holding out for term insurance.

Age arguments. It's cheaper to buy life insurance when you are younger, your agent will claim. Not so! Call his bluff by asking for a comparison of the total cost of two contracts providing equal death benefits—one starting at early age and another starting at middle age. With one major company, for example, beginning life insurance at age twenty-six sets your annual premium at $281, but by age sixty-five you've paid $11,000 in premiums. The same policy beginning at age fifty asks $675 yearly payments, but your total investment by age sixty-five is only $10,150—a 7 percent savings! Don't let bargain talk pressure you into wasting your money on premiums before you really need the coverage.

Double indemnity. Are you considering life insurance which pays double indemnity in event of your accidental death? While this coverage may only cost an extra $12 a year, it's money wasted on a mirage.

Your chances of accidental demise are only 6 in 100 and, logically, your family won't *need* twice as much money just because a mishap rather than illness caused your death. If your accidental death was the result of someone else's negligence, your kin already have the makings of a substantial lawsuit. Don't pay double-indemnity fees to insurance sharpies! Use the money to buy additional life insurance which you're *sure* your survivors will collect.

Flight insurance. A neighbor takes out $25,000 in life insurance every time she boards a jetliner. Somehow she feels safer, but her chances of dying in an air crash are exactly the same. The insurance booths set up in air terminals take her for $3 each time she travels!

You, we're sure, will laugh at offers of "low-cost" coverage for air travel, freeway death, or vacations. You're sensible enough to buy one life-insurance policy paying a set amount for any cause of death. The logical consumer recognizes flight insurance as double coverage that plays upon common fears to harvest travelers' dollars, yet rarely has to pay a claim.

State specials. In spite of the best efforts of a wealthy, well-staffed insurance-industry lobby, four states have enacted laws allowing their citizens low-cost insurance equal to or better than the coverage offered by high-priced commercial outfits. Three states—Connecticut, New York, and Massachusetts—allow banks to sell cut-rate life insurance, and anyone close to these states should take advantage of the bargain.

Wisconsin sports a state-operated company, the State Life Fund, that sells up to $10,000 in life insurance to anyone in the state at the time his policy is approved. So plan a vacation to Milwaukee after writing for information to Wisconsin State Life Fund, Commissioner of Insurance, 212 North Basset Street, Madison, Wisc. 53703.

HOME AND PROPERTY POLICIES

Homeowner's coverage. The homeowner's policy is by far the most comprehensive as well as the most economical policy on the market today. This type of coverage indemnifies against such perils as fire, explosion, vandalism, and theft, covering personal liability claims as well. In addition, a basic homeowner's policy provides coverage for such items as furniture, appliances, clothing, and other personal property at half the market value of the home, as well as limited coverage on valuables stolen inside the home and from your automobile.

Rates vary considerably from state to state. In California, for example, a $250 deductible homeowner's policy on a home that would cost $50,000 to rebuild costs $270 per year.

Tenant's policy. As a renter, you can obtain, through many insurance companies, a policy that will insure your possessions against theft, vandalism, and fire, up to a maximum of $10,000. Also included in the typical tenant's policy is $25,000 worth of personal liability insurance plus up to $1,000 coverage on valuables stolen from your automobile. Costs about $100 per year.

Federal flood floater. Homeowners can avoid high commercial rates for flood insurance by taking advantage of the government's Federal Flood Insurance Program. Flood-prone areas qualify for the program if they agree to land-use controls and apply for eligibility. If your city hasn't applied for this premium-saver, buttonhole your city councilman and demand this readily available insurance discount.

High-crime insurance. Since 1971, the federal government has underwritten an insurance program to provide coverage at a reasonable price to residents of high-risk (high-crime) neighborhoods. The Federal Crime Insurance Program offers up to $10,000 protection in those states where it has been accepted. Write the Federal Insurance Administration (P. O. Box 41033, Washington, D.C. 20014) to see if your state is among these. The government policies are easily obtained, low-cost and noncancelable. Burglary, larceny, robbery, damage to premises, mugging, and valuables stolen from your car are all covered. It's a fantastic buy for those living where private insurance companies refuse to sell policies.

Fur floater. Fur coats, sparkling jewelry, or other especially valuable items should be protected with a "floater" policy attached to your regular homeowner's coverage. A floater pays the full replacement value of these likely-to-be-stolen items, and leaves more protection for your other belongings under your home policy. In suburban areas, for example, fur floaters run about 50 cents a year, and jewelry floaters $1.50 a year, for each $100 worth of goods.

Homeowners' discounts. Homeowners can cut steep insurance premiums down to size by considering companies which offer an array of discounts to particular policyholders. Some, for example, slice your premium by 10 percent if you install a burglar-alarm system. Another grants a like reduction for marking your valuables with an engraving pen. Nonsmokers get yet another discount of 5 percent with some firms. Still others bill senior citizens at 15 to 25 percent below the going premium rate. Check to see if you qualify.

Club policies. Avoid homeowners' and personal-property insurance ripoffs by taking advantage of club or group policies tailored to protect you as a member. Some gun clubs provide low-cost coverage for firearms, boating clubs offer floaters on boats, and special-interest groups like the American Numismatic Association have established policies to protect their members' collections. If you've got money tied up in a hobby, a related organization often offers the most effective insurance deal at honest rates.

HEALTH POLICIES

Policy limits. The first health-insurance policy we ever bought promised "Surgical fees, up to $400 each operation." A closer look (too late) showed this was top dollar for one type of operation only—the policyholder's second and third heart transplants!

In studying which company's policy to switch to, we were extra-careful to find out what the *average* operation's maximum payable amount was. Here is our voice-of-experience tip: If the average limit is not given in the literature on a policy, figure it at one-quarter the top amount mentioned in the sales pitch.

Disability definitions. A California man, struck down by emphysema, could walk only 300 yards at a time, but was denied his $150-a-month disability-insurance claim because he wasn't technically "house confined." Will vague phrases keep you from collecting disability payments in event of a crippling injury?

Be sure of definitions *before* you buy. Ask your agent for examples of when the insurance company has paid disability claims (nature and extent of injury) and when it has not. Consider engaging a lawyer for advice on how difficult it might be to prove in court that any injury meets the policy's disability standards. Drop any disability-insurance setup with vague or confusing wording before you find yourself bilked of deserved payments by a language loophole.

Medicare. Many elderly citizens find enough gaps in the government's Medicare health-insurance plan to make them look for supplemental private health coverage. The trick here is to dodge the hoards of hucksters hawking worthless "supplemental" policies which do no more than duplicate Medicare measures.

Talk to your current insurance agent about converting your present policy to a Medicare supplement when you turn sixty-five. If that can't be arranged, find out exactly what Medicare takes care of by sending for free booklets entitled *Medicare/Medicaid* and *A Brief Explanation of Medicare* to the Consumer Information Center, Pueblo, Colo. 81009. Plan your extra health protection to plug Medicare's loopholes and you won't be plundered by useless premium payments.

First-day payments. A squint at the itty-bitty print of health insurance policies touting "Full benefits payable from the very first day" often reveals that these policies actually pay up only for sickness originating more than thirty days after the signing date. Heart diseases, blood diseases, and ailments of any reproductive-system organ aren't covered until the policy is in effect from six to twelve months. And any medical cost related to an illness incurred before your signing date—like a recurrent backache, an ulcer, or arthritis treatment —is excluded. About the only thing they will pay for from the first day is if you're laid low with acute perfect health!

Double coverage. A common ploy of the health-insurance hawker out to boost your premium (and his commission) is to sell you double coverage for health catastrophes without you even suspecting it. You'll be sold "major accident" or "serious illness" plans with benefits identical to your hospitalization coverage. Yet contract provisions prohibit you from cashing in on both coverages for the same accident. Check the health policy you now have, or plan to buy, for this and other double-coverage schemes.

Information on health insurance. If you have questions about the adequacy of your health-insurance coverage, complaints about questionable policy-selling practices, or gripes about inadequate payments for health expenses, write to one or both of the following groups: The Health Insurance Association of America, 750 Third Avenue, New York, N. Y. 10017; or the Health Insurance Institute, 488 Madison Avenue, New York, N. Y. 10022.

They can put the pressure on your company to pay up, or prevent such problems from arising by steering you clear of unwholesome characters.

CATCHY CAR CLAUSES

Cancellations. If your auto-insurance company has canceled your policy, for whatever reason, you will automatically find yourself in the assigned-risk category, which means a premium hike of up to *500* percent in every state but Massachusetts.

If you feel you have been unfairly canceled, check with your state insurance department. Some states—including West Virginia,

Florida, Michigan, Illinois, Minnesota, and California—will hear such complaints and force a company to continue an unjustly canceled policy, thus saving you the added cost of the all-risk premiums.

For further information, get hold of one of the following: *How to Keep Them Honest; Herbert Denenberg on Spotting the Professional Phonies, Unscrewing Insurance and Protecting Your Interests,* Howard Shapiro. (Emmaus, Pennsylvania: Rodale Press, 1974); or *Getting Your Money's Worth; Guidelines About Insurance Policies, Health Protection, Pensions and Professional Services,* Herbert Denenberg (Washington, D.C.: Public Affairs Press, 1974).

Sports cars. Owners of sports cars and other high-powered models pay a king's ransom in jacked-up insurance premiums. The only way to dodge this injustice is to look to the lower-horsepower buggies. Many now sport some pretty racy styles, with the engineering emphasis switched from acceleration to getting more miles per gallon. Don't let auto-insurance companies take advantage of your venturesome tastes despite a good driving record. You'll retrieve an average of $100 a year in premium-payment reductions—and tune-ups will be easier, too.

Good-driver discounts. These lowered rates for good driving records are glittery, but not as good as gold. You may get a small premium reduction, but the slightest fender bender and wham! Your insurance company can increase your annual rate by 40 percent or more. Many times the premium increase is more than the cost of the accident. Find out definitely how much your auto-coverage premium will climb if you report a crash. If rates will jump $200, say, in the next three years, you'll want to ignore scrapes and dents costing less than that amount, rather than be robbed by rate inflation.

High-risk insurance. A couple of ill-timed car wrecks will bring you the high premiums that high-risk drivers must pay major auto-insurance companies. Accident-prone drivers, lured by comparatively cheap payments, are prime targets for fraudulent insurance companies.

The officers of these fly-by-night insurance firms are nothing more than practiced embezzlers. They'll siphon your gas money, then declare bankruptcy before they are forced to pay claims. Don't suffer the double loss of premium payments *and* unpaid claims—check with your state's insurance department before signing that bargain policy.

Unauthorized drivers. One famous ruse of the fly-by-night insurance agent is the innocent-looking statement that the auto policy is no good if the car is used by an unauthorized party at the time of damage or loss. Of course a car thief won't be "authorized." When your wheels are filched, your insurance company will give you sympathy, but no money.

Don't end up on the losing side of a few well-chosen words. Read your policy before signing.

CHAPTER 11

Protecting your business

In both total dollars lost and number of people involved, crimes against businesses far outstrip crimes against persons—and business crimes are growing at an even faster clip. In 1976, for instance, employee theft and kickbacks bilked American corporations of more than $12 billion. Shoplifters walked away with another $5 billion in merchandise. Throw in substantial losses to holdup men, burglars, check forgers, blackmailers, and assorted other schemers, and the sum of stolen cash and products is astounding.

Consumers, employees, proprietors, and stockholders—*everyone* pays the price of business crime. Losses from larceny of all types add as much as 15 percent to the cost of goods and services. Furthermore, commercial ventures that fail because of business crime cost workers lost income from discontinued employment—not to mention the large amounts lost by the owners of these firms. Business crime is a problem for anyone who owns or works for any department store, supermarket, wholesale house, manufacturing plant, hotel, insurance company, bank, or corporation. And that includes more than 150 million Americans!

Within this chapter, you'll find hints, ranging from common-sense measures to intricate, computerized safeguards, to benefit any business from a Mom and Pop corner store to an international corporation. You'll learn to deal with the three major categories of business losses —theft from the outside, theft from within, and inadequate or violated procedures.

Some of the points made in the selections which follow are already known to top management, yet procedural violations, in many instances, continue virtually unchecked. Enforcement of adequate procedures is the most important factor. We urge you start immediately to crack down on your corporate losses by announcing strict policies, posting the rules, and enforcing them. Even the courts frown upon lax managerial practices and refuse to prosecute suspects when a lack of in-house rules makes business crime effortless and attractive.

Besides an extensive section on shoplifting, we focus on ways to stop cashiers who regularly dip into their registers, ways to nip dishonest truckers and loaders who make off with merchandise through loading-dock doors, and ways to foil such modern menaces as computer crime, looting, and bomb threats. A batch of ideas on bad-check passers, if implemented, should cut your company's paper losses to a bare minimum.

Those who don't own a shop or service outlet can check the security where they work against the following suggestions. If your place of employment needs improvements, pass along some of our ideas to your management. Chances are they'll appreciate the help and just maybe reward you with a bonus or pay boost. One thing is for sure: Businessmen who cut crime losses will increase company profits and can then afford to increase salaries of their loyal and honest workers, benefiting everyone—except the business criminal.

FOR FURTHER INFORMATION:

Booster & the Snitch, The. Mary Owen Cameron. New York: Free Press of Glencoe, 1964.

Combatting Shoplifting. Arthur C. Kaufmann. New York: National Retail Merchants Association, 1974.

Computer Security. Peter Hamilton. Philadelphia: Auerbach, 1973.

Computer Security: Equipment, Personnel & Data. June-Elizabeth Thorsen, editor. Los Angeles: Security World, 1968.

Detection and Prevention of Business Losses. Keith M. Rogers and W. G. Whitham. New York: Arco, 1962.

How to Stop Pilferage in Business & Industry. Charles P. Rudnitsky. New York: Pilot Books, 1961.

Internal Theft. Sheryl Leininger. Los Angeles: Security World, 1975.

Introduction to Security. Gion Green. Los Angeles: Security World, 1975.

Protecting Your Business Against Employee Thefts, Shoplifters and Other Hazards. L. Nader. New York: Pilot Industries, 1971.

Shoplifting ... A Manual for Store Detectives. James Brindy. Matteson, Ill.: Cavalier Press, 1967.

Successful Retail Security. Mary Margaret Hughes. Los Angeles: Security World.

Thief You Pay, The. Ron Mingus. Los Angeles: Security World, 1969.

SPOTTING AND STOPPING SHOPLIFTERS

The stuffer. This individual's trick is to hide small, expensive items inside or under larger, low-priced articles, which are then purchased in the normal fashion.

Jewelry, small tools and leather goods, cigarette lighters, handkerchiefs, ties, and socks can all be hidden in the pocket of an inexpensive jacket before it is brought to the checkstand. A folded shirt, blouse, or sweater can effectively hide a record album. Before a large can of motor oil is purchased, the cap can be removed and small tools slipped inside, with the oil silencing the sound as they fall. In fact, *any* large container can serve as a storage place for smaller items.

Insist that your cashiers check thoroughly through all merchandise *before* every sale is rung up.

The bagger. The bagger, as opposed to the stuffer, goes into his act *after* a purchase has been made. This bird will buy an inexpensive item, which he'll have the clerk bag. Then he'll wander through other areas of the store, filling the bag as he goes. If the ploy works, he'll be able to walk right through the front door, carrying your store's bag like any other good customer.

One way to reduce the effectiveness of this act is to have your cashiers staple each bag shut—with the sales receipt stapled on top. Then simply station an employee or security guard at the door to inspect the contents of any unstapled bags. However, boosters have been known to reopen stapled bags, deposit additional merchandise, then restaple the bags themselves with their own staplers. Beware.

Another type of bagger. But what if the customer enters your store carrying a bag from *another* store? What's to stop him from placing *your* merchandise in *his* bag?

You can't demand to rifle through customers' personal belongings when they leave. But what you can do is require customers to check all parcels upon entering your store. Place an identifying number on their packages and give them a claim check. Let them retrieve the parcels only when leaving the store.

The switcher. This individual's method involves confusing a young or inexperienced clerk to the point where the clerk will agree with just about anything the shoplifter says.

A common ruse is for the customer to return to the clerk or checker a few minutes after a purchase saying that she's changed her mind and would like to exchange the item for a more expensive item of the same type, or for something else. By shuffling the merchandise around and by using distracting conversation, the customer confuses the clerk and is able to walk out of the store without paying the difference for the higher-priced item. Or a customer may try to exchange or get a refund on merchandise he or she never paid for in the first place.

It's easy to outwit the switcher. Simply make it a rule that only you or your manager can approve exchanges and refunds.

The garment switcher. Last year, in a large Midwestern department store, detectives watched through one-way mirrors while a woman made her way from one department to another, systematically replacing her old blouse, skirt, sweater, purse, hat, and shoes with new merchandise from the store's display racks. They finally grabbed her after she had emerged from a dressing room wearing a new, racy set of underwear, having dutifully left her old undies behind.

One way to become sensitive to the wiles of this culprit is to train yourself and encourage your employees to notice what customers are wearing and carrying as they walk into your store. You'll also want every employee to become thoroughly familiar with *your* merchandise.

The fitting-room thief. The fitting room offers both amateur and professional boosters an opportunity to steal. Clothes from the store can be put on under the thief's own. Or, as we saw in the previous instance, new clothes can merely be substituted for old.

If your store sells clothes, you can't eliminate fitting rooms. But here's how to minimize fitting-room filching: Keep the entrances to these rooms curtained, rather than using solid doors. Have the curtains made of a slightly shorter width than the actual door opening. This way you, an employee, or a private detective can cruise the area —even "mistakenly" walking into a fitting room when necessary— keeping an eye out for boosters.

Or, if you have enough sales personnel, you can instruct them to wait on only one customer at a time, carefully noting what that customer carries into—and out of—the fitting room.

Another security measure involves stationing an employee at the entrance to the fitting rooms with a pencil and pad of paper. The employee checks and marks down the number of garments taken inside, then checks again when the customer exits.

The ticket switcher. This bird, as opposed to the run-of-the-mill shoplifter, prides himself on his imagined cleverness at taking a low-figure price tag and affixing it to a higher-priced item.

How can you outfox him? Use tamperproof gummed labels which rip apart when an attempt is made to remove them. Or you can staple your tickets on, using special staple patterns which are recognizable to store personnel. Also, you can conceal *extra* price tags elsewhere on the merchandise. For soft goods, you might attach your tickets with hard-to-break plastic string.

The package snatcher. Instead of stealing the store's merchandise, this thief steals *customers'* packages from counters. The victim may be legitimate or he may be working in cahoots with the thief. In either case the victim will demand that you either replace the merchandise or make restitution. If you're not sure of the situation, you'll probably want to comply in order to maintain good customer relations.

Aside from watching out for this type of activity, you might want to put up signs warning your customers to watch their packages at all times.

The till tapper. This crook can use any number of devices to throw a harried cashier off guard in order to grab a fistful of large bills—or a whole register tray—and run. Accomplices are sometimes stationed in the area to "inadvertently" block anyone trying to pursue the thief.

The cashier's attention to his or her open register may be diverted by an accomplice's question or argument. A split second's distraction is all that's required for the till tapper to make his move.

A tapper can also open an unattended register with a duplicate key. Some registers have a release lever which will open the drawer even when it's in a *locked* position.

Alert your cashiers to the till tapper's methods and keep a close watch on your unattended registers at all times.

The carry-out. Many times a busy cashier will be on the alert for stuffers, till tappers, and the like—but she'll ignore the obvious.

Realizing this, a shoplifter will pick up a shirt, blouse, or jacket from a rack, put it over an arm, and simply stand there with it while other goods are being checked out. Or jewelry, cosmetics, or a food package can be held in the hand. If the cashier spots the item, the customer can feign innocence and absent-mindedness. If the checker doesn't spot the merchandise, the booster simply strolls out the door with it.

Caution your checkers to make a visual check of every customer at the checkout stand.

The money changer. This fast-talking dude can easily make himself $100 or more per day by practicing his shifty specialty. Here's how he does it.

Approaching an inexperienced-looking cashier, the money changer will ask for change for a $20 bill. Then he'll ask for change for one of the larger bills he's received back. Next, he'll look at the small bills and decide he really doesn't need such small bills after all, and ask the cashier to please give him a larger one for them.

By this time the poor cashier is thoroughly confused and ripe for a big mistake—in the customer's favor!

Make it a rule that only one transaction per customer is allowed whenever your cashiers give change.

Business thieves. The wiles and ways of shoplifters, till tappers, short change artists and other such culprits are outlined in *The Hands Do the Stealing,* a pamphlet published by the Public Affairs Division of the Los Angeles Police Department. Get a free copy by writing them at 150 North Los Angeles Street, Los Angeles, Calif. 90012.

The bill marker. Here, the crook will work with an accomplice. First, the border of a $20 bill is inscribed with "Happy birthday, John," or simply with a name or number. The accomplice enters the store first and makes a small purchase, paying for it with the marked bill, then departs.

Some time later, his partner enters the store, makes a small purchase, and pays for it with a small bill. After counting his change, the customer claims that he gave the cashier a $20 bill. "Why, it was a birthday present and even has my name on it," he indignantly proclaims. Nine times out of ten an unwary cashier will be hoodwinked by this shenanigan.

You can avoid losses here by tipping off your personnel to this trick. Then, if they suspect it's being perpetrated on them, have them call you over. Offer to check the register readings against the cash in the register in the customer's presence.

The crotch crook. The female professional is able to secrete merchandise between her legs in any of several ways. Ropes containing hooks can be attached to a belt inside the skirt. Merchandise is then attached to the hooks, which dangle between the legs, concealed by the skirt. Or she may store the goods in a bag slung between her legs. Some professional crotch workers have perfected their walk so well that they can even carry goods held by the thighs alone without detection.

Since a fair amount of maneuvering is required for the crotch worker to get the goods into position, your best protection against these crooks is to be constantly on the lookout for any suspicious movements.

The rubberband ruse. A strong rubberband is attached at one end near the booster's shoulder. A paperclip or small spring clamp attached to the other end is hooked over a ring on the finger. The entire arrangement is hidden from view under a coatsleeve.

The shoplifter can easily and surreptitiously remove the clamp from his ring and attach it to a small item such as a ring or necklace. The clamp is released and zip! The stolen article disappears up the coatsleeve.

How to spot this tricky fellow? Again, alertness is the key word. Watch the hands.

The stockroom thief. These pilferers have no compunctions about walking into your stockroom and lifting everything in sight. Sometimes in order not to arouse suspicion, they'll sneak an employee-type smock into the store and surreptitiously don it just before entering the stockroom.

If you can't station a security guard at your stockroom entrance, or haven't installed alarms, mirrors, or other detection devices in your stockroom, then your best bet is simply to keep this area under lock and key at all times, with keys given out only to your manager and trusted employees.

The juvenile. Surprisingly enough, the professional booster accounts for only a small minority of all shoplifting losses. Fully 80 percent of all shoplifted merchandise is taken by juveniles and housewives, with most of the juveniles being thirteen to nineteen years old.

The value of most of the items taken by juveniles is under $5. Nevertheless, juvenile theft, in the aggregate, amounts to millions of dollars every year.

Today, in our permissive society, many kids treat shoplifting as a game. Many times, they'll invade a store in a large group, causing such turmoil and confusion that the detection of individual theft verges on the impossible.

How to cope with the problem? We'd hate to suggest the radical solution of barring everyone under twenty-one who is unaccompanied by an adult from your store, as many merchants have done. A more reasonable alternative might be to limit them to groups of two, only allowing one group in your store at a time.

In either case, watch the juvenile as carefully as you would any other age group. Shoplifters come in all ages.

The setup. This game is played by the elite of the shoplifting world. Not shoplifters at all, they'll *pretend* to secrete a small, expensive item in a purse or coat pocket. You or your security man sees them take it. Or at least you *thought* you did. What actually happens is that they take the article but, with a hidden hand, remove it from their person and drop it on the floor or stuff it in with merchandise on a display table.

Obviously, their scheme is to get you to make an arrest, then sue through a collusive attorney or make a big settlement with your insurance company.

The more sophisticated professionals will work with an accomplice who can watch you watching his partner, then signal the partner when to make the "lift" and the "drop."

False-arrest suits can be extremely expensive. Before apprehending or accusing anyone of shoplifting, consider whether a setup might be involved.

Duplicate merchandise. Here's another setup that'll be somewhat easier for you to avoid. A customer will pick up a piece of merchandise from your store, again purposely acting suspicious. "Aha!" you say. "Another shoplifter." When you confront her, she vigorously denies stealing the item, claiming she bought it at another store.

Not believing her, you decide to prosecute and, lo and behold! She surprises you in court by producing a sales slip for the same item from another store. Naturally, she's acquitted, and aside from incurring heavy attorney's expenses and court costs, you've just set yourself up for a fat false-arrest suit.

The only guaranteed way to outsmart this character is to mark every piece of merchandise in your store with some type of nonremovable identification. Otherwise, you'd probably be better off just letting the customer walk out the door with the article.

The handbag switch. This is another variation on the setup game. Two women with identical handbags will enter a store at different times. While she's sure you're watching, one of the women will snitch an item, putting it in her purse. Then, when you're *not* watching, the women will trade purses. Poof! There goes your evidence.

Now you can't possibly win. If you decide not to risk apprehending the woman you saw putting the article in her purse, you've lost some merchandise. If you *do* decide to apprehend her, you've not only lost your goods, but you'll have a false-arrest suit on your hands.

Obviously, a very important rule in store security is to watch suspects closely after they've taken the merchandise—until they're out of the store.

Multiple choice. Here again, a pair of thieves cooperate. One partner will ask a clerk to show him some watches, rings, or other small, expensive items. Eventually, he'll get the clerk to have, say, ten or twelve watches on the counter. At that point, the accomplice will casually saunter up to the counter, feigning interest and watching the clerk demonstrate the goods. The first partner will momentarily divert the clerk's attention. In a split second, the accomplice will have palmed and pocketed one of the watches. He or she will stick around for a minute or so, then casually wander off. The first partner will then continue to keep the clerk occupied until the accomplice is safely out of sight.

Caution your personnel against putting out too much merchandise at one time. In the above instance, having only two or three watches on the counter at any one time would have given the clerk much more control over the situation.

Mountains of merchandise. The oversize brassiere affords the professional female booster an excellent pair of containers for snitched merchandise. Such items as bottles of perfume, compacts, scented soap, watches, and rings can all be conveniently stuffed into an oversize bra. After trying on a valuable necklace, a woman can easily drop it into a waiting cup. Even small articles of clothing can be balled up and stored here.

You'll not be able to inspect the brassieres of customers entering your store, but by being aware of this dodge, you'll be better able to cope with it.

A pregnant ploy. Who would ever suspect that that attractive suburban housewife, apparently in her ninth month of pregnancy, who just walked in your store was carrying, not a child, but an empty fruit basket under that pretty maternity frock? Yes, the professional female booster will even go to this extreme in order to ply her trade.

Strollers. A baby stroller or carriage can have a false bottom. Soft goods can be secreted between the baby and its seat or in a paper bag inside the carriage. Also, mothers have been known to completely reclothe their babies while in a store, discarding their old garments under a counter.

Be alert to the merchandise-mulcting mother.

Brazen theft. A few years ago, two men wearing overalls walked into the sporting-goods section of a large department store, picked up a small fishing boat—with outboard motor attached—and carried it down three floors via an escalator and out the front door. Nobody knew where they came from or where they went.

Could this happen in your store? Caution employees, as well as your security guards if you have them, to watch for this type of brazen act.

Coats and jackets. One of the booster's most valuable aids is the open sportcoat or jacket. As the shoplifter leans over a counter or open display case, the coat can effectively shield his actions from you and your employees.

There's no way to prevent customers from wearing open coats and jackets into your store. But by being aware of this ploy, you can plug up one more leak.

The purseless female. It's a rare woman that goes shopping without a purse. The one that does may have the idea of picking up a purse in your store and unobtrusively walking out with it.

If you see a purseless female enter your store, watch her carefully around the handbag counter.

A good scare tactic. If I were a shoplifter about to pocket a coveted little trinket and suddenly heard over the store's P.A. system, "Will all security officers please report to area 341?" I'd sure think twice about going through with it.

You may not fool the professional with this tactic, but since most shoplifters are amateurs anyway, you'll scare enough of them off to make it worth your while.

Lock up those valuables! It may seem like simple common sense to you to keep your small, expensive merchandise items in locked display cases. But merchants lose hundreds of thousands of dollars worth of merchandise every year by carelessly leaving these items within reach of shoplifters.

Geometric displays. If you *must* leave your big-ticket items within reach of customers, keep these in geometrically designed showcases. Have a pigeonhole for each item and make sure that an alert employee

—who should always be stationed nearby—refills the empty hole immediately after each item is sold.

In this way you can tell at a glance if an item has been lifted.

Chaining down merchandise. Another way to guard against the theft of valuable items—especially larger ones—is to chain them securely to the counter. Here, however, you may encounter some customer resentment.

If this idea appeals to you, we suggest you try it on a small scale initially. Then, after a week or so, query your clerks as to customer reaction. If you've gotten no negative response, you can begin to chain down more of your merchandise.

Small items. Small items such as rings and earrings should be attached to cases and stands in such a way that the customer will have some difficulty in removing them. Then the customer's struggles to remove an item will attract a clerk's attention.

The eyes give it away. Know one of the best ways to spot a potential shoplifter? Watch the eyes. Most amateurs invariably give themselves away not only by their darting eye movements, but also by conspicuously craning their necks in all directions.

Professionals are not as obvious but nevertheless can betray themselves by their steadily shifting eye movements, as they watch for someone watching *them.*

Booster coats and skirts. A booster coat or skirt can hide such items as a belt containing hooks, pins, tape, clothespins, or other gadgets on which to hang or attach stolen items. A pair of bloomers can be worn under the skirt as a receptacle for merchandise.

How to tell a booster garment from regular ones? It's almost impossible. Again, watch for darting eyes, suspicious hand movements, and other telltale signs.

The greeting. In the days before supermarkets and huge discount department stores, every customer was courteously greeted at least once—usually several times—by store employees while shopping. Naturally, this practice engendered goodwill by making the customer feel noticed, recognized.

If you and your employees make it a point to greet every customer who walks into your store—either with a "hello" or with a polite "May I help you?"—not only will you build goodwill, but your shoplifting losses will drop significantly. Why? Several reasons. By greeting customers, you're putting things on a *personal* basis, and a shoplifter (remember, most are amateurs) can face his conscience a lot easier when he steals from a company, rather than from a person. Also, by recognizing the customer, you'll give him a distinct impression of being alert. And alertness is the shoplifter's biggest enemy.

The oblique approach. OK. You've seen an individual steal a tube of toothpaste or a package of hosiery and you don't want to make a big fuss over it, but you would like to retreive the merchandise. Here's what to do.

Casually walk over to the customer, pick up the *exact* same article as she's stolen, and, holding the item up, say, "You know, we sell more of this than any other brand. I'm sure you'll like it." Then walk away, giving the customer a chance to remove the object from her person without losing face.

Or wait till she gets to the checkstand, then hold up a duplicate of the stolen article and say to the cashier in a loud voice, "A lot of this is leaving the store without getting checked out. Better use the emergency buzzer, just in case." Naturally, there is no such thing as an emergency buzzer, but it sounds ominous enough to scare any amateur into either paying for the stolen item on the spot or leaving it in the store. Of course, this ruse will necessitate tipping off your cashiers in advance so that they'll play along with you.

Pickup departments. If your business is large enough to have a customer "will call" or pickup department, you'll want to watch here especially for the customer who picks up other merchandise in addition to his own. Or you just may get people in off the street who start helping themselves. Thieves have been known to back up a pickup truck to a loading dock, and after showing official-looking receipts, drive off with lawn furniture, sporting goods, appliances, and—in at least one instance—a fully equipped golf cart.

Staff your pickup department with alert, trusted employees. Let them release merchandise only to those customers who have receipts signed by the proper personnel. Keep signature cards in the vicinity so that, if in doubt, your employees can compare the signature on the receipt with the authorized signature on the card.

Employee bonus plan. A faithful employee, alert to the ways and wiles of the shoplifter, is worth his weight in gold.

Set up a bonus program, whereby an employee will receive 10 percent of the value of any goods recovered through his help in spotting and apprehending shoplifters.

Layout logic. If I were a shoplifter, I'd want all the protection against visual detection I could get. Therefore, I'd favor stores with tall displays and long, unbroken rows of display cases.

Although a series of waist-high, individual display stands would afford ideal shoplifter visibility, the cost of such wasted display space would be prohibitive. A wise compromise would be shoulder-high displays broken at, say, every 20 feet.

Too many exits. Extra unlocked doors on your premises represent a tempting invitation to the alert shoplifter. Fire regulations permitting, lock all doors not necessary for convenient customer usage.

Attach large "no exit" signs and noise alarms to those doors which must be kept unlocked. Check your noise alarms frequently, as the canny shoplifter has been known to jimmy these alarms in advance of his strike.

Unused checkout aisles. These represent potential escape paths for shoplifters and should be securely blocked off. Not with a chain or sign, but preferably with a large barricade-forming display.

If you allow your customers to check their own items out, chances are they'll put the payment in their own register!

The booster box. This is a container made up to look, innocently enough, like a freshly purchased package from another store. Professionals carrying booster boxes into stores account for losses of millions of dollars' worth of merchandise every year.

Several different devices are employed in the operation of these boxes. A hole or slit in which merchandise is deposited is concealed by the carrier's body. Sometimes a hinged door installed on one end can be opened by arm pressure on the box. A spring shuts the door after the article is inserted. A variation of this is a sliding spring door on the bottom. The door is opened and the box is set down on the counter over the desired merchandise. The spring then closes the door, concealing the article inside the box.

Aside from watching for general indications of any suspicious activity among parcel-laden customers, there are two main ways to protect yourself against these individuals. You can either require that they check their parcels at the door, or as a tipoff, you can watch for signs of smudge marks or wear spots on the supposedly new package.

Pocket slits. Men's overcoats and raincoats are frequently manufactured with slits cut in their sides just above the pockets. These allow the wearer access to his inside coat pockets without the necessity of unbuttoning the coat and reaching in from the front. Keeping his

207

hand inside the slit, the booster leans over a counter. With the open raincoat shileding his actions, items can be picked up and stashed in a coat pocket quicker than you can say "thief."

Now we're not saying that all your customers wearing these types of outer garments are shoplifters. But they *do* bear close watching.

The adhesive-tape trick. Two-way adhesive tape (tape with adhesive on both sides) provides another excellent tool for the determined shoplifter. The tape is affixed to the palm of the hand. When the booster spots a small item—a ring, pocket watch, cigarette lighter—on the counter, he simply lays his hand on the object and presto! You've incurred another business loss. Again, keep small valuable items out of the browser's reach at all times.

Watch the hands. Next to the eyes, watch potential shoplifters' hands. Notice where the merchandise is being placed. Has it been moved toward the edge of the counter where it can easily be slipped into a waiting purse? Did the hand just unbutton a coat or sweater in preparation for the snitch? And finally, did the hand actually perform that dastardly shoplifting deed?

Orderly displays. Keeping your counters and displays orderly not only will result in a more pleasant, relaxed atmosphere for customer shopping but will help your employees to watch for "disappearing" merchandise.

Purses and such. The purse, the large canvas shoulder bag, and the shopping bag make handy receptacles for lifted goods. The tipoff here is that the bag must first be opened before the merchandise is inserted. Therefore, be on the lookout for any such containers being toted into or being opened in your store.

Hoods. You wouldn't ordinarily think that the open hood of a hooded sweater worn by a customer could serve as a receptacle for stolen merchandise, but it can—and does. It may not happen very often, but this is one more trick you should be aware of.

Returns. Using this trick, customers virtually set their own prices on your merchandise and get away with it. Knowing your store has a "loose" policy on returned purchases, the sly shopper purchases two of the item he wants—say two lamps, one cheap, the other more expensive. The next day he returns the cheap lamp in the expensive lamp's box and gets a refund of the expensive lamp's purchase price. One sure way to avoid this swindle is to institute a "no refund" store policy. A less drastic answer is to have clerks check all returns against similar merchandise on the store shelves and not merely refund the price marked on the box.

Gift-wrap grifters. Gift-wrapping practices vary from store to store, but you'll be giving away your profits under fancy ribbons and bows if a crafty customer discovers your wrapping procedure lacks adequate safeguards. Require your salesperson or wrapping-desk cashier to carefully check the customer's sales ticket against the merchandise presented for gift wrapping. This practice stems a common ploy —presenting stolen goods along with paid-for merchandise for wrapping.

Mannequin stripping. Shoplifters sometimes disrobe mannequins and disappear with the display clothes, jewelry, and handbags. Such plunder is often taken openly, with the lifter impersonating an employee who is dismantling the display. In most cases, dummies are stripped near exits and stairways. If you keep displays where your workers can watch them and where sneak thieves can't make a quick getaway you'll see fewer losses and fewer naked mannequins.

Government advice. A publication put out by the Small Business Administration gives some valuable tips on how the business person can significantly cut down on his shoplifting losses. Entitled *Reducing Shoplifting Losses* (Small Marketers Aids no. 129), the pamphlet is available at any Small Business Administration office or by writing the Small Business Administration at 1441 L Street, N.W., Washington, D.C. 20416.

EMPLOYEE THEFT

Lunchbox lifters. The employee who steals from his company makes his getaway by strolling out the front door, chirping goodbye to the boss as he passes. The electronic calculator he's swiping is tucked in a lunchbox or wrapped in the jacket hanging over his arm. Stop this walkaway robbery by forbidding employees to bring their lunches or to take packages into their work area. Or issue "package passes" which must be returned as parcel-toting workers leave the job. As a last-ditch measure, hire a guard to inspect *every* container carried through the employees' door.

Safeguarding mail. Outwit sneaky employees by having company mail addressed to a post office box rather than to your shop. Pick up the mail yourself or assign a highly trusted assistant this duty. Have the mail-getter personally open the mail and record cash and checks received. Such a precaution will thwart the most common embezzlement tactic—the accounts-receivable clerk opening the mail, pocketing cash or money orders, and not recording a customer's payment.

Separate duties. One no-cost security measure to protect your business against theft by employees is instituting a strict separation-of-functions rule among your workers' job designations. For example, having one person count inventories and another record them will avoid intentional short counts with one worker taking home the difference. Or assigning one person the duty of opening incoming mail and informally recording incoming checks prevents the accounts-receivable clerk from juggling your books and dropping company cash in his pocket. Separation of employee duties means workers will be checking up on each other to protect their jobs and your cash.

Mail-clerk theft. A Los Angeles department store's mailroom clerk was recently discovered with $4,000 worth of the store's clothes in her apartment—she'd simply mailed them to herself. If your business does selling through the mails, you need to take extra precautions to make sure profits don't go out through the postage meter in a similar fashion.

Division of responsibilities is one way of averting the postal pilferer. Have one person receive and fill mail orders, another fill out a receipt ticket, and yet another clerk run packages (only those with properly verified receipts) through postal meters.

Embezzlement. It's a fact that a successful embezzler can send a thriving enterprise into the bankruptcy courts overnight. To help the business person reduce the possibility of such a crime, the Small Business Administration has published a bulletin entitled *Preventing Embezzlement* (Small Marketers Aids no. 151). Get your free copy at any Small Business Administration field office or write the Small Business Administration at 1441 L Street, N.W., Washington, D.C. 20416.

No days off. Computer criminals and embezzlers often get so snarled in their trickery they decline regularly scheduled vacations, never call in sick, and even eat lunch at the office. Why? Because anyone taking over their duties would likely discover their outrageous swindles through consumer complaints or miskept records.

Order employees to take their allotted days off, and see to it that all electronic-data-processing personnel plan their vacations for the end-of-the-month periods. This ensures that someone else will be double-checking their work during these frantic bookkeeping periods at least once a year.

Trash stash. Periodic spot checks of your trash bins are a must if you want to stop employee pilferage. A widespread worker rip-off technique is to toss tools, office supplies, and other goodies in the waste baskets and return to scrounge them out of the garbage pails after work hours. Crooked employee-garbageman teams have systematically drained some companies. Make sure your trash bins are as far as possible from storage sites and shipping or receiving docks. Consider padlocking dump bins to prevent unauthorized junk plundering.

Break-outs. Most businessmen concentrate on controlling burglar break-ins. Talk to them about preventing "break-outs" and they recommend an acne cure! But break-outs—employees hiding until after closing time, then leaving with armloads of loot—are a major problem.

Catch concealed crooks coming out by activating motion detectors or electronic eyes near all exits as you leave your shop. Or install metal gates on doors and windows which can be clamped together and locked as you leave. Take the keys with you and anyone hiding inside will still be there when you return in the morning.

Ins and outs. Obviously, the more doors your company building has, the more opportunities a dishonest worker has to make off with your goods. Take a tour of your plant today and note seldom-used side exits, doors opening onto the alley, and passages to the roof. Cut down on swiped supplies and filched inventories by locking up or bricking up unneeded entryways. The optimum safeguard is making all workers come and go through one door only. Chain and padlock loading-dock doors so no one can unload your wares while you're busy elsewhere.

Pilferage. The Small Business Administration publishes a free pamphlet entitled *Preventing Employee Pilferage* (Management Aids no. 209) which gives some solid advice to the business person on how to reduce internal theft. You can get a copy at your nearest Small Business Administration field office or by writing the Small Business Administration at 1441 L Street, N.W., Washington, D.C. 20416.

Engraving iron. A legitimate security expense for any business is the price of an engraving iron, available at any hardware store. Use it to etch the company name on typewriters, tools, furniture, and anything that could conceivably end up in a sticky-fingered employee's possession. Simply knowing the goods are marked discourages workers from stealing them.

Lending rather than losing. Following a rash of employee rip-offs, one manufacturer in Indianapolis instituted a policy of allowing workers to borrow tools for their home-repair jobs, provided they check them out and return them the next work day. Thefts declined dramatically as employees no longer had to steal to gain home use of tools they knew how to operate but couldn't afford to own.

Such a plan could be the solution to your worker pilferage problems. Why should an employee risk his job by stealing when he can legitimately borrow anytime he needs a tool?

Destroy damaged goods. Stop letting employees purchase merchandise damaged in shipment at discount prices! You lose with this policy, since once aware of it your workers may begin rough-and-tumble handling of packages, causing damage in order to buy the goods later at lowered prices.

Losses from beat-up merchandise declined by one-third, a Midwest retailer recently reported, when his company began destroying damaged items instead of offering them to workers at prices below cost. Do the same to protect your assets.

Fluorescent powder. A fluorescent powder invisible to the naked eye can be used to mark items an employee is thought likely to filch. For instance, in one case an ultraviolet light made the powder on the hands of a trusted porter glow purple—a sure tip that he was responsible for a steady loss of perfume bottles, some of which were dusted with fluorescent powder the night before. In another case, dusting a cash register resulted in glowing fingers and pockets of a night watchman who dipped into the till. Order the fluorescent powder from a chemicals distributor.

Loan books. A display man takes a $10,000 fur from one department to use in a window showing. The window display changes, but it's not until months later, at inventory time, that the fur is discovered missing. Who knows who has it?

You would if you'd instituted a policy of keeping "loan books" to record any passage of merchandise from one department to another.

For fashion shows, window displays, dressing mannequins, or any other purpose, require every item to be signed out with the authorization of the department head. And let it be known your policy holds the last person signing for an item responsible for its return, undamaged, at a specified time.

Incentives. Businesses can tighten their security belts by applying the psychological principle of positive reinforcement. Instead of just punishing wrongdoers, try rewarding loyal employees—especially those who help stem losses due to others' negligence or criminal intent. Stage suggestion contests and offer vacations, dinners, pay boosts, or bonuses as incentives. Also, make a company policy of offering an "appropriate" award and of offering confidentiality to employees bringing problems to the attention of company security personnel.

Hiring hints. Whenever possible, avoid hiring members of current employees' families or their good friends. Ties of kin and comradeship run deeper than loyalty to the company, and employee collusions can cost you plenty in losses to pilferage and embezzlement schemes. By the same token, occasional personnel transfers—switching job assignments or rotating shifts—will shake up the social circles that turn into employee theft rings.

Checking checkers. Examine the records of your loading-dock clerks to compare how many "shorts" and "overs" each lists. The checker claiming a large number of shortages could be changing numbers and taking merchandise home. The ones with noticeably fewer overages may be doing the same thing by not reporting "extra" deliveries. Also look for the checker with no shorts or overs to report. He may be okaying invoices without counting goods received—thus leaving the door open for devious deliverymen.

Insist on invoices. Demand that drivers present an invoice with all deliveries before unloading their trucks. This basic protection against short-changing by wholesalers is nevertheless often neglected. When bills arrive in the mail a few days later, you may find the firm charged higher prices than you'd agreed to or billed for items you didn't receive. When sending goods, attach typed invoices signed by a clerk in your billing department. Truckers without typewriters can't alter invoices to cover their thievery, since handwritten changes will be glaringly obvious.

Dock double-checks. Dishonest drivers will steal you blind with short-count deliveries if they learn your receiving routines are lax. Require that a count of goods delivered take place on the loading dock and that a receipt, in triplicate, be signed by your receiving clerk. One copy should be attached to the invoice, another goes to the person marking pricetags, and the third remains with the merchandise. Tell your clerks to check *inside* all cartons for their count. Crooked truckers are clever enough to open cartons, remove items, and reseal the boxes. Price markers should be made to double-check dock clerks by making their own count of items they tag. Compare markers' totals with clerks' counts to see whether you've hired thieves to unload incoming trucks.

Loading-dock security. Whenever possible, keep shipping and receiving docks physically separate. Fences or walls dividing a platform are acceptable substitutes when providing separate docks is not possible. Separation of intake and outflow functions prevents the confusion of cargoes which robbery-minded truck drivers and loading personnel use to their advantage. Also raise a gateless fence between loading docks and employee parking lots. Otherwise workers will whittle your profit margin by pirating goods from loading docks to their cars instead of leaving by way of guarded exits.

Beating the time clock. Post a notice above the employee time clock which reads, "If anyone is caught punching in or out for another person, both parties will be dismissed." Then enforce this rule to stop wage rip-offs caused by friends clocking in and out for each other to log extra work time. Allowing the practice will cost you thousands yearly in unearned wages. Be sure you keep your time clock in an easily observable location and require workers to punch their times in single file. Bunching up around the time clock allows a chance for unobserved payroll fraud.

Restricted areas. You'll want to keep some areas of your business under tighter security than others. In particular, such infrequently used places as stock rooms, marking rooms, and receiving and shipping docks are ripe for plundering by thieves. Fit these and other top-priority areas with locks the master key can't open. Keep the keys in a safe or in the manager's locked desk drawer. These restricted areas should remain locked when not in use and the keys should be given out only with official authorization and for a stated purpose.

Keys. In your business, as in your home, controlling who has the keys is as important as installing good locks. If locks to cash registers, drawers, vaults, and doors haven't been changed for a good while at your place of business and you don't know for sure how many keys are out, change the locks immediately. Keep a close count of everyone with company keys. When an employee in charge of one or more keys leaves the company, change locks again. Of course you must find a competent, honest locksmith and stick with him for all your key changes.

Payroll doctoring. Doctoring the payroll is one common way embezzlers keep business profits sickly. Relatives, friends, or fictitious names may be added to your company books, giving a crafty clerk two or three paychecks a week. Or he may issue more than one check to a fellow worker, keep the duplicate before checks are dispersed, and later forge a signature and cash it. To plug payroll leaks, make sure no one can be added to the payroll without your okay. If you have a personnel department, require it to approve additions to the payroll as a double-check. Rotate the job of paycheck disbursement to keep workers honest. Or have company paychecks printed in such a way that you or another trusted company official must sign them by hand. Unless you have more than fifty employees, the task will take only minutes monthly, and could save thousands yearly.

Setting an example. Take yourself for an example—your employees do. The first order of business security should be an ultra-honest image for the owner or manager of your shop. If you (or your store manager) "borrow" from your own cash register, pad your expense account, make personal long-distance calls on company phones, or use company funds for personal items, your workers will quickly pick up your loose traits. "The boss does it so I can do it" will be the excuse that'll cost you thousands of dollars in employee pilferage.

Fidelity bonds. In spite of your best efforts to stop embezzlers, your business may be victimized by these white-collar criminals. If the crooked employee was bonded, you may be able to recover your losses.

Any worker in a position to mishandle funds should be adequately bonded by companies which specialize in insuring employee fidelity. Such firms are listed in the Yellow Pages under "Bonding Companies." Their charges for this insurance service vary. If you make fidelity bonding a company policy, have workers share its cost.

CASH-REGISTER CAPERS

The bottom of the cart. Many shopping carts have, in addition to their main compartment, a shelf on the bottom near the wheels. Unless you carefully instruct your cashiers to check this shelf on *every* cart passing through the checkstand, your customers may just be carting off your profits.

Phone location. Mom and Pop are advised to install the shop phone near the cash register, since a favorite tactic of robbers who prefer small stores is to occupy the proprietor with a phone call while a conspirator takes cash from the register. With the phone close at hand, the register ringer can keep an ear to the receiver and an eye on his cash receipts.

Telltale no-sale. Frequent no-sale transactions appearing on the cash-register tape may indicate stealing by one of your cashiers. The no-sale markings mean the drawer is being opened for no legitimate reason—perhaps sales are going unrecorded as a nervous thief repeatedly checks to balance out his filchings. Investigate the clerk responsible for too many no-sale ring-ups, and if the problem continues, institute a policy requiring cashiers to okay no-sale transactions with managers before punching them into the register.

Over-ring okaying. Make it a store policy that a manager or department head must okay every over-ring as soon as possible after the cashier makes the mistake. *Don't* let clerks attempt to balance the cash register as they go along by not ringing up the next few sales! A little practice at that and your salespeople will get good enough to steal a few bucks without your knowing it. Instruct your managers to sign the over-ring slip and record the clerk's name and the amount in your cash log in order to adjust the next register reading.

Tape-check rules. Ordinary salespeople using the cash register should not be allowed to check the cash with the register tape or know the amount on the tape reading. When this happens, it's all too easy for the cashier to "correct" overages by dropping the difference in his pocket. Always have a manager or department head read and reset your cash registers—or perform this crucial duty yourself.

Register records. Chart your over-rings and shortages daily in order to spot any major pilferage that needs immediate attention as well as to look for trends that suggest petty thievery. For instance, if every Friday a certain register turns up with cash shortages of $5 or multiples of $5, you can infer that bills of that denomination are being stolen. Make monthly reports on the over-and-short records of each salesperson or cashier. Comparisons between clerks' "batting averages" will tell you who's making mistakes or stealing. In either case you'll protect your profits.

Refund rip-offs. Dishonest sales clerks use your store's refund policy to pad their pocketbooks after forging refund slips and keeping the cash. Make things tougher on these cash-register crooks by requiring a manager's or your signature on the sales slip before returns, exchanges, or refunds are allowed. Make sure you use a full signature, as initials are easily forged. Also, keep a list of those refunds you do okay and spot the embezzling cashier by checking your list against the refund slips collected with the day's cash.

Checking by mail. Another way to see whether your workers are stuffing the register with phony refund slips and pocketing the proceeds is to demand that the customer's name and address be written on refund and return tickets. Follow up on this by sending friendly letters to customers asking if the refund transaction was satisfactory. You may be surprised to find that there is no such address or that the customer did not ask for or get a refund. When this happens, call in the cashier who signed the refund slip and get an explanation or a resignation.

Register locations. Though it cuts down on available counter space, it also cuts down on shoplifting if your cash registers are set up between clerk and customer on your sales counter. If your cashiers must turn their backs to ring up sales, the dishonest shopper gains an unguarded second to grab items displayed nearby. Also, see to it that your registers are located in full view of doorways. When the cashier's view of exits is blocked, customers can slip away without paying for their selections.

Cashier testing. Here's how to test a cashier you believe is dipping into your register and not recording cash sales. Have two friends make purchases from the suspected clerk. The first should get change and a sales slip and make general observations. The second should pay the exact price in cash and leave quickly with the merchandise and no register receipt. If the clerk is crooked, he'll swipe this second shopper's cash and not record the sale on your register. Check his honesty by taking the first friend's sales slip and matching it to the register-tape record of sale. Is the second friend's purchase noted next on the register tape? If not, fire the cashier.

Separate change drawers. Each salesperson authorized to use the cash register should have a separate change drawer in order for you to pinpoint shortages and overages. Some registers have keys or codes which match the seller to the sale. Without some such safeguard, clerks can rip you off and dodge the blame by pointing at co-workers. Also, consider removable cash trays to be taken out and checked against register receipts when the cashiers change shifts. It's the only way to be sure who is taking your money and who isn't.

Open-drawer policy. Empty your registers at the end of the business day and store cash for use the next day in a moneybag locked inside a safe in the manager's office. Then leave your cash registers' drawers open. That way, any night prowlers will plainly see there's no money in the till without breaking into (and damaging) the register to find out.

BURGLARIES AND HOLDUPS

Gasing safecrackers. Make your safe more safe by installing a tear-gas device that sprays those who tamper with it. When a cracker touches a safe's dial or enters a vault, he'll trigger electronic sensors which set off chemical gas guns. A vault or entire room can be protected in the same manner. Tear-gas outfits can be installed for about $100 by one of the security specialists listed in your Yellow Pages under "Burglar Alarm Systems" or "Security System Consultants."

Night-call precautions. Your phone jangles you awake at 2:00 A.M. and the caller urges you to return to your store for some emergency —say a burglar alarm is ringing or a car has crashed through your business door. However plausible the excuse may sound, never go alone—it could be a thief calling you to unlock the doors so he can conk you on the head and rob you and your shop.

If you do get an emergency night call, always phone the police and arrange for a patrol car to meet you when you arrive at your store.

Routine holdups. Falling into a set day-to-day business routine is one way of inviting a gunman to hold you up. Robbers and burglars notice if you always take the day's cash to the bank at 3:30. Transferring expensive merchandise at a fixed time also catches their eye. Keep your routines varied and keep the holdup man guessing.

Side-door swipers. While his sweetheart busied the jeweler with deciding on $1.50 worth of gawdiness to hang on her ears, the daylight bandit slipped in an unguarded side door and made off with a $16,000 treasure. It only takes a second for a sneak to take advantage of your shop's rear and side exits. Protect yourself and your merchandise by keeping these doors locked and installing a pressure-sensitive floor-mat in front of the entry points. Rig the mat to blare an alarm to announce unauthorized intruders. Such mats are available from Ademco (165 Eileen Way, Syosset, L. I., N. Y. 11791) and other security-device distributors.

Squeeze attack. This assault on your merchandise and cash on hand is made by burglars small and clever enough to wedge their way through the unlikely openings the too-casual businessman fails to protect. Break-ins through coal chutes, freight elevators, trash chutes, skylights, and steam vents tag retailers with millions of dollars' worth of losses yearly. Take a tour of your business grounds today, noting any unguarded, narrow passageways to the outside world. Install locks, and alarms, if needed, on any opening big enough for a midget or trained monkey.

Burglary booklet. Doors, locks, lights, alarms, windows and safes—all relating to business security—are just a few of the subjects discussed in a free pamphlet available through the San Diego Police Department. For your copy of *Commercial Burglary Prevention,* write the San Diego Police Department at 801 West Market Street, San Diego, Calif. 92101.

Central-station systems. Central-station alarm systems transmit the alarm automatically to a security service (under "Burglar Alarms" in the Yellow Pages) or an answering service. These people then send in their own troops or call police or firefighters. Proponents of these central-station setups point to fewer false alarms and greater burglar apprehension rates.

But keep in mind, when arranging central-station coverage, that your system will be only as good as the electronic detectors, wiring, and devices installed at your store. Make them too simple and any burglar will beat you. For example, a system using the company phone to alert an answering service can be blocked if the intruder keeps the company line busy.

219

Direct-connect systems. These systems include automatic phone dialers and other setups that transmit directly each alarm to the police or fire department. Properly installed, a direct-connect system beats all others in speed of reporting and in number of crooks caught. Improperly installed, they turn in false alarms that dull police enthusiasm and response time. This type of alarm is best for businesses which are frequent crime targets—liquor stores, banks, gas stations, and so on.

After-hours security. State Farm Fire and Casualty Company has a lot of good reasons to promote business security. Perhaps that's why they've published the informative booklet on the subject entitled *How's Business... After Hours?* It's free upon request, and you can get a copy by writing to State Farm's Public Relations Department at 112 East Washington Street, Bloomington, Ill. 61701.

Local systems. This alarm system is a noisemaker, and so it depends for effectiveness on whoever, if anyone, is within earshot of your alarm and responds to it. As night guardians, these sirens, horns, bells, and buzzers are far from foolproof, since most are familiar to the professional prowler. But inexpensive local "noise" alarms offer adequate protection when used in conjunction with a night patrolman service, or where the idea is to make the amateur burglar or holdup man scared enough to run. Get together with your security consultant before buying to determine if one of them fills your protection needs.

Proprietary systems. You'll need at least a small full-time security force to protect your business with a proprietary system. The prime advantage is that you are given the discretion to call police or not, and thus avoid false alarms. Your workers monitor alarm and detection devices and either alert your security guards or call police or firemen. The expense of a monitoring room and equipment and personnel makes this system worthwhile only if you have a good-sized business with substantial security problems.

Less loss. Preventing Burglary and Robbery Loss (Small Marketers Aids no. 119), a free booklet published by the Small Business Administration, shows you how to significantly reduce such losses at little or no cost. Available from any Small Business Administration field office or by writing the Small Business Administration, 1441 L Street, N.W., Washington, D.C. 20416.

Holdup foot alarms. Any store alarm system can be adapted to include a behind-the-counter foot rail switch. A cashier's upward toe movement activates the alarm, be it silent or siren. Once tripped, a special key is needed to stop the alarm. Ask your local security-equipment dealer to order No. 266 in the Ademco catalog.

Wireless cash-register alarm. Trip the store's alarm right before the holdup man's eyes by simply handing him all the money in the cash register! When the crook's caught and wonders what hit him, tell him about the Wireless Money Clip alarm switches you keep in each register drawer. A $5 bill trapped in this clip device breaks an electric circuit. When removed (only in a robbery situation) the circuit is completed and a radio signal beams to a receiver elsewhere in the store, causing an alarm condition. The signal can set off your choice of a silent alarm alerting neighbors or police, a telephone dialer, or a loud siren. Ademco, 165 Eileen Way, Syosset, L. I., N. Y. 11791, is one distributor (Item No. 1623).

Computerized locks. IBM has come up with an ingenious lock for companies with rooms where high security is essential. Installed at entrances, these locks record on tape the time of entrances and exits. The tape can be checked for unauthorized entries. Furthermore, keys are alphabetically identified as to the person issued the key. Thus you'll not only find out when doors were opened but who did the unlocking. Call your local IBM representative, listed in the Yellow Pages under "Data Processing," and ask about this security device.

Battling the burglar. The Los Angeles Police Department aims to put the burglar out of business by keeping him out of your business. Their booklet *Protect Your Business from Burglary* describes and illustrates ways in which you can foil even the canniest crook. It's available, free, by writing the Los Angeles Police Department's Public Affairs Division, 150 North Los Angeles Street, Los Angeles, Calif. 90012.

Avoiding holdups. Some good tips are outlined in the brochure entitled *Robbery Prevention,* published by the San Diego Police Department. The material is free and can be obtained by writing to the San Diego County Task Force, Prevention Team, P.O. Box 1431, San Diego, Calif. 92101.

If you're robbed. Even if you've done everything you can to avoid a holdup—without success—there are still many ways in which you can work toward the apprehension of the thief. These are described in the free pamphlet *Will You be His Next Customer?*, published by the Los Angeles Police Department. For a copy, write the Los Angeles Police Department, Public Affairs Division, 150 North Los Angeles Street, Los Angeles, Calif. 90012.

BOUNCED CHECKS

Two-party checks. Bad-check passers thrive on this kind of paper—checks written by one person to a second person who endorses it so that a third person may cash it. Forgers steal blank checks, fake the first and second person's signatures, then sign the check over to themselves so they can use their own signature and identification when cashing the bogus document. In a simpler but still common two-party check fraud, a legitimate check is cashed by the third person, then the maker quickly cancels payment on the check at his bank. Businessmen are stung so often by bouncing two-party checks that their only foolproof defense is a store policy: Don't accept *anybody's* two-party check.

Bad check passers. In an effort to help stem this rising tide of deceit, the Small Business Administration has published a booklet entitled *Outwitting Bad Check Passers* (Small Marketers Aids no. 137). You can get a free copy by visiting your nearest Small Business Administration field office or by writing to the Small Business Administration at 1441 L Street, N.W., Washington, D.C. 20416.

Government checks. Checks issued by federal, state, and local governments are frequently stolen from mailboxes and cashed illegally. Unless you know the endorser or she or he has an account with your business, don't cash government checks. Refer a suspected forgery of a U.S. Government check to the local Secret Service field office. Police divisions of other government levels should be contacted in the event that a bad-paper pusher shoves one of their official checks across your counter.

Payroll checks. Payroll checks are issued by companies to employees for their wages or salary. Such checks, often printed entirely by a check-writing machine, are a forger's delight. Some simply steal check-writing machines and issue themselves paychecks from imaginary companies. Others fake or swipe blank business checks and type in their name and amount.

Avoid giving good money for these worthless scraps of paper by refusing any handprinted, rubber-stamped, or typewritten payroll check. On machine-printed checks, call the company to see if they employ the person trying to cash its check. Or safer still, refuse all payroll checks unless the customer has an established credit account with your business.

Rubber stamps. Cashiers casually accepting checks is the major reason stores get stuck with bogus paper. Make your clerks check-conscious by requiring them to initial each check they accept. Every time the bank returns a bad check, take it to the cashier who accepted it and go over your store's check-cashing policy again, pointing out where the cashier went wrong.

One way to make employees alert to possible check frauds is to buy a rubber stamp to print a form on the back of each check which the clerk must fill out before cashing it. The salesperson's initials, customer's address, identification numbers, amount of sale, and manager's signature should be on the rubber-stamp form. Buy standard check stamps at stationery or business-supply stores for under $2 each.

Checking identification. Identification cards can be forged as easily as checks, but you should still demand at least two good IDs from a check casher so you can locate him if and when his note bounces. Current driver's licenses, car registration cards, charge cards, government passes, and military identification cards are all good IDs. Use IDs to *compare*—verify the signature on the check with that on an identification card. Compare the person standing before you with descriptions on driver's license or other card. Does the person look like the current picture on an ID? If these comparisons don't check out, throw the check out.

The nonforgery racket. The businessman on guard against bad-check passers is caught off guard by this schemer's routine. Dressed shabbily, he saunters into your showroom and quickly makes a major purchase, writing a check for the entire amount due. Of course you're suspicious, so you call the trickster's bank and, sure enough, the check checks out all right. The con man then takes the merchandise to another storeowner and tries to *sell* it to him. This second businessman, alarmed to see brand-new goods resold, calls you and by now you're *sure* you've nabbed a forger. You call the cops and bank officials. When the dust settles, the trickster's check is still a good one and the next paper he passes to you is a court summons for a false-arrest suit.

Spotting forgeries. You'll take in fewer bad checks if you instruct your cashiers to stay alert for smudged checks, misspelled words, and poor spacing of letters or numbers. These are calling cards of an inept forger.

Other things to check: Is only the current date given? Is it drawn on a local bank? Are the numerical and written amounts the same? Is the check legible and free from erasures and written-over amounts? Is it properly signed and/or endorsed? Is the check for amount of purchase only and under your store's limit? Making sure each check you cash passes each of these tests can reduce your bad-paper intake by more than 50 percent.

Phony phone calls. One bogus-paper routine employed by a team of counterfeiters to slip bad checks to businessmen starts with a call from a man claiming to be an executive of a local company. His assistant is on the way, the caller says, and would someone tell the aide to call the company when he arrives? The assistant walks in, gets the message, and makes the call. Having thus created an illusion of identity, he is allowed to purchase goods with (or cash) a forged check bearing the local company name. Sidestep this scheme by phoning the company to get authorization before accepting its check. Get the phone number from the book, not a counterfeit number from a crook.

Travelers checks. A crook disguised as a customer enters your business with a booklet of stolen travelers checks. Before arriving he's carefully forged countersignatures on all but the top check. (Anyone can do a passable job of copying a signature if given enough time.) While you watch he quickly signs the top check, then by flipping that check up and cupping his hand to block your view, he goes through the motions of countersigning the other checks. He then palms the top check and hands you the pre-forged checks for cash or merchandise. You'll be duped unless you make sure you see pen touching paper during the signing of every travelers check you accept.

Taped checks. Don't cash "mended" checks stripped together with cellophane tape. A favorite forger's ploy is lifting a signature from a canceled check by peeling the handwriting off with tape. A blank check is then torn near the signature line and the "borrowed" endorsement stuck in place.

Easy does it. Take great care when apprehending a customer you suspect is trying to pass a bad check or use a stolen or forged credit card—your business assets can be ravaged by a false-arrest lawsuit. Clue your employees in on a plan of action, similar to the following.

If convinced of a violation, the salesperson should remain courteous and cautious and continue writing the sales slip but delay as much as possible.

Summon the store's manager or security chief to "okay" the check. A prearranged code word will tip the manager that foul play is suspected. Only when the manager has made an exhaustive investigation and is prepared to file charges should police or security personnel be summoned to make the arrest.

Fingerprinting. One way to discourage bad-check passers is to post a sign near each cash register proclaiming "Check cashiers will be fingerprinted." The sign itself will dampen most forgers' fast-buck fantasies, and enforcing the policy will only cost you pennies. Just buy an ink pad like those used with rubber stamps and get a lesson from a local cop on fingerprinting techniques. Then instruct your cashiers to take the right thumbprint of each stranger cashing a personal or payroll check. If the paper bounces, you'll have an identification that will hold up in court.

Credit cards. As long as your salespeople follow three rules, your business can't be held liable for losses resulting from your accepting bad credit cards—the issuing company or owner who has lost the card will pay for your losses. First, make sure every credit card is current by noting the expiration date. Then insist that the customer's signature match the signature on the card. Finally, if the card-issuing company has mailed you a list of bad credit-card numbers, check your customer's card against the list of stolen ones. Refuse to honor any credit card that fails on one of the above points and your store will get its due credit.

Checking bills. Your cashiers can spot all but the very best counterfeit jobs if they examine the bills closely. Tell them to look for the fine lines. These are distinct, clear, and unbroken on genuine money. On counterfeits the sharpness, contrast, and detail are generally missing. The quality of paper is another tip to bogus currency. Real money is printed on paper shot through with actual fibers of red and blue thread. Printing red and blue lines—not fibers, but lines—is as close as counterfeiters get. Most don't get that far. If you notice a bill lacks these fiber colors, don't try to make the counterfeiting arrest yourself. Pass the buck to the United States Secret Service.

SAFEGUARDS, CHECKUPS, AND SECURITY SERVICES

Shopping services. Can your employees spot and stop shoplifters? Do they forget the safeguards you've instituted to nip bad checks? Do human errors leave your merchandise open to the plundering of burglars and other crooks? You can get answers to these questions in writing by periodically employing a shopping service. These firms, which use undercover techniques to test the honesty, efficiency, and courtesy of retail employees, are listed in the Yellow Pages.

Security switching. Unless you record and periodically check the identification numbers on your stock certificates, you may be the unwitting victim of a slick security-stealing manuever. In this swipe-and-switch tactic, a 100-share certificate of ABC Company is stolen from a broker or forged. It's then substituted for a 100-share certificate of ABC Company from your vault. The original security loser is issued a replacement bond. But if your auditors check only whether the number of shares noted on inventory records corresponds with the number of shares counted during a physical inspection, your loss will go unnoticed. Auditors must check the numbers on your securities, not just the number of securities, to fully safeguard your investments.

Private detectives. Businessmen and investors stand to lose large sums of money if they aren't sure whom they're dealing with in routine and special transactions. The surest way is to hire a private detective firm to investigate people with whom the firm negotiates major deals. Such agencies specialize in confidential reports on the character of a man and his past record; on the status of a company and how substantial it is; and on the validity of claims made. Rates vary with assignments. Find private eyes listed under "Detectives" in the Yellow Pages.

Deliberate errors. One effective auditing method is the input of deliberate errors. What, for example, will the shipping clerk do when more goods than the shipping order calls for reach the loading platform? Divert the surplus for his own use? Load the extra without even noticing the excess? Or return the intentional oversupply to the storeroom? If you withhold an invoice from the accounts-receivable clerk, will he or she notice it? Such sly management puts critical employees to the test. Honest or dishonest? Alert or asleep? Adding errors can help you find out.

Investigative operations audit. A routine audit of your firm's financial workings will not uncover the clever embezzler or employee fraud. It merely checks to see that your company complies with generally accepted accounting principles. If you suspect book juggling, engage an outside accounting firm to conduct an investigative operations audit, the kind designed to let management know whether honest procedures and controls are being followed and where the problems are. Merely knowing such a thorough audit will be conducted at regular intervals (yearly at least) will deter most white-collar crooks from dipping into your company till.

Defective goods. As the seller of goods, your customers look to you to make good on guaranteed items, and, to be accommodating, you may make replacements from your stock, planning to deal with the manufacturer of the defective merchandise later. Don't!

Putting off the return of guaranteed articles lets the manufacturer pin his losses on you. Most guarantees stipulate that the merchandise must be returned within a specified time or makers won't honor the warranty. It's a fine-print clause designed to catch the seller. Don't get caught! Assign someone the duty of shipping out all defective, returned items at least once every week.

Embezzlement deterrent. Preventing and detecting embezzlement is no easy task, since the typical embezzler is a trusted employee who considers himself foxier than the boss. The best way to discourage and discover this white-collar thievery is to enlist a public accountant to set up an adequate accounting system, with internal controls, checks, and safeguards to protect your business assets.

Skilled, certified accountants are listed in the phone book. Their fees vary with the size and complexity of your business venture. Demand an accounting system that provides you with at least monthly statements to advise you of the firm's current financial status. Any unusual or unexplained month-to-month variations can pinpoint your losses to a particular department or employee.

Unit controls. One way to detect shortages due to shoplifting and other retail theft is to institute unit controls in suspect departments. Do this either by attaching special tags to all merchandise or by making cashiers tally each item sold. Tags should be torn off at time of purchase and saved by clerks to be counted later. Cashier listings should be signed and dated. After a week, count your stock and compare the decrease in merchandise to the number of tags or listings which note sales. More merchandise gone than sales account for indicates shoplifting or employee theft within the department. Apply anti-shoplifting and anti-pilferage strategies to these troubled departments.

Collection agencies. Don't write off bad-credit losses before putting a collection agency to the test. These bill collectors will chase down skips and missing persons for a (usually large) percentage of the amount due you. Most accounts *can* be collected, and these agencies have the resources and experience to bring in overdue payments. Not only will you keep bad accounts from being a total loss, but hiring a collection service may turn up evidence of dishonesty among your own bookkeepers. Time and again company collection clerks write off paying accounts as "no good." They make the collections, but your money is pocketed instead of reported. Collection agencies can confirm whether the accounts have been paid.

Business insurance. Nearly every business needs the following insurance protection: car and truck, employee health and accident, workman's compensation, fire, theft, burglary, surety, and fidelity. In addition, you can protect yourself from losses in lawsuits by purchasing additional coverage. This legal-losses policy is often available at group rates through the industry-wide association in your retail field. Coverage includes damages for libel, slander, invasion of privacy, false arrest, false imprisonment, false accusation, assault, detention, and malicious prosecution. If your business group doesn't offer such a policy, urge them to negotiate one with a broad-based insurance group such as Lloyds of London.

Inventories. The quickest and surest way to pound the security message home with every single employee is to order an exacting inventory conducted by an outside firm. Have the auditors give you a book inventory and a physical inventory of merchandise and assets on hand. The book inventory starts with your opening balance and adds purchases, markups, and returns, to equal the total merchandise handled. Subtract from this the sales, discounts, claims, markdowns, markouts, cancellations, known losses, and damages. That remainder is how much you should have. It will seldom match the number of items tallied in the actual physical count, however. Thievery and embezzlement are among reasons why not. Demand that all discrepancies be explained to your satisfaction.

Pre-inventory count. A good tool for spotting where your business losses are coming from is the pre-inventory count. Stage the count unannounced in only a few departments and use trusted personnel from outside the department to do the counting. The pre-inventory totals will show up discrepancies in your regularly scheduled inventories and point the finger at managers or employees who doctor inventory figures to cover their shenanigans.

Loading guard. Larger stores and plants should post a uniformed guard in the shipping and receiving area to stop carriers from carrying off company goods. Guards should be charged with inspecting each leaving truck to make sure it's empty (unless the load is scheduled, checked, and sealed). Another duty for the dockside inspector is breaking up confidential chats between drivers and loaders or shipping clerks. Such private talks are the starting point of schemes for ripping off the company and splitting the loot.

Protection departments. One possibility for your business security is starting or hiring a "protection department" assigned the duty of protecting company interests at all levels. Such a department combines the duties of watchmen, shopping services, and store detectives in curbing crimes by customers and employees alike. Store security will be systematically enforced and new protection needs met by a flexible, in-house force. Contract these services with an outside agency or advertise for an experienced police investigator or law-enforcement academy graduate. Make the person head of your newly formed protection department and let him devise a program to meet your unique security needs.

Patrolmen. If money for security is a problem, small businessmen should consider banding together with their neighbors to hire a night patrolman—guard dog optional—to make the rounds checking the outsides and insides of buildings on a block or smaller area. These uniformed, armed security forces will check your store's doors to see they're locked and look for signs of forced entry. They'll spot smoke, break up loitering groups, and investigate suspicious sounds and sights. Hire an established local security-patrol service and split the cost with the stores next door.

Watching the watchman. Hiring a lazy or crooked night watchman can be worse than hiring no watchman at all. A thorough background check by a private investigating company and a bonding firm are musts for all night security men. Make sure the watchman has enough duties to keep him occupied. Long periods with nothing to do make the guard drowsy or allow him time to rip you off. Require that he tour your grounds at irregular intervals and file reports, stamped by the time clock, several times each night. If you employ more than one night watchman, rotate duties and make spot checks now and then to spot sleeping guards and check pilfering by watchmen.

Contracting outside guards. Okay, persistent shoplifting or an outbreak of employee thievery has you determined to hire a guard. Do you start a company security force or engage an outside service? We recommend hiring a well-established, reliable outside firm. A uniformed and trained security guard will command the respect of your employees, and as outside employees, they won't show favoritism to bosses or buddies. Besides, training, equipping, and deploying your own security brigade is risky work for a beginner and is no bargain compared to the fees of outside guard services.

Pick a few companies from among those advertising in the Yellow Pages and compare fees and services. Ask for names of businesses the guard services now protect and check to see if these customers feel secure and satisfied.

COMPUTER CRIMES

Computer buddy system. Theft by computer is the dirty work of professionally trained persons who are quite shy about being discovered by coworkers, since it could mean the end of their careers. Thus, an effective deterrent to computer crime is a company policy that at least two people must be present whenever electronic data processing equipment is in use. Require workers to log their use of computer time and include the name or initials of another employee present at time of use.

Computer security after hours. Since the computer manipulator often does his digit dupery after hours, one way to stop him is to cut off the electricity going into the computer room at closing time. Throw a circuit breaker or loosen a fuse, then lock the fuse box. Make computer personnel get explicit, written permission before operating your electronic hardware on overtime hours. If you do allow after-hours data processing, insist that all daytime rules be followed.

Lockwords. A tactic which the computer-terminal user can employ to keep his file from being read and misused by others is the lockword. Before leaving a file, the user encodes a new lockword, which must be repeated before the computer allows the file to be reopened. The system can be made to record unsuccessful attempts by other terminal users to gain entry to the computer, and users trying an invalid lockword can be automatically disconnected. Thus research data, marketing plans, and trade secrets are secured from business spies.

Computer codes. Company secrets and highly sensitive data should be coded or scrambled in your computer as a safeguard against industrial espionage agents who electronically tap data systems to discover trade secrets. Coding a particular computer program is a relatively simple matter. For greater security, the codes can be changed or rotated on a regular basis.

Sign-out safeguard. Terminal users who forget to sign off jeopardize their company's records by leaving the computer open to whatever accounts they last worked on before walking away. To compensate for employee forgetfulness or crooked intentions, program your business computer to disconnect terminals after a specified period of inactivity by a terminal user. You might also consider requiring users to indicate when they will return to the computer controls. Those who attempt to gain access to files before the declared time can be flagged as impostors.

Computer ID cards. Restricting access to highly sensitive computer files will enhance your protection against theft of money and information. Among devices accomplishing this aim are machine-readable cards and badges by which terminal users identify themselves to the data system. Lock up these cards at the end of the work day. Passwords and security codes, written into the computer program, do the same thing and can be periodically changed. Or you may consider new gadgets which when added to your computer system will identify terminal users by their fingerprints or hand dimensions. Consult your computer-company representative for prices of these electronic safeguards.

Adding sequential numbers. A way to control both the number of records processed and the accuracy of the processing on your business computers involves adding check numbers, purchase-order numbers, account codes, or stock-order numbers and comparing the totals at different stages of the processing function. Omissions and duplications will be readily apparent and gaps in sequential numbering (such as payroll-check numbers) can be pinpointed. Providing for a computer programmer to make periodic comparisons of these "hash" totals can tell you at a glance if and where someone is bilking you through your own data system.

Original records. Keep original copies of receipts, payroll records, and other data even after you've logged this information in your company computers. Storing them for a one- or two-year period should be sufficient. Your objective, of course, is to catch computer crooks who may be altering your firm's data banks to cover their larceny. Investigating auditors can check the original copies against the computer printout to detect illegal tampering.

Computer checkups. Appropriate tests, checks, and "threat-monitoring" can be built into computer programs vital to those applications that can be fraudulently manipulated. With these precautions added when the program is made, suspicious changes from normal patterns can be detected and brought to your attention by automatic computer "exception reports." For example, if your weekly payroll is $100,000 but the total next week comes to $150,000 the previously rigged program would note this deviation in a special report.

Program pilfering. A stolen computer program can cost your company plenty in lost trade secrets and confidential earnings reports, or in replacing the programs themselves (costs run into the thousands of dollars). One way to deter data-program thieves and to facilitate the program's recovery is to make sure a statement of ownership is written into the data bank. A reliable computer programmer can encode such a statement in a way that is both undetectable and unalterable.

ASSORTED SCHEMES AND SWINDLES

Blackmail. Most blackmail attempts don't start with a mysterious letter demanding thousands of dollars. Instead, they begin with a "loan" request from someone you know and most likely work with. The request is accompanied by a thinly veiled threat of blabbing some personal secret if the "loan" is withheld. Take action at this first hint of an extortionate demand! Tell the dirty dealer it takes more collateral than a threat to get a "loan" from you and that you are unafraid of his story-spreading intentions. Make a note of the time, date, and wording of the demand and let the blackmailer know you're recording this information. Then drop a lightly cloaked threat of your own— telling him the fines and prison sentences possible from a blackmail conviction.

Riots. When your business is Duffy's Roadside Motel and Restaurant and you share a highway intersection with three Georgia cottonfields, don't worry about protecting against business loss from riots—boll weevils present a greater danger. But if you run a jewelry store in downtown Detroit, you'd better have a riot plan. Fire and looting are your biggest problems. Consider installing a hose to reach the roof, plenty of fire extinguishers, and sliding steel gates or awnings to protect street-level doors and windows. Have a battery-powered citizens-band radio handy to communicate with police if phone and electric lines go down. Provide for protecting workers and customers in a written riot plan which you distribute to each employee.

Bomb threats. A relatively new, and serious, threat to a business's reputation and profit is the hidden-bomb scare, whether or not terrorists have actually sabotaged your buildings. Do you evacuate employees and customers from your store? Your answer must be based on whether you believe the bomb threat is genuine. Keep this in mind: A sincere bomb tipster will be trying to help save human lives and will provide necessary details regarding the bomb's location, when it will explode, and so on. If the call's a hoax (most are) the anonymous phoner may sound vague, incoherent, drunk, childish, or bombastic. But bomb or no bomb, *always* notify police. And when in doubt, get the folks *out!*

Defusing accidents. If a customer falls down, is hit by a falling object, or has some other accident on your business premises you should immediately get the names and addresses of any witnesses in case the customer tries to take you to court. Fraudulent accident claims give you a bad reputation, raise your insurance rates, and cost you money. Insist that the injured person be examined by a doctor at the time of the accident, even if he insists he's not hurt. The medical testimony will be invaluable in fighting trumped-up negligence charges.

Bust-out plots. The usual planned bankruptcy or "bust-out" scam works with con men starting a "company" and depositing a modest amount in a bank account to establish credit. They order merchandise from suppliers and pay for it in cash. Gradually they increase the quantity of orders while decreasing the percentage paid and upping the amount "on credit." Finally they place one final large order, charging truckloads of goods to their established accounts. The merchandise is sold or hidden, the money withdrawn from the bank, and the "company" files bankruptcy—thereby bilking creditors.

Manufacturers can lessen the damage caused by these schemes by setting a cut-off point (say $500) at which a credit check is conducted before goods are shipped.

Ownership changes. Another bankruptcy scheme, this one a favorite of organized crime lords, starts with underworld characters buying controlling interest in an established company with a good credit rating. Before suppliers realize the ownership change, the new management uses credit cards issued to the company before their takeover to charge large orders. They ditch the goods, claim theft, and simultaneously file bankruptcy and insurance claims.

Fight this fraud by telling your salesmen to report immediately any change in a customer's management. Then run a thorough credit check on the new owners and treat the company as cautiously as you'd treat a new account.

Phony branch offices. For the price of a telephone answering service, confidence plotters will set up a "branch office" in a nearby city, using the same name as your company, or one nearly identical. The self-proclaimed "branch manager" then begins ordering merchandise, using your name and credit rating with suppliers. He absconds with the goods, leaving you billed and your supplier bilked.

Skirt this scam by centralizing your ordering process and telling suppliers all orders must have your (or a specified company official's) authorization. Wholesalers can guard against this type of fraud by always checking with the parent company on branch-office orders and by looking for incongruous orders—such as an auto-repair shop requesting a load of stereos. The reason for such a strange request might be legitimate, but it could be criminal.

White collar crime. A 92-page booklet entitled *A Handbook on White Collar Crime* is available that explains such subjects as embezzlement, pilferage, credit card fraud, computer crime, bribes, and kickbacks. For your copy, send $2.50 to the Chamber of Commerce of the United States, 1615 H Street, N.W., Washington, D.C. 20006.

CHAPTER 12

Prevention and protection potpourri

Would you believe "Bows, Bow-Wows, Self-Guards, and Credit Cards?" That tongue-twister was almost the title of this chapter—which is a hodge-podge of hints that defy conventional groupings. Included here are subjects which may relate to several of the preceding chapters or topics but don't easily fit into any of them.

Ingredients in this stew of suggestions are ideas to foil dognappers and boat burglars, outwit credit-card coppers and check kiters, deal with obscene mail and phone calls, and circumvent campsite perils.

BOAT SECURITY

Preventing boat theft. One no-cost way to discourage the theft of an inboard motorboat is to pry off the distributor cap, remove the rotor, then replace the cap. For outboards, most of which have magnetos rather than distributors, replace your spark plugs with "dummy" plugs—plugs which have had the inner and outer electrodes filed off. Naturally, you'll have to replace the above parts before you'll be able to start your boat.

Registration numbers. If your boat is stolen, you can bet your sea legs that within twenty-four hours your registration number will be changed. To counteract this, scratch or paint your registration number on a hidden part of the inside of your hull.

Loudspeaker alarm. A unique anti-theft device for yachts has recently been developed which automatically sets off, over a loudspeaker, a prerecorded, repeating message such as "There is an intruder aboard this yacht. Call police immediately."

The alarm, called Auralarm, is expensive—about $400 including installation—but offers excellent protection against theft and vandalism. The unit is available through Eaton Corporation, Lock and Hardware Division, 401 Theodore Fremd Avenue, Rye, N.Y. 10580.

Electronic policeman. A relatively low-cost ($140) anti-intrusion alarm for boats, the Electronic Policeman, protects all doors, hatches, and ports and also includes a trip switch that tells if someone is trying to remove the outboard motor. To make sure unwanted shipmates don't show up unannounced, order the maritime alarm from Protective Services Corporation, North Plainfield, N.J. 07060.

Sound-wave alarm. The Bourns Model MA-2 ultrasonic alarm system uses sound waves to protect your boat (it can be rigged to guard camping trailers, too). Sound-wave beamers powered by the boat's battery cover from 6 to 18 feet. Connect the $108 alarm to the boat's horn, or add a weatherproof bell ($10) or siren ($44). Ultrasonic boat alarms can be triggered by outside noises, so don't use one in a noisy marina.

Horn and light alarms. One type of boat burglar alarm uses the vessel's shipboard horn and lights as warning devices—thereby cutting the cost of the entire security system. Polstar Industries, Inc., P. O. Box 142, Nyack, N.Y. 10960, sells a do-it-yourself unit for $90. When a thief triggers the device, horns blare and lights flash aboard your floating fortress. For an additional $20, you can get a device that warns if your bilge is filling.

Mooring lines. Most small boats afloat are tied to their home docks with nylon or manila mooring line. Any thief with a sharp knife can steal your boat. A light, case-hardened steel chain, secured to the hull and padlocked to the dock, is a must.

Boat-trailer drydock. Maybe you lugged your pleasure boat up the driveway or into the garage or even put it in the back yard to weather out the gales until next boating season. But if you left your boat mounted on your boat trailer, you're likely to return home someday to find that someone with a trailer hitch on his car or truck has stolen the whole thing.

To squelch such plans, remove the wheels from your boat trailer and prop it up with concrete blocks.

GUN SECURITY

Trigger locks. The possibility that you or a member of your family will be injured by the accidental discharging of a gun kept in the home is far greater than the possibility that you will use your gun against a burglar. Better play it safe and lock all your guns with a trigger lock, available at gun shops for $6 each.

Shotguns for protection. The squabble between those who would curb crime by banning handguns and those who claim they need handguns to defend their lives and property ignores authorities who assert that the shotgun, not the handgun, is the most effective defensive firearm for the average home or apartment.

Experts recommend a 12-gauge, single-barrel shotgun for its operating ease, accuracy at the short distances involved inside a home, and intimidating presence. Prices start at about $40. Saw off the barrel at slightly over 18 inches (legal minimum length) to make the gun more compact, faster-handling, and easier to store. Keep the gun in a bedroom security closet and use it as a last defense against burglars or intruders.

Handguns for protection. Many people wouldn't feel safe with a handgun in the house, but if you wouldn't feel safe *without* one, the most practical gun to get is a Colt or Smith & Wesson .38 Special double-action revolver with a 4-inch barrel. Fully loaded, this pistol can be fired only by deliberately pulling the trigger with considerable pressure, thus making accidental shootings less likely. The barrel length improves pointing accuracy without being cumbersome. You'll have six shots in a rotating chamber with this model that sells for about $100. Use lightly loaded, flat-nosed lead bullets for reduced wall penetration, less recoil, and greater accuracy.

Shotgun ammunition. Next you'll want to know the best kind of ammunition for your home-defending shotgun. The best load for inside-the-house shooting is the standard skeet or trap shell with No. 8 or No. 9 shot. These have a lot of tiny pellets with little penetration power—so innocent bystanders won't be hit by shot going through your wall. Such shells throw a wide pattern which will compensate for poor marksmanship. Skeet shells usually won't kill a person more than a few yards away, but even a partial hit will take an intruder out of action completely and instantly, often without killing him.

Target practice. Owning a shotgun or handgun will do you no good unless you're familiar with your weapon and can load and fire it quickly and accurately, even when panicked. Your life and the lives of your loved ones are in serious danger if the handgun you bought six months ago but never used jams in your inexperienced hands in the face of a threatening prowler.

You'll need target practice to be confident and ready to shoot—at least one session with a shotgun, many more for a pistol. Most gun shops offer or know where you can get shooting instruction. Or get a friend or neighbor to share his knowledge of guns.

CHECKS AND CREDIT CARDS

Direct deposits. Arrange for dividend, interest, and social security checks to be sent directly to your bank for deposit, rather than to you. By having these checks take a direct route to your bank, you'll greatly reduce the chances of loss through mail theft.

Registered mail. Never send a letter containing a sizeable check or money order by ordinary mail—always register it. Each piece of registered mail is numbered, shipped separately from ordinary mail, and signed for when received, providing excellent protection against loss and theft. The fee is only $1.25, which automatically insures the contents for up to $100.

For an additional 20 cents, you can get a return receipt showing that your party received the letter.

Deposit-slip giveaway. Forgers have been known to pick up a crumpled bank checking account deposit slip, copy the name and account number, then forge a check in the individual's name. Therefore, if you make a mistake on a deposit slip, don't just crumple it up and throw it away. Rip it to shreds first. If you really want to be safe, take it home and burn it.

The check raiser. This fellow plies his trade by adding an extra digit to a check where a blank space exists—adding a zero to $65, for instance, making the amount $650. To guard against such knavery, leave no such spaces adjacent to a numbered or spelled-out dollar figure.

Check count. By continually comparing the number of the last check you've written with the number of the next blank check in your book, you can—and should—keep a constant eye out for any missing blank checks. The maid, the babysitter, or anyone can quickly tear a blank check from your book, forge it, then cash it. If you find a check missing, notify your bank immediately.

Check cover. Never send a check through the mail "bare"—that is, without folding it in at least two pieces of paper. For if the check can be seen when held up to the light, it could get snatched from the mails, then cashed by the thief.

Signature impression. If you make out and sign your checks while they're still in your checkbook, then lose the book, it's extremely easy for someone who finds the book to trace or write over the impression of your signature, then simply fill in any amount he desires. To prevent this, get into the habit of tearing out each check as you need it, filling it out over something other than your blank checks.

Bank statements. What a pushover the average checking account is to even a novice forger! He merely dips his hand into your mailbox the day your bank statement arrives. The criminal copycat then has it all: your account number, the balance in your account, your style of check, and most important, your signature.

To guard against this bird's antics, have your bank hold its statements for you to pick up in person.

Pocket check. Our neighbor was relieved that there was only 47 cents in her purse when some kid broke into her car to swipe it. But like many, many people, she had forgotten about the blank check she kept folded in her wallet to meet emergencies. Even if she'd remembered it, she couldn't have reported the missing check to her bank—she hadn't recorded the check number when she put it in long ago. Sure enough, the thief used her identification cards and her check to slip $150 out of her checking account.

Carry emergency blank checks, if you must carry them at all, in a pocket, in a car glove compartment, or *anywhere* but in a wallet.

Credit-card numbers. In the event of loss or theft, you'll want to have the numbers handy for all your credit cards and charge plates. The easiest way to do this is to simply put them all face down on a copy machine. Then make three copies—one each for your home and safe-deposit box, and another to carry on your person, separate from the wallet in which you carry your credit cards.

Watch your credit card. Unscrupulous store and gas-station clerks will try to get more than one charge out of you. Here's how they do it. While validating your charge tickets, they stamp one or two blank ones with your account number. Later, they trace your signature through one of the thin charge-slip copies and fill in some additional items. You get the bill for those items the crooked clerks take home.

The only preventive medicine is to always keep your credit card in sight. Don't let cashiers take your charge plate to a back counter or inside a gas station. Follow them if they try.

Credit-card switch. When using a credit card, always check to make sure that the card returned to you is really yours. Unscrupulous clerks have been known to give a customer someone else's outdated or invalidated credit card, then charge goods to the customer's card.

Extra credit cards. Many credit firms automatically issue two credit cards, even though only one may be needed. If this is the case with you, destroy the extra card upon receipt.

Don't leave credit cards lying about the house.

Credit-card insurance. Insurance is the last line of defense to keep you from losing cash if your credit card is stolen. At $3 per year for the minimum coverage of $1,000 ($6 per year for $10,000 coverage) the protection is worth it. The coverage will pay for your legal liability if the thief runs up your bills and will pay the cost of your attorney if the company issuing the card decides to sue you.

Credit-card protection service. A large number of credit cards crammed in your purse or wallet will mean a tremendous headache in the event of theft. Check your Yellow Pages under "Security System Consultants" for one that offers a credit-card protection service. For $5 a year such a firm will notify pay-later plate issuers of theft in time to save you the $50 deductible per card. You'll have to furnish the firm with your credit-card serial numbers in advance—then just keep its number handy and make one local phone call to take care of reporting loss of all your credit cards.

Credit is a right. Banks, savings and loan associations, department stores, and credit-card distributors used to be able to deny you credit at their whim. Maybe you were too old or the wrong sex or race to suit them. You couldn't scream foul play because these business institutions didn't have to tell why they rejected you.

But now they do. A new Federal Reserve Board ruling requires every creditor to fix the reason credit is denied and spell it out in writing. Regulations ban discrimination for reasons of race, color, religion, sex, or age. Welfare recipients and married persons seeking independent credit records are also protected. Ask for your denial reason in writing and take it to your attorney if you suspect someone is monkeying with your power to buy now, pay later.

Credit-card liability. Is a credit-card company trying to pressure you into paying for the hundreds of dollars worth of charges a thief rang up under your name? Simply knowing the law will help you fight your creditor's pressure tactics. New federal legislation limits the liability of card holders to the first $50 of improper use of the credit card. And you may not even have to pay that much for charges on your stolen card! If the issuer failed to provide you with a self-addressed, pre-stamped notice to be returned when the card is stolen or lost, you owe him nothing.

PETS

Pet protection. Guard your pet against loss by purchasing an engravable identification tag at any pet-supply outlet. Then send it in to the address given to have your address and telephone number engraved on it. Costs just $2, which includes engraving.

Tattooed ID. A new government agency has been created to help return pilfered pooches to their rightful owners. For a $5 registration fee, the Canine Bureau of Identification (17 Battery Place, New York, N. Y. 10004) will send you a special identification number and a dog tag.

Your nearby veterinarian or humane shelter will tattoo the ID number on your pet's right thigh or ear for a small fee. The process is permanent and painless. The tag warns that your dog is registered and instructs the finder to send CBI a collect telegram. The bureau then calls you and your stolen or lost dog is returned.

Maximum-security pen. The dognapper's usual method is to steal the animal from its pen, kennel, or run. These dog-keeping enclosures are usually located in a secluded part of the house lot and rarely have locks on gates or roofs.

If you have valuable pets, they won't be entirely safe until you construct your pen of hardened-steel (chain link) fencing with an overhead cover, install adequate locks on gates, and make sure the pen's steel end posts are embedded in concrete. Even with this, a dog thief can still use bolt-cutters to get at your pet, but he can't return the dog for reward or ransom claiming it "escaped" and he "found" it.

Dog thefts from cars. Your dog should be left locked in your house or with a neighbor while you go grocery shopping. Owners who leave their pets in the car with the windows slightly open in parking lots are among the dognapper's most frequent victims. The cracked car window allows anyone with a coat hanger to get in, and many cooped-up pooches go along willingly just for the fresh air. Treat your pedigree-holder like any other valuable—don't leave it in plain sight, unattended in your car.

Mutts. That $250 pedigreed puppy whose ancestors won blue ribbons at dog shows is a rip-off and a dognap hazard if all you're looking for is a playmate and love object for your children. Mixed-breed and mongrel dogs are given away at animal shelters and in newspaper want ads, and mutts are every bit as playful. And, since dognappers look for exotic breeds that have higher resale value and whose owners are more likely to pay large rewards or ransoms, you can save yourself and your youngsters the trauma and expense of a pet stealing by buying a mutt.

Noseprints. Trying to prove the dog you see really belongs to you but was stolen can be difficult. New "owners" will have changed the tags, and dognappers are expert at forging pedigree papers. One surefire way to establish ownership of a valuable dog is to keep a record of its noseprint. Since no two dogs' nose-ridge patterns are the same, noseprints identify dogs as fingerprints do humans. Have the veterinarian press and sign a print and keep it to protect against possible dog theft.

Barking dogs. The family pet that yelps up a storm at strangers and may even nibble an intruder's pants leg can be an effective household burglar alarm and the cheapest of canine guards. For best protection, you'll need to keep your pooch in the yard or house at night and train it in obedience and to restrict its barking. These dogs are more economical, since they don't require the special training of guard dogs or attack dogs. You can do your own dog teaching with the help of a book or two on the subject, available at bookstores and libraries.

Include lessons on not accepting food from strangers—drugged meat and poisoned food are common ways for prowlers to silence barkers.

Guard dogs. These large dogs are costly, professionally trained animals which require special care and handling, a fenced-in yard, and daily owner-dog workouts. Breeders charge upwards of $200 for trained canines, and care and feeding costs will easily add $50 a month to the tab.

Trained to patrol a certain area and attack anyone but the owner who crosses the boundaries, guard dogs are most effective protecting large, private grounds such as barnyards or estates. Often-robbed small businesses, such as service stations and liquor stores, may profit from dogs stationed near cash registers at night. Since these dogs can be trained to protect persons rather than places, the elderly, invalids, or others needing an edge in personal security will be well protected if they can afford a guard dog.

Attack dogs. Attack dogs are highly trained, highly dangerous weapons and must be used with a handler to be effective. They are practical only for the richest homeowners with lots of loot to guard. For business security, these animals programmed to chase, fight, hold, and release anyone on the handler's command are more useful. Several shops can band together and share costs of a security guard/attack dog patrol team. Or service-station attendants and night clerks can also be trained as dog handlers. Training costs vary from $250 to $1,000.

Buying dogs for protection. It's easy to fall for a dog seller's line about the security value of a canine, and many will take your cash while giving you an ill-trained dog at an exorbitant price. Don't believe the shyster selling a "special breed" of barking dog—any size or kind of canine can make a suitable four-legged alarm. Buy them from pet dealers or animal shelters and train them yourself. For a guard dog or attack dog, go to the experts listed in the Yellow Pages under "Dog Trainers." Never buy someone else's guard or attack dog without immediately retraining the animal. You won't be able to control the dog, and such large critters, taught to be vicious, pose a serious safety hazard.

A GRAB BAG OF CAUTIONS

Tenant patrol. In New York City, many apartment-house dwellers have successfully decreased or eliminated crime in their buildings by forming tenant patrols. Male tenants volunteer to work in pairs, patrolling the premises around the clock.

Some of the better-organized patrols provide a bright blazer with identification badge for each man. Although weapons are not carried, whistles and flashlights are standard equipment.

If your building is prone to burglaries, muggings, and the like, you'll be wise to organize such a patrol. Start by contacting your local police department, which will provide you with valuable tips on such an undertaking.

Auxiliary police. Because of the crime rate, the New York City Police Department now augments its regular force with several thousand volunteer Auxiliary Police.

The program includes both men and women, each of whom is provided with a uniform, nightstick, and whistle, but not a gun. A brief training session is given each volunteer.

If your community has a high crime rate but a short-handed police force, you'd do well to encourage local residents to become involved in such a program. To generate support, work through your mayor, police force, and local newspaper.

Crime prevention file. Over 1,300 Exchange Clubs across the land have valiantly joined in the anti-crime battle by helping to implement a variety of prevention activities. Upon request, they'll mail you a Personal Crime Prevention Action File which gives handy information on protecting your car, home, and family. It also has blank spaces for emergency telephone numbers and other vital information. For your free copy, write The National Exchange Club, 3050 Central Avenue, Toledo, Ohio 43606.

Eavesdropper safeguard. The Phone Guard, because of its special built-in circuitry, effectively prevents anyone from eavesdropping on your telephone line. The gadget takes just minutes to install on the end of your phone cord.

Available at $7.95, it can be ordered from Viking Electronics, Inc., Box 91, Hudson, Wisc. 54016.

Privacy protection. Invasion of privacy is a serious matter. For if your personal and financial affairs are open to public and governmental scrutiny, facts about your life may be used against you in any of many possible devious ways—from blackmail to bunco schemes.

Find out how to protect yourself from invasion of privacy by subscribing to *Privacy Journal*, Box 8844, Washington, D.C. 20003 ($15 a year).

Foul phone calls. Obscene telephone calls come in all shapes, sizes, and colors. Your caller may scream vulgarly at you or simply pant passionately into your ear. Naturally, your best defense against the first such call is to hang up. But if you get persistent calls of this nature, you may have to go to the extreme of changing your number and getting an unlisted telephone.

First, however, try tapping the receiver with a key or coin, then saying, "This is the caller I told you about, officer." Your caller may think he's being traced and hang up.

Thefts are deductible. Victims of burglars, muggers, car thieves, or cattle rustlers can find some solace in a specially tailored tax loophole. You can deduct the value of stolen items from your gross income for tax purposes—but only if these items are listed in an official police report. Staple a copy of the report to your income-tax return. It's better to recover 25 to 50 percent of your loss than nothing at all.

Naturally, this only applies to theft losses not reimbursed by an insurance company.

Policing the police. On the seamy side of the street lurk enough toughs to rough you up and shake you down. But where do you turn when the person pushing you around or giving you hassles wears a badge and blue uniform?

Many cities have a Community Relations Department which will go to bat for citizens with gripes against cops. Find out if your town has such a department. If so, you'll know how to cope with trouble from the boys in blue.

Operation good morning warning. For years now, "Operation Good Morning" has worked successfully for senior citizens in many communities throughout the land. Aged participants call a police complaint officer or senior citizens' club staffer each morning before breakfast (some groups take calls just before bedtime, too) to exchange good cheer and let someone know they've made it securely through the night. Switchboard operators keep a checklist, and if you haven't called by 9:00 A.M., they call you. See if such a safe-and-sound system is operating in your area. If not, start one!

Letter bombs. You don't have to be a foreign ambassador or a corporate bigwig these days to get mauled by mail—specifically by a letter bomb. These postal explosives are often book-sized packages or large envelopes which are unexpected or from an unusual source and feel somewhat lopsided. You may feel a springiness (bomb padding) around some heavier object in the envelope. Wires may be noticeable, there may be greasy marks from explosive sweating, or the parcel may rattle slightly when shaken gently. If you receive such a packet, put it down, stay clear of it, and call police to defuse the device.

Electric failures. Give a crook the cover of darkness and you give him a hefty advantage, but when he also gets the cover of an electrical outage—as in modern "blackouts" and "brown-outs" in the cities— he becomes particularly dangerous. When the power fails, immediately check that all windows and doors are locked. Keep an oil lamp or candles handy to shed light on your situation. If caught without candles, make one from a cup of margarine by soaking a shoestring or pipe cleaner in the margarine in the cup and leaving a wick-length tip above the surface.

Obscene mail. Unsolicited porn in the postbox isn't always the pleasant surprise its distributors seem to think it is. You needn't tolerate repeated unwanted mailings of material objectionable to you. Simply go down to your post office branch, fill out the proper form, and your postmaster will screen your mail for undesired ads, brochures, and packages.

Camper thefts. You can really get close to the great outdoors—a whole lot closer than you'd want—if some crook cops your camping trailer while you're hiking a trail. One natural way to avoid this is to secure your home away from home with a $15 lock which fits over the trailer hitch when your camper is unhooked. These Master Lock Company camper securers are sold by many campground operators and outdoor-equipment stores.

Snakebite. If you, your child, or your companion is bitten by a poisonous reptile (check for fang marks atop regular snake-tooth patterns), stay calm, but get medical attention immediately.

If you're more than one hour away from the emergency room, apply a constricting band about 4 inches above the wound. Loosen it for a few seconds every fifteen minutes. Keep the victim quiet, with the bite lower than the rest of the body, to slow absorption of the poison. Practice with the snakebite kit you bought at a drug or sporting-goods store before venturing out into the wilds. Know how to use

246

it and how to apply a tourniquet *before* wandering out of reach of civilization.

Campsite cautions. Each year more and more people hit the camping trail to savor the freedom of the great outdoors, and more and more crooks follow to gather the outdoor equipment and other valuables many campers leave casually strewn around their supposedly safe campsite. Nowadays it is no more safe to leave unattended property in the wilds than in the city. We suggest that large wooden or metal boxes, fitted with padlocks, be used to pack camping stoves, lanterns, and other supplies to the campground and to secure these valuables in when you take to a nature trail.